THE NEW SHADE GARDEN

KEN DRUSE

STEWART, TABORI & CHANG   NEW YORK

CONTENTS

PART 1

INTRODUCTION

NEW WORLD (DIS)ORDER: NATURE'S HARD TIMES

PREVIOUS SPREAD Plants like white foamflower (*Tiarella* spp.) and tufts of grassy *Carex morrowi* var. *temnolepis* 'Silk Tassel' grow beneath small-leafed rhododendrons in the Azalea Garden at the New York Botanical Garden.

ABOVE, CLOCKWISE FROM TOP Plants of the world's forests: Welsh poppy (*Meconopsis cambrica*) from the British Isles; a navelwort selection (*Omphalodes cappadocica* 'Cherry Ingram') originally from Turkey; variegated fairy bells in fruit (*Disporum sessile* 'Variegatum') from Japan.

OPPOSITE Garden in the Woods, home of the New England Wild Flower Society, with understory trees like silverbell (*Halesia tetraptera*) and eastern redbud (*Cercis canadensis*).

S hade is looking good to twenty-first-century gardeners. No one needs to be sold on the idea of finding shelter from the heat and sun anymore. As global average temperatures continue to rise, we have more reasons to seek a retreat in the shadows. Our gardens, and the world, are changing.

In the early 1990s, when I first started writing and lecturing about shade gardening, people used to ask questions like "How can I get rid of the shade on my property?" Shade was seen as a curse. "Nothing can grow in the shade" was the oft-heard lament. People tried a couple of ferns or an astilbe, if that.

This was a time when the sunny English flower border captured the imagination of American gardeners with tints and shades of soft lavender, pink, and blue. In those days, far-north Britain was never too hot. Gardens there basked in bright daylight, with soft sun for long hours in the summer while the temperatures remained cool. In a given season, flowers would last many times longer there than in the United States, and one might come upon lilacs blooming with roses. In most of the United States, lilacs are long gone by the time the roses begin to flower.

In time, my audiences recognized that planting away from full sunlight under trees presented opportunities to grow some of the most exquisite and precious wildflowers that come from the world's temperate forests—and incidentally, not from England, because the last ice age scraped away much of Great Britain's flora. On the other hand, the southeastern United States is second only to China in the number of indigenous cold-hardy species.

Fortunately, we are no longer talking about suffering with shade, or heaven forbid, getting rid of it by cutting down valuable trees. More people are trying to create shade instead. Who wouldn't want to find a spot in the summer garden that could be 10 to 20 degrees cooler than its counterpart in the sunny flower border? We are adding canopies and awnings, pergolas and gazebos, and planting more trees for now and for generations to come, not only to help create shady places but to also reduce our carbon footprints, since trees absorb and store carbon dioxide, or CO_2, a primary greenhouse gas. (We'd have to plant a lot of trees to make up for our very big American feet. It's no secret that since the days of the Industrial Revolution, fossil fuels like coal, oil, and gasoline have been burned at ever-increasing rates, leading to a rise in atmospheric gases like CO_2 and methane from industrial livestock production. Since the 1800s, CO_2 has risen by 40 percent.)

Evidence of the effects is everywhere and is always apparent. Have you noticed that summer heat waves seem to happen nearly every year? Temperature swings are more extreme than in years past? That rainy days are less frequent, but often have much heavier downpours? That normal dry weeks in August may now stretch into months of drought? Even hurricanes act abnormally, for example, when Irene took a sharp turn to the west in 2011 or when, the following year, Sandy led to ocean surges and destruction in areas where such events were rare to unheard of.

The forecasts for a changing climate said we would begin to feel the effects of global warming by 2050. To longtime gardeners such as myself, though, it feels as if the changes hit around 2005, and they keep on coming. The projection for sea-level rise continues to be updated, and by 2100, climatologists predict the ocean will be 3 feet (1 m) higher than it is today, threatening coastlines around the world. Right now, hundreds of millions of people live in these places, but many will become uninhabitable, and some island nations will completely disappear.

How do we, as home gardeners, push ahead in the face of so much change?

A Call to Rethink

The garden of the future will be a shade garden. There are many reasons: fiscal, historical, environmental—and for the sake of our health and of the planet's. In many ways, this is an older notion of landscaping—it's planting for generations to come. It won't happen overnight, though. For one thing, it means planting trees.

Since 1989, I have published several books with *natural* in the title. I used that word to mean naturalistic—a design style that was friendly to nature in its appearance, planting, and maintenance. *Natural* doesn't always mean "native," or what would have lived on this continent in the years before humans arrived.

Picture the land thousands of years ago—cleared by lightning-sparked fire or Native Americans. Viable seeds in the ground would sprout once exposed to warmth and sunlight. In sunny open spaces, these seeds would most likely be meadow plants in the East and prairie plants in the Midwest. If there was enough rainfall, shrub and tree seeds would germinate as well, and in time, those woody plants would grow tall and cast shade on the meadow plants, which would gradually fade away. Eventually, a deciduous forest might take hold. This is the succes-

sion of plants that leads to forests and savannas—plant communities dominated by trees. The leaves of the trees would filter sunlight. There would still be enough light in late winter and spring, however, for the woodland ephemerals such as trillium, bloodroot, and mayapple to thrive. These are the new (old) models for our gardens.

This kind of gardening requires planning, thought, and effort—and some adjustment of expectations. There may not be masses of frothy color under the trees, but I promise there will be a good show. Just look again at the plants of the forest floor: They have little time to gather light, bloom, attract pollinators, and set seed, so they pack every precious bit of energy into a few spectacular blossoms. Some of the flowers, like those of the jack-in-the-pulpit and wild ginger, may seem more grotesque than showy; the plant's energy has been put into reproduction, but not into creating something we might consider pretty the way Japanese wood poppies (*Glaucidium palmatum*) are. Out in the sunny garden, bees (and people) may favor fragrant flowers. In the shady realm, beetles and ant pollinators might not care. To me, all of these shade-loving plants are beautiful, stars of the botanical kingdom and among the most fascinating hardy plants of the natural world.

What else will be different as we increasingly take to the shade? It's a given that you are not going to have a burgeoning rose garden or colorful annuals for cutting, and shady spots will not produce food for a family of four. Those kinds of horticulture will happen in other parts of the landscape developed for these purposes. But the shady spots won't be dull. You will be able to grow some remarkable species in places of serene tranquility and enchanting freshness.

Our sheltered plantings might be the most down-to-earth versions of horticulture we can practice. Unlike the transitional meadow, perennial borders, or vegetable gardens, our adaptations of the natural woodland can be the most sustainable and enduring habitats of all. Today, though, the areas surrounding our homes are more likely to be monoculture lawnscapes than natural or habitat-like, so that is where our thinking—or rethinking—must begin.

OPPOSITE The exquisite cold-loving white Japanese wood poppy (*Glaucidium palmatum* 'Album') grows well far north, at the Montreal Botanical Garden.

ABOVE A meadow is a transitional plant community. This one is on the edge of a savanna in the Midwest. If there is enough moisture, and if it is not grazed, burned, or cleared for development, the meadow will become a woodland as tree and shrub seedlings slowly take hold.

MAKING SHADE, OTHER THAN WITH TREES

I could have put more places in my garden where you could stop and rest or sit, but that's something we gardeners rarely do, or only do for two seconds. When a gardener sits down, he or she inevitably sees a weed that needs pulling, or a plant that has flopped over and needs some propping. Then we're up in a flash. Benches, swings, and chairs are for regular people.

But as temperatures grow warmer and there is less natural protection from sunlight, when planning for outdoor recreation spaces and for entertaining, consider covers—awnings, canopies, and constructed structures such as pergolas and trellises—so you and your guests can be in the shade for at least part of the time.

Each year, there are more cases of skin cancer diagnosed than breast, prostate, colon, and lung cancer combined, and the rates are climbing. According to the National Cancer Institute, the rate of new melanoma cases among American adults has tripled since the 1970s, from 7.9 per 100,000 people in 1975 to 23.8 in 2010. A person's risk of developing melanoma doubles if he or she has had more than five sunburns. The Skin Cancer Foundation recommends staying out of the sun completely between 10 A.M. and 4 P.M.

ABOVE In the garden of Noel Gieleghem and Brandon Tyson, jungle orchid cacti (*Epiphyllum* spp.) hang from a pergola that shelters them from full sun.

OPPOSITE The 1915 lath Botanical Building at Balboa Park in San Diego, California, transforms the brilliant sun to a softer filtered light. Photograph by Diana E. Ruark.

Lawnscapes, or Sustainable Landscapes?

Lawn grass is a plant, and like all plants, it removes CO_2 from the atmosphere. But the antilawn movement has shifted into high gear, meaning that many of us are thinking about living with less lawn or even eliminating it altogether. Grass lawns are not natural—humans invented them, and they are very hard on the environment. Cutting the grass takes human energy; keeping it weed-free and making it green often involves chemicals and fertilizers; producing and transporting those products uses energy; and synthetic fertilizer is actually *made* from fossil fuel, adds nitrogen to the atmosphere, and affects waterways through runoff.

It's not easy to break the water-feed-grow-cut-repeat cycle, and for the sake of full disclosure, I admit I have some lawn, although it is only half grass and none of that is of the care-intensive blue-grass variety. I do not water or feed the lawn, aerate it, or dethatch it, but I do cut it when it gets about 4 inches (10 cm) tall.

In general, mowed lawn is the only living ground cover that stands up well to foot traffic, so it remains a useful surface to let us move through the garden. Lawn fights erosion, and at least it is alive—better than asphalt or impermeable surfaces. Like a garden, turf soaks up heat and disperses it, which is especially useful in urban areas, where buildings and asphalt absorb and radiate heat into the air and onto us. Even just looking at green spaces feels invigorating, reduces stress, and elevates mood. But how about reducing the stress on the environment?

Mowing and fertilizing a lawn most likely produces enough CO_2 and nitric oxide to negate all the possible advantages. Gardens have all the benefits of turf and many more, and depending on the level of one's chemical dependency, next to none of the drawbacks. Replacing a high-maintenance lawn with other plants is one of the best things you can do, and that brings us back to shade gardens—and the potential to shift some of that wide-open, sun-soaked turf into something more diverse, something inviting, natural, and sustainable. Sheltered from the heat, these places require less frequent watering than sunny gardens and no potentially hazardous chemicals.

The Reality of Season Creep

As the planet warms, winters may be milder and springs may arrive earlier. We're already starting to see this phenomenon, which is known as "season creep." I remember that it wasn't that long ago when the weeks of blossoms in my woodland garden filled May with the beaming flowers of Virginia bluebells, wood poppies, and bright white trillium wake-robins. These days, the white trillium usually bloom in late April. One April, not too long ago, I went off to lecture in California. When I left, those plants were not yet in bud. I returned a week later to find faded flowers.

Tracking the blossom dates of plants, and especially their timing in relationship to weather and climate, is part of a science called phenology. I've noticed that the date for the cherry blossom festival at the Brooklyn Botanic Garden, Sakura Matsuri, which was set years ago at a time when the trees were at peak bloom, is now more a celebration of blossom fall (which it kind of is supposed to be), year after year. I remember being in Washington, DC, around 2005 for its annual cherry blossom

festival celebrations. Thousands of tourists flocked to the capital that year to find they'd missed the blooms by more than a week.

Perhaps we think a longer growing season is a good thing—more days to spend in the garden, right? But warm days in late winter are almost always followed by a cold snap. The apple and peach growers are more nervous than they have ever been, and more than once in recent years, they have lost an entire year's crop to a frost that hit when the trees bloomed too early in spring.

Not all species are adjusting at the same rate. Some birds might migrate to their summering grounds only to realize that their favorite food source has changed its schedule. Crossbills fly east from California to as far away as Pennsylvania, now that the warmer climate has reduced the availability of the pine nuts they used to find closer to home.

Plants are moving as well. If seeds from a local plant fall to the ground, perhaps the ones that germinate farthest south will not survive, and the ones that sprout a bit north will. Slowly but surely, the population of growing things that like cool or cold temperatures will creep ever northward, to a cooler climate. Even the oak trees are moving northward, with the help of the squirrels.

Some viticulturists are happy about global warming; certain familiar wines are developing more alcohol, because the grapes are growing in higher temperatures than in the past. Vintners in far north Britain and Scandinavia can produce wine now as well.

OPPOSITE My woodland garden in New Jersey used to peak in mid-May. Now, it blooms early—sometimes as early as April—with white trillium wake-robin, yellow wood poppy, and Virginia bluebells.

ABOVE A path in late summer is flanked by hostas and flowering Japanese anemone hybrids/ windflowers (*Anemone × hybrida*) at the State University of New York in Farmingdale.

AMERICAN LAWNS BY THE NUMBERS

NASA has calculated from satellite images that as many as 40 million acres in the United States are planted in grass lawn. Lawn is the single largest irrigated "crop" in the nation. In addition to eliminating food and habitat for native pollinators, grass lawn maintenance guzzles water and spews smog and harmful chemicals. According to EPA findings, the average American household consumes about 320 gallons (1,200 L) of water per day, a third of which is used outdoors. It is estimated that some 200 gallons (750 L) of potable water per person per day are used on lawns during the growing season. Although regulations are being reexamined, as of 2013, one gas-powered lawn mower running for one hour produces the same amount of pollutants as a typical car driven 45 miles (70 km). Enormous amounts of gasoline are used for mowing, but it is estimated that approximately 17 million gallons are spilled when filling mowers and other garden power equipment per year.

Of the 90 million American households with yards, it is estimated that 45 million use synthetic fertilizers, 46 million use insecticides, and 47 million use chemical weed killers. These chemicals damage natural habitat, can seep into the ground, run off in rainstorms, and contaminate our drinking water.

ABOVE Grass lawn is a living ground cover that can take heavy foot traffic and is best planted for recreational use or on pathways. Limited patches of lawn may be useful as design elements in contrast with adjacent plantings.

OPPOSITE Grass lawn is best reduced to the smallest area. This narrow path framed by two Wave Hill chairs requires just one pass with the mower.

Some insect pests wake up earlier than in the past, just in time to destroy the emerging growth on their hosts. Invasive plants, which are often cold-season species, get going earlier to take over land before our warm-season North American plants have a chance.

In 2012, the US Department of Agriculture amended its Plant Hardiness Zone Map to reflect the country's warmer temperatures. I used to grow plants in USDA zone 6; now, it seems, I may be gardening in zone 7 (although with weather anomalies being the new norm, I am afraid to test that). We gardeners need to think about strategies for coping with the inevitable.

When I looked back at my 1992 book, *The Natural Shade Garden*, I discovered that I had written a chapter on global warming. Were we talking about this that long ago? And still some Americans do not agree with the current scientific conclusions that humans have contributed to rises in CO_2 and other greenhouse gases that are the cause. What people often *can* agree on is that we do not like spending billions on sea-surge mitigation or suffering from air and water pollution, and that we all need to pass a healthy environment on to the next generations. What we can also agree on: as gardeners, we can make decisions and take actions that contribute to that goal.

Extending a Guiding Hand

When human meets earth, a partnership is struck. A garden is a place where people interact with plants. It is this collaboration that makes a garden a garden, indoors or out, in the ground or at the windowsill.

Every garden is unique; I've never seen two that are alike. Some appeal to me more than others. When I visit a garden, I can often tell in an instant whether I am going to enjoy the experience. The plot may be small or vast, wealthy or poor. The thing that attracts me is what I call the evidence of a guiding hand—the soul of the garden. I've seen this caring in a humble tire planter, and I've missed it while touring a grand estate. As garden makers, our hope is to create a work that is filled with self-expression—that reveals our souls.

Although some paved outdoor spaces, especially in urban settings, may be thought of as gardens, I can't see how these plant-free, nonporous constructions enhance nature, which is another prerequisite to my definition of *garden*.

We can enhance or help nature mostly by lessening the stress on our bit of earth. Rather than fighting the site with wildly inappropriate constructs, like a water-guzzling golf course in the desert or even simply too much front lawn, we would be better served to learn from nature's model and use plants that will do well in our environment with minimum intervention. We hope to leave the places we've come to just as we found them, if not better off, and we strive to work with nature in the garden, not to tame—or taint—it. I hope that's what I have been doing along the way in my own gardening journey.

It's a lot to think about, so we'd better get started. And please turn the lights off when you leave the room.

OPPOSITE LEFT A salamander, once common in my New Jersey garden, has become a rare creature.

OPPOSITE RIGHT In 1992, I published *The Natural Shade Garden*, a book that documented the creation of my city garden (foreground, from above). My naturalistic style was apparently contagious as it inspired the plantings of the late garden designer, Bill Fidelo, next door. His seating area is seen beyond the trees of my garden.

ABOVE Gardens that appeal to me most are expressions of their makers' personality, which is the soul of the landscape. Kathy Fries has a "funnel garden" where a collection of found objects illustrates her inventive style.

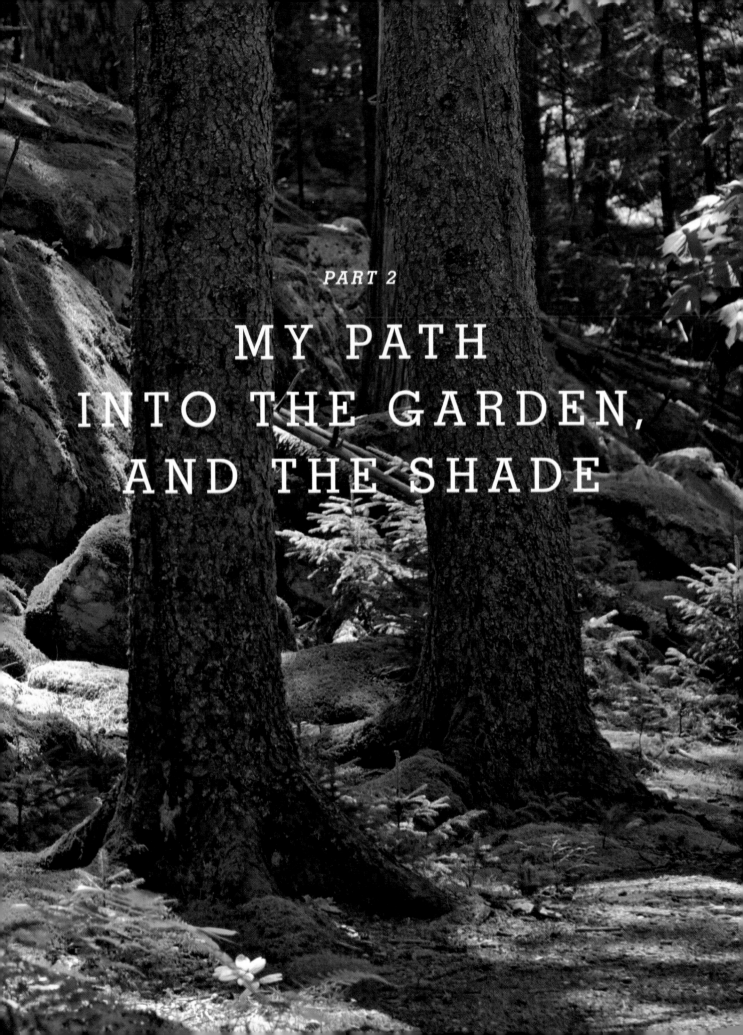

PART 2

MY PATH INTO THE GARDEN, AND THE SHADE

INTO THE WOODS

Trees have been making shade for millions of years, and most of those trees have lived together in forests. Nature's model tells us that the woods are not scary. But for millennia, people believed the woods were dangerous. Fear and forest went together. Remember those fairy tales where children in peril skipped to Grandma's cottage (or the witch's house) in the woods? People tend to like, and feel most safe in, open space—pastoral landscapes often made by man and grazing animals—bright-green expanses with nary a tree. Unfortunately, many people think that is what nature looks like. To be fair, woods can be dangerous, as they offer plenty of places for predators to hide. Clear the land, and you can see for long distances—see where predator (and prey) might be lurking.

Why, then, did wooded places have a special appeal to me from such a young age?

I have often recalled and written about a vivid memory of being introduced to a wildflower in the shade by my mother, who had a great love of nature. We stopped in the dappled shade along a path to see a strange flower with an even stranger name: jack-in-the-pulpit. She explained that the name came from the image of a preacher standing in his pulpit with a canopy above his head. I probably didn't know exactly what she was talking about, but the magic of the meeting wasn't lost on me, and I've never forgotten it. I never thought of the forest as being scary. For me, the woods were where the cool things were.

Natural woodland, with plenty of trees spaced far enough apart for the plants of the floor to grow, offered enclosure and endless fascination. There might be orange fungus on a fallen log, a salamander (in the days when you could still see such a creature in the woods), big insects and little ones, plants with every shape of leaf, precious flowers made more special by their scarcity. I know that today, anyone who takes a child outdoors when he or she is very young and fearlessly turns over a rock to reveal a bug, or looks at the shapes of the tree leaves in autumn, or sees the face in the moon at night might make a convert to the love of life outdoors—and maybe even counter the lure of the digital screen.

A Sheltered Childhood

Children seem to always be able to discover an outdoor hiding place. I suppose grown-ups forget about that need and what it felt like to be in such places. I think any reader can imagine being in a pleasant private space, and remember what it was like in childhood when you found a secret spot where you ruled the cool air and damp earth.

I grew up playing in the dirt. My interest (at five years of age) was not necessarily to garden, but to push soil around and observe tiny critters. Occasionally, little plants would play roles. A seedling became a tree under which my toy truck could park. These activities always took place in the shaded spots around the outer edges of my parents' property in north-central New Jersey.

PREVIOUS SPREAD A moss-covered rock outcropping along the Shoreland Trail at the Coastal Maine Botanical Garden.

ABOVE The American jack-in-the-pulpit (*Arisaema triphyllum*) made a strong impression on me as a child and inspired my love of native plants and naturalistic design.

OPPOSITE Take a walk on the wild side at Jennings Environmental Education Center in western Pennsylvania. Visits to protected and managed parks and other areas will provide inspiration for your own garden and an overview of plants that grow in your area, like the white speckled wood lily (*Clintonia umbellulata*).

In one area, I had a handsome fort under an aged hemlock and a cluster of enormous rhododendrons. I remember a faded photograph of my father in cap and gown when he graduated from law school. He was standing in front of those ancient blooming rhodies, which were much taller than he was.

Those old shrubs were all that was left of a garden surrounding a burned-down mansion that once stood on the quarter-acre lot where my parents built their ranch house in 1951. There were several of these grand old dwellings in the neighborhood, which were considered white elephants by the early fifties and far less desirable than the spiffy new chunk of brick and clapboard we called home. Of course there were newer attempts at horticulture, such as the ubiquitous green fringe of foundation plantings surrounding our house. In the front, a plump evergreen yew threatened to block the view from the big square picture window. The concrete walk from the street to the door parted our green sea of lawn. It was unembellished—simply the shortest distance between two points—nothing fancy, just the facts.

The former mansion's shrubs grew right next to the sidewalk on the south edge of the property. There was a huge mountain laurel concealing a U-shaped path that ducked into the shrubby thicket. I could go inside the laurel, and although I was right next to passersby on the concrete walk, I was invisible in my sheltered bushy fort.

In winter, my best friend (who later became the chairman of a nature conservation nonprofit) and I would pile snow into a high mound, carve a tunnel entrance, and scoop out the inside of our annual snow-dome *quinzhee*. We'd crawl in for warmth. One year, we built our igloo in the shape of a giant whale with a wide-open mouth for the entrance. That shelter got its picture in the local paper.

Whether it was winter's cold or summer's heat, we kids always managed to find or make shelter from the snow or sun.

My New Jersey Garden: Shelter from the Coming Storm

My devotion to gardening in the shade—and no longer just playing in it—began when I moved from a sunny container garden on part of an 8,000-square-foot (750-m²) rooftop in the SoHo section of Manhattan to a small backyard in Brooklyn. I found myself with a garden space shaded by the brownstone buildings on the block behind my 21-by-45-foot (6.5-by-14-m) outdoor space; by my own townhouse; and also by several weed trees, including Norway and sycamore maples. There was morning sunlight in summer between 8 A.M. at the front of the lot and 2 P.M. at the back of the space, with dappled shade from the neighboring trees through the day. The garden was in various degrees of shade most of the time.

I was thrust into the shade, but that felt like home to me, and it was home to the plants that I have always found most fascinating. Who could resist the weird but lovable plants that attract me as much as they do beetles and other bugs? We (the bugs and I) are attracted to the same flowers that summon the bees, ones that are colorful and sweetly perfumed, but we cannot deny the appeal of strange brown flowers that smell funky. I am attracted to the view from soil level, and it seems I am not the only gardener who is eager to crouch down to peer into the nodding blossom of a snowdrop or crawl in the duff to discover the tiny flowers of spring-time. Perhaps this pursuit harkens back to the days when I played in the shadows beneath those giant shrubs in suburban New Jersey.

In 1995, I added another place to garden, one I have also written about extensively. This spot is an island in a river in the northwest corner of New Jersey, a place that looks quite a bit like New England. When I bought the property as a weekend retreat, I kept records of the temperatures. After all, we gardeners, like farmers, are weather-forecast junkies. The daytime temperature in an exurban garden is often as high as it is in New York City's Central Park, where the weather station is located. In the early days, it was usual for the nighttime summer temperatures to drop some 30 degrees. The plants and I loved it. Today, I have to have air conditioners in the windows, and it is rare for the numbers to dip like they did in the old days. Things have changed, sometimes quite violently—for example, hurricanes that blew inland, record-breaking snowfalls, rains, and droughts.

I have come to realize all too clearly that my garden in the northwest corner of New Jersey exists only at the pleasure of nature. But is what we call nature in the twenty-first century natural? When people face the events of the recent past, like tornadoes in Brooklyn, record-breaking droughts, or thunder snow in Kansas and lament, "Well, that's Mother Nature," I feel bad. It doesn't seem fair to blame her at all.

While people were suffering calamities, I had my own losses. I lost some old

trees, my woodland wildflower garden, and other plantings to floods from a hurricane and a tropical storm in 2011. Although my garden *is* on an island in a river, nothing of this magnitude had occurred in records I could find, and I hadn't seen evidence that pointed to anything as devastating having damaged old structures, trees, or land in the neighborhood.

There was a mill from the 1700s that straddled the river across the road from me. The mill burned down in 1936, but the stone foundation remained intact until 2011, when half of it was pushed over by the floodwaters. What to do?

The Australians have developed a progressive strategy for dealing with climate change: "protect, redesign, rebuild, elevate, relocate, and retreat." I am not sure which of those words I can embrace, but I might add one more: *proceed.*

Do One Thing

But where does one begin after such unexpected havoc? I've realized that when faced with an overwhelming problem (or just the annual arrival of spring, when everything in the garden is screaming for attention), one thing you can do is "one thing."

Pick a simple task, like repotting a plant from a broken container. Soon, you'll be on to the next thing, and then the next. For me, instead of looking at the devastation in its entirety after the flood, I turned my back on all of that and did my best to cover the roots of a young tree that had been exposed, then I repaired some cracks in the wall that helps to keep the river at bay.

After bad things happen, like a freak ice storm, I'll get out there and start to clean up, pick up fallen branches, turn debris into compost; one step at a time. Cleaning up makes me feel part of the life in the garden, a participant, a friend, and softens the sadness of loss. And doing one thing, then another, then another adds up.

A Gardener's Code of Ethics: Chemicals and Weeds

In relatively uneventful moments, when the weather is "normal" and the season progressing as hoped for, the act of gardening puts us at various crossroads where a decision must be made, and a path taken—or not. With climate change come new pressures from invasive species, many of which, whether plants, insects, or diseases, we've never seen before. For example, disease-carrying insects that formerly were held in check by frigid winters have killed whole areas of northern forests. And I have evidence, albeit anecdotal, that warmer-than-usual temperatures have allowed a few weeds to thrive in my gardens that the climate used to keep in check.

We gardeners are in a unique position to improve our environment. Certainly if we are making new plantings, we'll do that with an eye toward good health and vigor: plants, soil, and our health, too. You may consider developing your own code of ethics, as I have, as to whether to use chemicals and synthetic fertilizers.

I strive to go organic, using organic practices first. I feed plants with compost, kelp, and other nonchemical sources. As for problems, I go organic there, as

ABOVE The arched bridge in my New Jersey garden (pages 2–3) nearly disappeared during Hurricane Irene in 2011. No other event of this magnitude had been recorded in the area.

OPPOSITE ABOVE My garden is situated on an island in a river in the northwest corner of New Jersey. An 8-foot- (2.4-m-) high stone wall keeps the land in and, for the most part, the water out.

OPPOSITE BELOW The aftermath of the great flood caused by Irene was 2 feet (60 cm) of sand covering much of the plants and beds in my garden, mixed with stones, twigs, and chunks of wood.

well. Sometimes, thankfully rarely, I come up against an issue for which the cure is beyond my arsenal of "natural" remedies.

The subject of chemical usage—spurred by the wish to "fix" a problem, to feed and overfeed for a hoped-for outcome via artificial means—is probably one of the trickiest decisions a gardener will have to make. Organic gardening does not allow for any synthetic fertilizers, insecticides, fungicides, or herbicides. That does not mean there is no way to handle problems, but the cures must be "natural." For example, you might use vinegar as a weed killer or attack insects with a bacillus that infects and kills them.

I am almost organic (about 95 percent), almost pure. (Is almost organic like almost pregnant?) If I have exhausted organic curatives for a problem, I turn to another protocol, of which enlisting the least hazardous remedies is the primary tenet: a program known as Integrated Pest Management, or IPM.

The Tricky Topic of Chemical Intervention

The last thing you want to do is bring things to your garden that might compromise its health and biological integrity—like potentially hazardous chemicals, whether insecticides, herbicides, or fungicides. I, like many gardeners, have also added synthetic fertilizer to the list of harmful products.

I like to think (hope) that the day when homeowners turn to chemicals even

LEFT The sphinx moth is a fascinating visitor despite being the adult form of the voracious tomato hornworm. If you love birds, butterflies and moths, you've got to accept caterpillars.

RIGHT When allowed to take its course, nature keeps things in balance. In my own garden, a wasp controls the hornworm, and a particular black snake in my garden helps to keep rodents in check.

OPPOSITE ABOVE One of garden writer Margaret Roach's green "frogboys."

OPPOSITE BELOW Many shade gardeners are thwarted by slugs, but my island garden is bugged by snails. The mollusks love hostas, and there are times when the damage they cause has to be conscientiously managed.

before there is a problem is dying away, but many people see those weed-and-feed lawn grass commercials and still believe that so-called preventative measures are necessary, at least when it applies to their turf grass. Americans use an estimated 78 million pounds of insecticides, fungicides, and herbicides on their lawns, gardens, and homes per year, and this figure does not include commercial pest control and lawn-care professionals. Seventy-four percent of the households in the United States employ some kind of pesticide, and that number is increasing. In one recent study of children living in metropolitan areas, traces of horticultural chemicals were found in 99 percent of them.

Modern humans who prefer the no-kill route may go organic or at least adopt the principles of Integrated Pest Management, or IPM. I remember when this acronym meant nothing to most people, but now, gardeners, farmers, arboriculturists, and many homeowners recognize it. It's right up there with the doctors' philosophy of "first, do no harm." Following IPM guidelines can help reduce that staggering pesticide figure. As mentioned, unlike pure organic gardening, IPM allows for some pesticide use, but only as a very last resort.

The idea is observation first—to discover a potential problem before it gets out of control. Manage it early so you won't have to nuke it later when it probably is too late. If something shows up, turn to the least-toxic curative first, which might mean physical remediation—mechanical removal. You can pull out weeds by hand or squish a bad bug, and even a jet of water from the hose can be a pretty good way of dealing with many early onslaughts.

The use of chemicals, even organically based pesticides, should be the last choice, after all safer options fail. I mention organically based because a chemical that comes from a natural source is not necessarily safe. I can always tell/smell when someone has sprayed with pyrethrum, for instance; it is derived from a daisy-like flower. Natural or not, it will kill good and bad bugs alike (and maybe a philandering husband).

Before we act, or buy, we need to know the impact of the products we use in our homes and gardens, and choose carefully. Many people shop without even knowing that chemical formulations have labeling codes telling you what is scary to deadly. Look for these so-called signal words in order from lowest to highest toxicity: *caution*, *warning*, and *danger* (with *poison* also added on the scariest labels).

I have another suggestion in developing a strategy for pest and disease control: Get over it! I can live with some powdery mildew, unsightly whitish covering on leaves that rarely results in the death of a plant. Holes in hosta leaves? I can ignore a few of those, too.

Mollusks often attack plants in shade gardens. Slugs might be one of your issues. In the Brooklyn garden, I put old wood boards down on the path in the evening. The slugs sought refuge in the moist covering under the boards, and by morning, I could lift these and knock the slugs into the pond where they were quickly dispatched by the goldfish. Feeding the fish mitigated some of my guilt, and this helped to keep a balance between hostas, holes, and slugs.

I do not have many slugs, perhaps since they are outcompeted by the snails that live in the canal that connects the two branches of the river running around the island. When snails (my serious problem) get completely out of control—for instance, in one of those super-wet Junes—I turn to an actual pesticide. The pesticide contains iron phosphate, which breaks down into organic fertilizer and can be used safely around pets and wildlife. This control does not work as well as the conventional compound, metaldehyde, which as the package says is not safe around children or pets. I'm okay with knocking back most, if not all, of the snails and sparing the pets, kids, and me (snakes, frogs, and toads love slugs, by the way).

I do not want to get rid of all the bugs—in fact, most of us welcome wildlife to our gardens. If you love butterflies, please tolerate caterpillars and even plant their larval food along with flowers that attract adults. And, as my friend Neil Diboll of Prairie Nursery says, "Like birds? Then you better get used to bugs." Baby birds need protein, and the source of that is bugs. According to entomologist and author Doug Tallamay, chickadees catch between 6,240 and 10,260 caterpillars to fledge a single clutch of young. Consider that for a bird that weighs about a third of an ounce, something equivalent to four pennies.

Then there is the whole idea of beneficial insects—not the kind you buy and release, because that's another story, but the ones that come when conditions are right. Tomato hornworms often show up in my garden, the caterpillars that are the larva of the glorious sphinx moth, a pollinator that hovers like a hummingbird around flowers in the summer. Braconid wasps parasitize the voracious hornworms in no time. The wasp lays white eggs on the backs of a caterpillar, which immediately stops feeding. The eggs hatch and kill the larva. (Consider this: the tomato plant emits a hormone signal into the air that summons the wasp.)

Insecticides, though, are rarely pest-specific like that wasp. Kill the bad guys with sprays and you might be annihilating the good guys that come to help defeat the bad ones. So, you have to give even more thought to using a product that may eradicate the insect invader, but also harm the insect you welcome to your garden.

ABOVE Dried and brown in winter, the annual Japanese stiltgrass is the worst invader that has ever descended upon my garden. Preventing invasive aliens from becoming established—whether mile-a-minute, garlic mustard, kudzu, or other pests—is among a gardener's greatest challenges.

OPPOSITE ABOVE Not all aggressors are foreign. Poison ivy can be a problem, but it has a purpose—fighting erosion and bearing nutritious berries for wildlife.

OPPOSITE BELOW It's important to keep thugs in check, even if it is a native plant like *Anemone canadensis* with its invasive underground runners.

Weeds, Endless Weeds (A Tale of Two Invaders)

I have my weedy crosses to bear. I suspect you do, too. How can we sensibly, sanely fight back?

When I first came to my house in New Jersey, garlic mustard (*Alliaria petiolata*) was the major unwanted colonizer. I dispatched those biennial weeds by hand pulling, and if I had failed to dig any before they began to set their flower buds, I went around the garden with scissors and cut their flower heads off. I actually have been able to control this monster this way.

But many new weeds have moved into the garden, perhaps with the help of the changing climate. Japanese stiltgrass (*Microstegium vimineum*) does not show up, like the mustard, as an occasional seedling in a planting bed. This annual grass grows as thick as lawn and invades everything. It turns the roadsides in my county thick and shaggy tan in autumn. I've had floods in this garden (that probably brought more stiltgrass seed). While floods try my resolve, this weed was the first thing that made me consider giving up gardening.

Stiltgrass grows in dry soil and sunlight, but best in well-drained, moist sandy loam and shade. The grass grows in lawns, fields, and roadside ditches, and on stream banks—places disturbed by mowing, tilling, scouring, foot and hoof traffic, and flooding. Deer do not eat it, and since the deer have reduced populations of the naturally occurring local plants, there is less competition and more open area for the grass to take over. It is said that the plant has the allelopathic potential to chemically inhibit the germination of the seeds of neighboring local plants. Stiltgrass has wiped out most of the trillium that the deer missed in the mid-Atlantic states.

As with garlic mustard, it is best to know the weeds that come to your garden and understand their cycles. The wispy bamboo-like stems of the stiltgrass cannot be weed-whacked or sprayed in planting beds without harming desirable plants. The only way I can get rid of stiltgrass in garden beds, among precious plants, is by hand pulling.

Any missed plants should be allowed to grow and then pulled late in the summer, before they go to seed—because each plant can produce hundreds of seeds that remain viable in the soil for up to seven years. New plants will germinate from those seeds as soon as the soil around them is disturbed by weeding. So my first attack begins in spring by tweezing out the sprouting seedlings or scratching them off the surface with a hand cultivator. I then leave the overlooked plants alone until late in the summer.

I am amazed that my perseverance is helping; I can see that the weed is slowly being pushed back from the garden, although I realize I will never be completely free of it. Unfortunately, I look across the river and see that all the ground is still blanketed with stiltgrass. Yet there may be a hint of promise through a form of biological control. A very rare butterfly lays its eggs on the plants and the larva feed on it. It is my dream for the future, but the population of these insects is still very low. I live in hope.

Space Invaders: The Weed Wars

An "acclaimed horticulturist" has said, "Gardening should never be taken seriously. There are no rules."

I am sure that sounds reassuring to new gardeners, and I agree that gardening should be fun. But no rules? I've already proposed that one rule is to avoid chemical usage, or at least follow the guidelines of IPM. And here is another one: Never knowingly introduce a potentially invasive exotic species to the landscape. Not only would this be bad for the environment, it could mean a lifetime of weed work to eradicate a botanical monster.

A couple of brutes are perfect examples of this directive, and at the time of this writing were still sold at nearly every garden center and nursery: the chameleon plant (*Houttuynia cordata* 'Chameleon') and goutweed (*Aegopodium podagraria*).

Sometimes plants brought home from the garden center or even well-meaning gifts can be a menace. Most people like the idea of "pass-along plants." If someone has too much of a plant and begs you to take some, you can be pretty sure the plant is a brute. I call them "pass-along pests." Someone once brought me a pot of a coveted plant from his garden. Along with the desired plant in the pot was a sprig of green goutweed, and so: into the trash.

It is worth noting that both of these thugs—the chameleon plant and goutweed—are not native to the United States. *Houttuynia* originated in East and Southeast Asia, where it is used in cooking (another way to dispatch it, I suppose?). *Aegopodium* hails from Eurasia. Most of the botanical monsters I have encountered over the years have been accidental or intentional imports like these.

If I lived next to a wooded lot, state forest, or land preserve, I would stop my garden far short of that boundary, because garden plants have no place in a natural or mostly wild area. The places closer to my house are for the exotic plants—those I want to keep an eye on for their beauty and behavior. In all cases with exotics, I avoid those that have berries or are aggressive climbers, sprinters, or self-sowers.

But, I admit, not all aggressive plants are imports. There can be overly zealous plants that are technically local to your environment (for example, trumpet vine, which is local to my garden). However, one person's weed is another animal's lunch. Poison ivy has the greatest value of any woody vine: birds are attracted to the subtle edible white berries by the leaves' vivid autumn color. In the "wrong" place, the path, for instance, poison ivy is a scourge to humans—we are the only animals allergic to the vine. But the very fact that this "weed" creeps onto the path is its ecological importance. The vine has evolved to colonize disturbed land and fight erosion. We probably wouldn't have the sand dunes of Cape Cod without poison ivy.

So, should we welcome this plant and leave it be because it lived on our site before humans ever walked there? It's a decision we all have to make. I remove poison ivy (wearing disposable gloves) and discard it in the trash if it is in a planting bed or by the path, but I let it grow elsewhere. I have no second thoughts about dispatching a nonnative weed, but as for a native thug? Call me prejudiced, but I leave the indigenous local species whenever I can.

ABOVE I consider "native plant" to be a broad term. If I am looking for a plant that grows, or at one time grew, near my garden, I think "local," like doll's eyes (*Actaea pachypoda*), which grows within a ten-mile radius of my garden in New Jersey.

OPPOSITE ABOVE LEFT Some purists do not welcome selections or varieties of wild plants, like the white form of the eastern redbud tree (*Cercis canadensis* 'Alba'); they want species only.

OPPOSITE ABOVE RIGHT One reason I seek local plants is their relationship with the animals they coevolved with, for example bumble bees feeding on the nectar of the nodding or fragrant lady's tresses orchid (*Spiranthes cernua* var. *Odorata*).

OPPOSITE BELOW Gardeners in a suburb of Sydney, Australia, connected hedgerows of native plants (bush) at the rear of their properties to create wildlife corridors for creatures like the koala bear.

We all can make a difference by starting in our own backyard. By planting local species in our gardens—even if not exclusively—we encourage the wildlife that coevolved with these plants—indigenous insects, birds, reptiles, mammals. A continuous site could be created for these animals if neighbors banded together to create concentrated areas with local plants, and even better, if these places were connected to make even more beneficial highways and flyways.

Native or Not: Taking a Stand

You'd think the word *native* was black and white, native or not. But we have to accept that this is a bit fuzzy, as are all the terms referring to origins of plants. To many people, natural and native are synonymous. Is it contradictory for a garden that claims to be natural to be filled with exotic creatures? As I've said, natural to me is a style, and even the word *native* needs clarification.

There are native-plant purists in the United States who insist on growing North American species exclusively, and a few who stipulate that they be only local—those plants that have grown in a very limited area for thousands of years. Those who are wholeheartedly committed to native plants tend to not tolerate any mingling of native and exotic species. Some of these folks may reject cultivated varieties and certainly hybrids of native plants. (Many native-plant people have vegetable gardens, and most vegetables are not native to the places where they are cultivated—but that is a conundrum for another day.) The backlash gardeners who tend to mix native with exotic may judge the evangelists, as well, calling them "native-plant geeks."

I admire the devotion of the purists, and it is certainly a worthwhile thing to do. I'll do my best to at least tell you where I stand. I am a native-plant geek, but truth be told, I am a plant geek—period. If I could, I might try to have an all-local-plant garden. It is a noble thought, but there are just too many fantastic plants that feel comfortable in my surroundings and are too wonderful to resist growing. My horticultural compromise for not going wholly "native" has been to devote one area of the garden exclusively to local plants. Many indigenous species share the rest of the garden with cultivars (cultivated varieties) and well-behaved exotic species.

In the area I've set aside for local plants, I have some small shrubs and trees, ferns, and beloved woodland ephemerals. I like to say "local" when a plant is one I know grows or used to grow within a 10-mile radius of a site. So, the doll's eyes (*Actaea pachypoda*) in my woodland garden is indigenous to northwest New Jersey, and local to me. I cannot say that I have the actual identical genetic material in most cases, because I may have purchased the original plants at a nursery or from a catalog, but the plant is the same species as the ones that were once local, and I hope have similar provenance.

It can be important to know the location of the source, the genotype even within a single species. If you live in a cold climate and buy a native red maple, a plant that grows all throughout the eastern states and into Canada, but one that was propagated from trees in Florida, it may not thrive in your home site. The opposite,

ABOVE Local plants, such as American wintergreen (*Gaultheria procumbens*) can often be purchased at plant-sale fundraisers for conservation groups and botanical gardens.

OPPOSITE The late gardener Evelyn Adams of Wellesley, Massachusetts, taught Margaret Roach and me how to propagate trillium, turning one plant into many. She dug them up while still in flower, cut the root, and reset each piece with a growing point in the soil.

of course, is true with plants that are used to cold, sweltering in the heat of a southern location. I do my best to buy regionally indigenous plants from a source as close to my location as possible. If you are growing plants from seeds, do not collect them from the wild, but try to acquire them from a source in your area that has ethically and organically produced the seeds from propagated plants. You can collect seeds from your own plants, and propagate them in other ways, of course. Think global, shop (and prop) local.

Some Policies on "Wild"

What's wrong with a pretty alien plant invading? Only one plant can live in one spot at one time, so wherever that Queen Anne's lace or daisy or purple loosestrife is, something else isn't, and that original plant might have had a lot of other organisms depending on it. Purple loosestrife (*Lythrum salicaria*) is attracted to moist places, but it lifts the soil out of the water, which dries up wetlands. That means animals like amphibians could lose their breeding places because of an invading alien plant. The food and environmental chain leads right up to you and me.

When I came to northwestern New Jersey in 1995, there were woods with trees up to 150 years old. There was an active shrub layer at the edges, and in places that had not been cleared for farming or houses, there was a rich forest floor with many species of ferns and spring-flowering herbaceous plants. I used to visit a rocky outcrop along the river not far from here where there was a living catalog of some of the plants I love and hoped to grow.

Fifteen years on, those plants were gone. The rock had been covered by creeping myrtle (*Vinca minor*), which came from an adjacent property. In other parts of the woods, the deer browsed, nonnative earthworms destroyed the surface layer of duff, and weedy invaders finished the job. Worms came by accident—hitchhiking in plant soil, as ballast on ships, perhaps, or more recently when fishermen toss their leftover bait. Like many exotic invaders, they flourished without the natural checks and balances of their homeland. Now to see native flora, I have to visit a state forest preserve or a specialized botanical garden.

How does one discover what was or is local? There has been documentation of plants for specific areas across most of the United States. Some of the information has been digitized. Most is still in books in libraries. You can check with your state native plant society. There are surveys in my state of habitats and plant communities like the hardwood woodland of the mountains in the northwest, or of the wetland habitats of the Pinelands National Reserve, 1.1 million acres in the southern part of New Jersey.

If you find a list of indigenous plants for your particular area, you can narrow your options by learning about the plant communities to find the ones that will thrive in the shade and soil and moisture conditions of your gardens. For example, a survey of a nearby woodland might focus on moist places, rock outcroppings, or perhaps even vernal pools, which are wet in spring and dry for much of the year.

Making More Shade Plants

When I began my first shade garden, the palette of plants was pretty narrow, and the really interesting ones—the responsibly propagated woodlanders (ones that were not collected from the wild) were priced far out of reach. A gardener couldn't afford an instant drift of anything.

I've learned so much in the garden and continue to every day. I know what good soil looks and feels like. I know when and how to prune. I've gained skills for propagating the plants I want more of—taking one thirty-dollar wildflower, for instance, and making it into three or more. One version of that skill was handed down to me by a great gardener.

Years ago, writer Margaret Roach and I visited the late amateur gardener, Evelyn Adams, for our book *The Natural Habitat Garden*. We witnessed around a thousand blooming white trillium (*Trillium grandiflorum*) in her woodland garden. We asked Ms. Adams how she developed this stunning vision. It turned out that she began with one plant rescued from the old foundation of a ruined barn. Every year, she dug up some of the plants and divided the horizontal rhizomes by cutting them and replanting each section that contained a stem or "eye," a growing point for a future stem. Since the plants go dormant and disappear after they flower, finding the dormant roots later in the season would be difficult, so Ms. Adams propagated them while they were in flower.

Simple math—one plant becomes two or three. Two become four, eight, sixteen, and so on. I've tried that method for propagating these plants myself, digging them up while in flower, cutting or breaking the rhizome, and transplanting and watering them immediately: it works.

There is another reason that propagating special plants is important: We do not want plants that have been stolen from the wild, or even rare ones that have been collected from privately owned land (it is usually legal to dig up rare plants on one's own property to sell). When you acquire a species that has been legitimately propagated by a reputable nursery or native plant society member plant sale, you can make more, which not only saves you money, but also helps to reduce the demand on the wild.

Some native plant societies have rescue groups that collect species from land that is about to be developed. These plants may be offered for sale at fund-raisers. And who knows, you might be so successful at propagating more plants, you will be able to contribute some to the next wild-plant sale in your area.

Not Our National Floral Emblem

Trillium are among our most wonderful wildflowers. Species grow from coast to coast. Shouldn't this genus be our national floral emblem? Years ago, there was a proposal to select a living symbol. Senator Everett Dirksen (the "Honorable Mr. Marigold") nominated his favorite flower. However, a long-stem red hybrid tea rose was the winner.

A "NATIVE" GLOSSARY OF TERMS

The terms we use to refer to the origins of our plants, such as *native*, *indigenous*, *local*, *wild*, *alien*, and *exotic*, can be a bit fuzzy, not to say confusing. Unfortunately, except in the case of *local*, the words are used widely, generally, casually, and often in a variety of ways. You might hear that a plant is native to a very specific locality, but more commonly, to a continent. "I'm a native New Yorker," someone may say, but visiting China, the same person might say, "I'm American."

Local is specific. "Alien" and "exotic" mean that a plant did not come from the place where it currently resides; it's foreign in origin. The word *alien* is usually used disparagingly to describe an unwanted invader. *Exotic* is synonymous, yet it does not carry the same bias. There are some exotic plants we might *like* to have in our gardens: hostas, for example.

Native plant: The phrase *native plant* is often applied to species that originated in the forty-eight contiguous states, or most of North America into Canada. That is too broad to be a useful guide. A shrub from California, like flannelbush (*Fremontodendron californicum*), probably has less business being planted in a Kentucky garden than one like Japanese kerria (*Kerria japonica*)—see the box Botanical Cousins, page 41.

But the word is also used generally. For example, "this plant is native to Asia." In this case, to a broad part of the world, a continent.

Indigenous: I usually refer to indigenous plants as those originating in a specific region and climate. For instance, I would call plants that come from the mountains of the southeastern United States indigenous to that location and habitat type. *Indigenous* is a term to express regionality—to communicate a place of origin, or homeland. For example, "This plant is indigenous to the Mediterranean region." Informally, however, the word is used broadly, much like *native*: "All cacti are indigenous/native to the western hemisphere."

Local: I find the word *local* most specific and appealing. For want of a standard horticultural definition, I'd say plants described as local are ones that have inhabited a limited area, perhaps within a 10-mile radius of a specific location, for as long as we know—thousands of years or longer. It doesn't mean the plant only grows in that limited area, but it grows or grew near to your garden.

Wildflower: I hear the word *wildflower* used in the most casual ways, and I might do that in conversation as well. *Wildflower* or *wild plant* is a generic term, like *posy*. Plants that grow on their own in places that are not cultivated are generally called wildflowers. The word can also be applied in conversation to a precious local woodlander like a slipper orchid or concurrently to "naturalized" citizens from other continents, like oxeye daisies (*Leucanthemum vulgare*) and Queen Anne's lace (*Daucus carota*) from Europe, or escapees like the common orange daylilies that originated in Asia, went to Europe, got away from colonial gardens, and now grow along the roadsides. The packagers of wildflower seeds tend to be loose with their terms. They may call Queen Anne's lace wild. I call it invasive.

OPPOSITE The short-lived American columbine (*Aquilegia canadensis*) loves to seed itself in little rock crevices, gravel, or moss in light shade to filtered light. When happy, the plant will self-sow to become a perennial cluster that returns year after year.

A FEW OF MY FAVORITE THINGS

The place in New Jersey where my garden and I live is an islet, a little island in a river. The river valley, at 500 feet (150 m) above sea level, is nestled within some of the highest, oldest mountains (what Coloradans call *bumps*) of northwest New Jersey. The spot is eccentric, to say the least. The island in a wooded mountain area hosts several kinds of natural habitat types and plant communities. There are the river and canal, flood plain, swamp, and woodland shrub edge on less than 3 acres in a mixed hardwood forest.

Some of the animals that have visited the island include black bears, kingfishers, beavers, great blue herons, raccoons, opossums, spring peepers, pileated woodpeckers, green frogs, leopard frogs, toads, salamanders, blacksnakes, milk snakes, garter snakes, mourning doves, ruby-throated hummingbirds, goldfinches, gray catbirds, northern flickers, robins, blue jays, Carolina wrens, cardinals, chickadees, titmice, bluebirds, phoebes, northern orioles, mallards, wood ducks, wild turkeys, cedar waxwings, gray squirrels, chipmunks, brown bats, and to my consternation, woodchucks, Canada geese, and white-tailed deer. And this is two and a half miles from the Walmart.

The area in New Jersey where my garden lives has the greatest diversity of damsel- and dragonflies in the United States. There are 472 dragonfly species in the country (6,000 worldwide), and 145 have been observed in my county. These predators can fly forward and backward at up to 35 miles per hour (55 km/h) and hover for up to a minute. Eggs are laid in or near water, and the larvae, also called nymphs, may remain aquatic for up to four years, feeding on other insect larvae and even small fish. Living on an island, like many things in life, is both a blessing and a bane: I experience the beauty of the river as well as the exasperation when floods bring tons of sand, debris, and weed seeds.

Among the native trees that I can see from the house are green ash, sycamore, white pine, maple (red, sugar, and silver), black willow, sumac, alder, hornbeam or ironwood, dogwood, American elm, box elder, eastern hemlock, American linden, butternut, hickory, pignut, black cherry, and black walnut.

There is a huge list of herbaceous plants that grow in the shaded woodland understory in my area (and many of which are in my garden). Here are just some examples: arrow arum, false hellebore, skunk cabbage, lizard's tail, mayapple, jack-in-the-pulpit, perfoliate bellwort or merry bells, wild oats, toothwort, bloodroot, Virginia bluebell, columbine, Dutchman's breeches, cinnamon fern, dogtooth violet or trout lily, bigroot geranium, goldenseal, aster, trumpet honeysuckle, slipper orchid, great blue lobelia, northern maidenhair fern, false Solomon's seal, starry false Solomon's seal, rue anemone, miterwort, partridgeberry, phlox, spotted wintergreen, rattlesnake plantain, smooth Solomon's seal, spiderwort, spring beauty, impatiens jewelweed, trillium wakerobin, trumpet creeper, twinleaf, and a couple of violets.

An insect visitor and local plants in my garden include:

1 The male ebony jewelwing (*Calopteryx maculata*) is one of dozens of species of damselflies and dragonflies that live in my part of the United States.

2 Creeping partridge berry (*Mitchella repens*, detail)

3 Goldenseal (*Hydrastis canadensis*) in fruit

4 False Solomon's seal (*Maianthemum racemosa* [syn. *Smilacina racemosa*])

5 Starflower, star-flowered Solomon's seal, starry Solomon's seal, or little false Solomon's seal (*Mianthemum stellatum* [syn. *Smilacina stellata*])

6 Double bloodroot (*Sanguinaria canadensis* 'Multiplex', detail)

7 Spring beauty (*Claytonia virginica*, detail)

Plant cousins, or analogous species, from North America and Asia:

1 A variety of the North American smooth hydrangea, *Hydrangea arborescens* var. *radiata*

2 Fall color on a cultivar of *Hydrangea serrata* from Japan and Korea, and similar to the big-leaf hydrangea (*H. macrophylla*)

3 Twinleaf (*Jeffersonia diphylla*) from the eastern United States

4 Cousin Asian twinleaf (*J. dubia*)

5 *Pachysandra procumbens*, commonly known as Allegheny spurge, with fragrant flowers in spring

6 The variegated cultivar of Japanese spurge, *P. terminalis* 'Variegata', is better behaved than the vigorous species.

7 North American mayapple (*Podophyllum peltatum*), photographed on a wild part of my property

8 The colorful spring leaves of the Chinese mayapple (*Podophyllum delavayi*)

··

BOTANICAL COUSINS

A magnolia collector I know showed me a fossil of a leaf that was 15 million years old. The fossil was found in the United States, and the leaf closely resembled the sweet bay magnolia (*Magnolia virginiana*). Magnolias are ancient flowering plants believed to have appeared before bees. There are around eighty known species. Some originated in North, Central, and South America, and many come from Asia.

You may have noticed that lots of our shade-garden plants come from Asia, with very similar counterparts in North America. In many cases, like the magnolias, these plants have been categorized as being two species in the same genus. The list of analogous plant species is huge, with cousins growing here and, often, in Japan.

One logical conclusion is that these landmasses were once connected. The best known among the super-continents of the past was Pangaea, which broke apart during the Cretaceous period, between 145 and 66 million years ago, when the continents we recognize today began to appear. Many plants share common lineage, probably dating back to the days before continental drift.

Temperate climates are in between tropical and polar regions. Technically, frost-free subtropical areas like coastal Florida and California are temperate, but I'm mostly referring to places that have cold winters and warm summers. Northeast China has the most diverse number of plant species in the temperate world. The area with the second most species is the ancient mountain ranges of the southeastern United States, such as in the Great Smoky Mountains. A special example of botanical cousins could be the only two species on earth of twinleaf, or *Jeffersonia*. One is *J. diphylla* from eastern North America (Tennessee up to Ontario), and the other is *J. dubia* from China (Manchuria east to Korea and Japan). Consider the common pachysandra as well. The Asian *Pachysandra terminalis* is Japanese spurge. Allegheny spurge, *P. procumbens*, is from the eastern United States.

Below is a list of some familiar genera with species found in both Asia and North America.

You may be surprised by how much Latin you already know: Many common plant names are also the scientific names, which are all in Latin, of the plants. For example, rhododendron, hydrangea, and magnolia.

Acer—maple
Adiantum—maidenhair fern
Clematis—clematis
Cornus—dogwood
Hydrangea—hydrangea
Juniperus—juniper
Lilium—lily

Magnolia—magnolia
Pinus—pine
Polygonatum—Solomon's seal
Rhododendron—rhododendron
Sambucus—elderberry
Trillium—trillium
Viburnum—viburnum

TRILLIUM AND *PARIS*

The genus *Trillium* gets its name from the tripartite nature of the plant, which has leaves, sepals, and petals in segments of three. These precious woodlanders are found in most of the United States, with the greatest number of diverse species in the Southeast. All have the form that gives them their name. The flowers have three petals that may be white, pink, red, cream, brown, or green. The single flower rises in a whorl atop the three-part leaves, either directly, as in the stemless sessile group, or on short or nodding stems. The leaves may be solid green or handsomely mottled.

There are more than three dozen North American trillium species and one from Japan, *Trillium camschatcense*. Closely related genera include several species of *Paris* from Europe and Asia, and *Daiswa* and *Kingugasa* from eastern Asia (some taxonomists consider these to be in the genus *Paris*, as well). Instead of leaves in a set of three like the *Trillium*, these allied genera usually have four leaves and tiered multiples of four.

Trillium albidum
Trillium angustipetalum
Trillium apetalon
Trillium camschatcense
Trillium catesbaei
Trillium cernuum
Trillium chloropetalum
Trillium cuneatum (1)
Trillium decipiens
Trillium decumbens
Trillium discolor
Trillium erectum (red form)
Trillium erectum 'Alba' (white form) (2)
Trillium flexipes (3)

Trillium foetidissimum
Trillium gracile
Trillium grandiflorum (4)
Trillium grandiflorum 'Flore Pleno' (5)
Trillium grandiflorum 'Roseum' (6)
Trillium kurabayashii
Trillium lancifolium
Trillium ludovicianum
Trillium luteum (7)
Trillium maculatum
Trillium nivale
Trillium ovatum
Trillium ovatum 'Klinger Double' (8)
Trillium parviflorum

Trillium pusillum
Trillium recurvatum (9)
Trillium rugelii
Trillium sessile (10)
Trillium simile
Trillium stamineum
Trillium sulcatum
Trillium tschonoskii
Trillium underwoodii
Trillium undulatum
Trillium vaseyi
Trillium viridescens
Paris polyphylla (11)
Paris quadrifolia (12)

RIGHT Red trillium (*Trillium erectum*) in my woodland garden's local-plant bed with companions, including the pink flowers of *Geranium maculatum*, which has common names like spotted, wild, or wood geranium and cranesbill (for the shape of its dry fruits).

PART 3

GOT SHADE? TAKING A CLOSER LOOK

DEGREES OF SHADE

PREVIOUS SPREAD Sunlight streams through a spider web in the needles of a white pine tree.

TOP A vivid crimson rhododendron among the hybrids in light shade at Rocky Hills in Mount Kisco, New York.

LEFT A hybrid Solomon's seal (*Polygonatum × hybridum*) in filtered light is a cross between *P. multiflorum* and *P. odoratum* and is more floriferous than either species.

RIGHT Unlike other malodorous species for light to medium shade, the elegant *Arisaema candidissimum*, which may flower white or pink by individual, has a vanilla scent.

OPPOSITE Small trees and large shrubs in a Brooklyn version of the understory include a pink-flowered variegated dogwood (*Cornus florida* 'Cherokee Sunset') and white double-file viburnum (*V. plicatum* f. *tomentosum*).

We know what sunlight is, and many of us gardeners have grown vegetables or annuals in a sunny cutting garden. Full sunlight is 100 percent during the daylight hours—there's no variation, or degree, of full sunlight. But what about shade? Is shade simply the opposite of sun?

I once gardened on an exposed "tar-beach" rooftop in SoHo, which felt like the plains of Georgia in summer and a Colorado mountaintop in winter. Then I moved to a shady backyard in Brooklyn. Back in the eighties, there were only a few books on shade gardening, and I read them. I also referenced mail-order catalogs and nursery tags that had printed symbols representing the light needs of plants, from full sun to shade.

I quickly discovered that the Brooklyn garden had more than one kind of shade. The plants taught me. In one area, flowering perennials did pretty well, but in another, the same plants grew tall and leggy and did not blossom at all. In those shadier places, some other plants thrived, but in other areas of the garden, the same plants wilted during the middle of the day, and the leaves turned brown. I wasn't dealing with the opposite of sun; I was experiencing various degrees of shade.

Unlike that single intense full sunlight, there are many kinds of shade to be encountered and understood, each with its distinct set of possibilities or limitations.

Learning the Light

Labeling in some nurseries can be misleading. Optimistic commercial growers make reference to light with symbols: sun (open circle), partial shade (circle, half

THE FOREST HIERARCHY

When considering the shade, we look to woodlands as our model. Plants in deciduous forests grow in layers—categories based mostly on their height and plant type and whether they are woody or herbaceous. The stems of the woody plants get hard as they mature, and leaves emerge from the previous year's growth. These deciduous plants do not die to the ground in autumn; they stay alive and go dormant in winter. In the spring, they add new growth, and this goes on year after year. The herbaceous plants have soft tissues, and they melt away when the frost comes. The herbaceous perennial plants return year after year.

The **canopy**, the uppermost part of the forest, is the treetop layer. Various combinations of hardwood species dominate the forests of the eastern half of the country; trees growing from 60 to 100 feet (20 to 30 m) in height include oak, maple, beech, hickory, linden, walnut, and sweet gum (and, in the past, elm and chestnut—both decimated by disease). In Vermont, you'll find lots of sugar maples, but in Virginia, there may be many more oaks. There might also be evergreens like pines and hemlock and vines that use the trunks and branches of their hosts for support.

Collectively, the plants below the treetops are referred to as the understory layers. The next layer beneath the canopy is made up of young sapling trees, as well as smaller species like serviceberry, sourwood, dogwood, birch, and redbud. Mingling with the smaller trees and growing beneath them are the bushy woody plants of the middle, or **shrub layer**. These plants have multiple stems coming up from the ground—for example, deciduous species like viburnum, witch hazel, shrubby dogwoods, hydrangea, azalea, and fothergilla. There are acid-soil-loving mountain laurel, azalea, and blueberry.

Next layer down are the herbaceous perennials that grow through the warm seasons. There could be plants in a clearing, ones that want a bit more sunlight and grow 1 to 2 feet (30 to 60 cm), or even taller. These might include certain ferns, sedges, and late-spring-through-autumn-blooming forbs: nongrass, flowering herbaceous plants like asters and goldenrod.

The very bottom of the woodland understory, the **forest floor**, is the place for creeping, ground-hugging covers, mosses, and moss-like plants. In spring there are plants that appear and blossom early, before the leaves on the deciduous trees of the canopy have fully emerged. These "spring ephemerals" are among the most precious jewels of the shade we hope to grow, nurture, and cherish.

OPPOSITE The hierarchy, from top to bottom begins with the tall trees of the canopy, then beneath them, the small understory trees and tall shrubs like pink-shell azalea, (*Rhododendron vaseyi*), and closest to the ground, the ferns and woodland ephemerals of the forest floor.

white, half black), and shade (black circle), but unwitting consumers might be easily misled by such generalizations. One could believe that a black circle means the plant doesn't need any light at all. Plants can't grow in the dark, of course; every plant needs light for photosynthesis. Unfortunately, I've seen tags for this full-shade situation on plants that I know from my own garden love sun. They may be able to survive with less, but I am certain they will not thrive without any direct sunlight.

All-day sun in summer could be fourteen hours. Does that mean that the half-blackened circle represents a half-day of sun, seven hours? Imagine a clearing in the woods with just a few trees allowing seven hours of direct sunlight to reach the plants. That would be some pretty sunny shade. You could grow roses there. But I have read that situation simply described as "shade." So confusing!

If you ask someone how they would describe filtered light, you might hear anything from what's beneath a canopy of tree leaves to what is viewed through frosted glass. What is partial shade? That's more baffling still. I could refer to "high shade" under trees that have had their bottom limbs removed. "Indirect sunlight" could denote the slanted bands of light early in the morning or late in the afternoon, or as the sun sets low in autumn and winter, slicing below the limbs of an evergreen tree.

Count on this: The characteristics of shade in your garden will change throughout the year. You have to remember the constantly shifting conditions through the seasons, that things will change over time, and you must make adjustments when possible. Plant a little tree and you will have a little bit of shade from it, but as that tree grows, the shade grows too. If a plant that was doing well beneath the growing tree begins to struggle, you can move it to a place with more light. If a tree that shaded your garden comes down in a storm and instantly turns a shady spot into a sunny one, plants may have to be moved.

And the quality of these types of shade will be different depending on the part of the country where your garden lives. The mountains, with clear air, may feel the sun more powerfully than city gardens. The sun is stronger the closer one gets to the equator, and that will even be noticed in variations between the southern and northern parts of the United States. Sunlight in Maine might not be as strong as it is in Louisiana. But far-north gardens may experience longer hours of daylight and bright light in summer, if not intense sun and heat. It's very important to take into account that light is cumulative—a little bit of direct sun, reflected light, and hours of bright light add up to a good amount of photosynthesis for a plant. But wherever you are, full midday sun is more intense than early-morning or late-afternoon sun.

The degrees of shade in the garden tell you only the amount of light an area will receive—one factor that can support or challenge a plant trying to establish a foothold and grow successfully. Of course there are other considerations, such as moisture, or lack of it, in the soil. Again, dry shade is the bane of the gardener who plants near trees. Some deciduous trees—for example, most maples—have shallow roots that steal much of the moisture. On the other hand, oaks tend to have deep roots and plants growing beneath them will have less competition for moisture. In the end, your own observations will guide you to your garden's actual qualities of light.

There are many more variations of shade than those nursery tags describe—

partial shade and full shade. Those symbols on plant tags should not be taken as end-all-be-all guides. Before planning a new planting, think about what might be called the degrees of shade. I hope the following will be a helpful guide for describing the types of light you might encounter. At the least, my intent is to be more specific than the black and half-black circle and more representative of what you might actually have.

Light Shade (LS): Around six hours of direct sunlight at the height of summer. These places might look like the open edge of the woodland. Or they could be washed in hours of unobstructed morning and afternoon sunlight and none at midday.

Filtered Light (FL): Four to six hours of sun, or light that passes through the foliage of a tree with broadly spaced branches and delicate pinnate or bipinnate feathery foliage, such as a paloverde or mimosa. This might be a place under a few high-limbed deciduous trees or below an open structure like a pergola with widely spaced crossbeams.

Medium Shade (MS): Two to four hours of direct sunlight, or light all day beneath a translucent cover, screen, or shade cloth (which comes in varying densities blocking different percentages of light), and in a garden beneath a grove of limbed-up trees

ABOVE The place where the meadow meets the forest is home to a wide variety of flowering and fruiting shrubs. In the home landscape, that equivalent area might be the edge of a lawn, where light shade and filtered light pass into the shady depths.

RIGHT Tiny fluttering leaves like the bipinnate dark red feathery mimosa's (*Albizia julibrissin* 'Summer Chocolate') allow light to reach plants below.

BELOW In Jeanne Will's former garden, areas of varying light were home to plants that liked those conditions, and sometimes more light was welcomed into the scene in the form of a chartreuse Japanese forest grass (*Hakonechloa macra* 'All Gold').

LEFT A botanical symphony of herbaceous perennial, bulb, shrub and fern genera in filtered light, including *Lilium*, *Paeonia*, *Podophyllum*, *Rhododendron*, and *Lamprocapnos*, prepare for their crescendo at the Elisabeth C. Miller Botanical Garden in Seattle, Washington.

BELOW The walk to the front door of Mark Veeder's home in New York is gloriously enhanced by light-to-medium-shade plants beneath high-limbed trees.

(see the box, Modifying Shade, Amplifying Light, page 64). This kind of light could be found under a lath house roof over a structure in a sun-exposed site with a ceiling made of slats of wood evenly spaced with openings to the sky. As the earth turns, sunlight streams across the lath, creating moving shadows on the foliage below. Medium shade might also be found beneath a pergola when it is covered with a small-leafed vine like American wisteria (*Wisteria frutescens*). We might think of this as dappled shade where the light is constantly fluttering.

ABOVE The mesh used for window screens can be stretched over structures to gently filter the sunlight. Commercial greenhouse shade cloth (shown) which comes in various densities and percentages of diffusion, can also be used to soften the light.

BELOW Translucent fiberglass will filter light while keeping an area dry for some potted plants and entertaining.

OPPOSITE ABOVE Grapevines on an elevated frame produce medium to full shade for a cool spot in landscape architect James David's Austin, Texas, garden.

OPPOSITE BELOW A pergola with widely spaced horizontal members creates a minimal filter of sunlight while adding an architectural element to the landscape.

Shade (full) (SH): Two hours or fewer of direct sunlight, or up against the north-facing side of a building, or places in the corners of buildings, grottos, and the like. (The very deepest shade is a challenge to plants, and, of course, none can grow in the dark.)

Urban locations often have buildings all around, but they might still enjoy an unobstructed passage to the sky. Add to that brightness by painting surfaces pale colors to reflect light back to the plants throughout the day (see the box, Modifying Shade, Amplifying Light, page 64).

Woodland Shade (WS): Areas under deciduous trees, where sunlight is full from midfall through winter and into midspring before tree leaves have fully unfurled, but then in shade for the rest of the season. Some of the shade-tolerant broadleaf evergreen shrubs, such as aucuba, skimmia, and rhododendron, may also thrive in woodland shade. Such evergreens, especially those growing in warm climates, like camellias and tea olive (*Osmanthus fragrans*), can absorb light and photosynthesize during the winter whenever the temperatures are above 45 degrees Fahrenheit (7 degrees Celsius).

OPPOSITE Exterior walls can be painted pale colors to reflect light, which is particularly useful in urban locations. A small-leaved *Magnolia grandiflora* is espaliered on the painted brick side of a house.

ABOVE The north-facing side of a building can be challenging with only bright light, but this variegated *Hydrangea macrophylla* thrives a few feet away from a low building wall.

ABOVE Woodland shade is the best place for some of our most precious wildflowers, like orchids. Hybrid tulips provide temporary color and typically only bloom the first season after planting.

RIGHT Woodland shade in early spring allows sunlight to reach the ephemerals before the leaves on the trees of the canopy have emerged. Many of the forest floor plants grow, blossom, make fruits, and ripen seeds by the time the light is filtered by a full leafy cover.

PUBESCENCE, A HIGHLIGHT IN SHADE

Most of us are familiar with the appearance of plants at the end of the growing season, what botanists call senescence. We love the brilliant fall colors of deciduous trees, and the faded parts of herbaceous plants can be attractive elements in winter as well. For example, the seed heads of some perennials after a killing frost in autumn, or fertile fronds of certain ferns.

Too few gardeners notice new growth on plants in the garden, and especially the shade garden. Along with the emerging woodland plants in spring, there are many perennials, shrubs, and later, trees, that exhibit often-overlooked colorful foliage and interesting shapes. Although these aspects of the garden are fleeting, they are nonetheless worth looking for, and perhaps planning for, to begin your visual enjoyment even earlier in the year than peak spring. The new growth of rhododendrons, especially subtropical species, is often exquisite; it may be downy or furry or even colorful. *Disporum cantoniense* 'Night Heron' grows from 3 to 5 feet (1 to 1.5 m) tall and has small chartreuse to yellow flowers, but the attraction is its new growth in spring—deep maroon. And nearly every fern's emerging bishop's crook crosier is fascinating from the moment it appears and unfurls in spring.

LEFT A selection of *Disporum cantoniense*, found and named 'Night Heron' by plantsman Dan Hinkley, has maroon-brown new growth and chartreuse flower buds.

RIGHT Many rhododendron species have spectacular young foliage early in the growing season, especially subtropical species like *R. kesangiae* in Richie Steffen's zone 8 garden.

LEFT Epimediums are chosen for flowers and foliage, which in some varieties lasts through the winter—both of which are evident in the hybrid *E*. × 'Pink Champagne'.

RIGHT Perhaps the most challenging situation for a gardener is dry shade, where the roots of the trees casting the shade are also stealing moisture. Among the best plants for this situation are species and varieties of *Epimedium*, like *E*. × *cantabrigiense* surrounding *Leucojum aestivum*, the spring flowering bulb paradoxically named summer snowflake.

Dry Shade

The bane of the shade garden and shade gardener is dry shade, usually caused by competition from nearby trees. The fine roots of established trees take moisture from the soil and they will be a lot better at doing this than the new plants we'll be installing around them. One of the most challenging places to garden is in the shade of evergreens, and especially those with low-hanging branches. In this spot, where both light and moisture are limited, your choice of plants for the understory will be limited, as well.

I have an old Norway spruce in my New Jersey garden. I removed a few of the lowest branches and pruned a few others back so I could make my way beneath them. But in the dry shade there—a very challenging type of shade—I have managed to find plants that have done well. For example, I grow dainty fairy bells (*Disporum sessile*), wild ginger (*Asarum canadense*), the vigorous ostrich fern (*Matteuccia struthiopteris*) and blue cohosh (*Caulophyllum thalictroides*) in the spruce's shadows.

Plants with water-storing adaptations in their leaves and stems, like succulents, aren't available in the shade, for the most part. There are plants, like bulbs, that store moisture in other ways. Some plants might surprise us, like the aggressive ostrich fern. Perhaps this is the place where trial and error is the guide. Opposite is a list of some plants to try in this challenging situation.

Plants for Dry Shade

PERENNIALS

Acanthus hungaricus—acanthus, bear's breeches

Acanthus mollis—acanthus, bear's breeches

Acanthus spinosus—acanthus, bear's breeches

Actaea rubra—red baneberry

Asarum canadense—wild ginger

Asarum caudatum—wild ginger

Brunnera macrophylla—Siberian bugloss

Convallaria majalis—lily of the valley

Dicentra formosa—western bleeding heart

Disporum spp.—fairy bells

Epimedium spp. and varieties—bishop's hat, barrenwort

Euphorbia amygdaloides var. *robbiae*—wood spurge, Mrs. Robb's Bonnet

Geranium macrorrhizum—bigroot geranium

Helleborus spp.—hellebore

Heuchera americana—coral bells

Iris foetidissima—stinking iris

Ophiopogon spp.—mondo grass

Oxalis oregana—redwood sorrel

Pachyphragma (syn. *Thlaspi*) *macrophyllum*—pachyphragma

Polygonatum spp.—Solomon's seal

Rohdea japonica—rohdea, lily of China

Saxifraga stolonifera—strawberry begonia, strawberry geranium

Sedum oreganum—Oregon stonecrop

Sedum ternatum—wild stonecrop

Maianthemum racemosum—false Solomon's seal

Maianthemum stellatum—starry false Solomon's seal and others

Thalictrum occidentale—western meadow rue

Thalictrum pubescens—tall meadow rue

Tolmiea menziesii—piggyback plant

Trachystemon orientalis—Abraham-Isaac-Jacob

Trillium spp.—trillium

Vancouveria hexandra—inside-out flower

SHRUBS

Aucuba japonica—Japanese aucuba, spotted laurel

Azara microphylla—boxleaf azara

Berberis darwinii—Darwin's barberry

Buxus sempervirens—American boxwood

Camellia japonica—camellia

Cornus alba—red-twig dogwood

Cornus stolonifera—red osier dogwood

Eleutherococcus sieboldianus 'Variegatus'—aralia

Euonymus fortunei—wintercreeper

× *Fatshedera lizei*—tree ivy, aralia ivy

Fatsia japonica—fatsia, glossy-leaved paper plant

Garrya elliptica—silk-tassel shrub

Gaultheria shallon—Oregon wintergreen

Ilex crenata—Japanese holly

Kerria japonica—Japanese kerria

Lonicera nitida—boxleaf honeysuckle

Luma apiculata—Chilean myrtle

Mahonia spp., varieties and hybrids—grape holly

Myrica californica—Pacific wax myrtle

Nandina domestica—heavenly bamboo

Osmanthus spp.—sweet olive

Paxistima myrtifolia (syn. *P. myrsinites*)—Oregon boxwood

Pittosporum tobira—Japanese pittosporum, Japanese mock-orange

Rhododendron macrophyllum—Pacific rhododendron

Rhododendron ponticum—common rhododendron

Ruscus aculeatus—butcher's broom

Sarcococca spp.—sweet box

Skimmia japonica—Japanese skimmia

Vaccinium ovatum—evergreen huckleberry

Viburnum opulus 'Nanum'—dwarf American cranberry bush

Xanthorhiza simplicissima—yellowroot

BULBS

Arum italicum—Italian arum

Cyclamen coum—hardy cyclamen

Cyclamen hederifolium—ivy-leaf cyclamen

Cyclamen purpurascens—purple cyclamen

CONIFERS

Chamaecyparis obtusa—hinoki cypress, Japanese cypress

Cryptomeria japonica—Japanese cedar

Podocarpus spp. and varieties—yew pine, podocarpus

Sequoia sempervirens 'Prostrata'—prostrate coast redwood

Taxus spp.—yew

Thuja plicata—western red cedar

Tsuga canadensis—Canadian hemlock

FERNS

Blechnum chilense—Chilean hard fern

Dryopteris spp.—shield fern

Gymnocarpium dryopteris—western oak fern

Osmundastrum claytoniana—interrupted fern

Polypodium spp.—common polypody

Polystichum spp.—Christmas fern and others

SHADIEST OF THE SHADY

Those most challenging spots, versions of full shade (SH), aren't just encountered on the north side of a house or under trees, but can also be found in the shadows of the leaves of shrubs and perennials.

While I was trimming a dwarf-climbing hydrangea that had covered the dry-stone wall in the gravel garden, I uncovered a strawberry begonia (*Saxifraga stolonifera*). I had planted it in a bit of soil among the rocks, and years later, it is thriving (in the age of climate change). This plant was growing without a lick of sunlight, with barely any bright light. Even more amazing, it was blooming. Not long ago, I would only have thought of growing this plant indoors, since most books claim it will not be hardy in the garden.

Glass filters light waves so plants that we have growing in our homes near windows, even in bright sunlight, are generally shade tolerant in the outdoors, and any cold-hardy ones could possibly be candidates for the outdoor garden.

Ivy varieties, for example, are incredibly shade tolerant, but remember that the species English ivy (*Hedera helix,* not including many well-behaved varieties) is an invasive thug and should not be planted near any open woodland (or trees or houses) where it will take over the forest understory and climb up anything vertical. Stay away from other *Hedera* ivy species, as well, for instance: Algerian ivy (*H. canariensis* var. *algeriensis*), Irish ivy (*H. hibernica*), and colchis ivy (*H. colchica*).

OPPOSITE The shadiest spot is next to and underneath the deck in garden designer Bill Fidelo's Brooklyn garden.

LEFT Strawberry begonia is one common name for *Saxifraga stolonifera*, which is growing and blooming here in the dense shade of a dwarf climbing hydrangea.

CENTER Dwarf variegated ivy (*Hedera helix* 'Goldheart') tolerates deep shade and does not have the invasive characteristic of the species from which it was selected. It has been gently growing on this ash tree for more than fifteen years.

RIGHT One of the best evergreen shrubs for dry shade is *Aucuba japonica*. There are many varieties, such as those with slender or wide green leaves; green leaves edged in yellow or yellow leaves edged in green; leaves splashed in gold; or some combinations of all of the above.

MODIFYING SHADE, AMPLIFYING LIGHT

Shade comes in various forms, as we've seen, but it can also be modified in many ways. You may want to create more shelter from the sun by planting trees. Or you might care to open up some places that have nice trees but seem a bit too close and dark. Deciduous trees may have their lower limbs removed by a professional to let more sunlight stream in from the sides. The term for this is "limbing-up."

You can also amplify the light. For example, I set up some mirrors to reflect the light in the darkest parts of the Brooklyn garden, but experience has shown me that pale-colored paint works even better. Rather than reflecting a little ray of light, or the green plants back to themselves, the paint bounces and spreads any ambient light into the larger area.

Some commercial paint companies list the reflection ratings of products in their descriptions. It might surprise you that the ratings of some colorful pastel tints of paint are actually more reflective than some popular whites. A reflective pale tint of terra-cotta could be as beneficial as bright white.

Plants are mostly green because that is the color of visible light that they reflect. The leaves absorb the colors we do not see when we look at them. Logic tells me that if plants reflect green light, they do not need it, and instead, want the light waves seen on the opposite side of the color wheel: the complementary color to green. That hue is magenta or red. But there are plenty of light waves that we humans do not see that plants might. We can boost red light for plants, as some people do with red plastic film used as reflective mulch below their tomato plants.

ABOVE There are ways to modify shade, for example when the lower limbs of trees are pruned away to let in more light.

OPPOSITE In shady gardens, pale painted walls can function as reflectors of light onto plants like this near-black columbine hybrid.

Testing the Degrees of Shade

Of course, we want our plants to not just survive, but to thrive, to grow strong and larger every year and to produce lush leaves and flowers. How can we tell which plants will tolerate shade and which version of shade is right for them?

Just as plants grow in various climates around the world, they thrive in various conditions in our gardens. We gardeners want to and may even need to test them by pushing and prodding them into surviving (if not thriving) in less light or more or less moisture than they like in nature. The results may not be what we hope. In general, plants pressed to grow in less light than there was in their natural environment, or even in the sunny rows of the nursery, will stretch, grow leggy, producing thinner stems with more space between their leaves. Some of these plants that stand straight in sunlight, such as the sky pencil Japanese holly (*Ilex crenata* 'Sky Pencil'), may grow toward the source of the brightest light and need staking in shade.

It is unlikely that we will be pushing a deep shade lover into light shade. If that happened, the plant might grow more compact, but the leaves would likely wilt, and in some cases burn, their edges turning brown. In the worst case, the plant could crisp up and die. If we really ask too much of a plant, stress may make the individual more susceptible to diseases or insect attacks. We have to be realistic.

You may have to learn more about your situation by observation and perhaps testing the shade. You could assess the intensity of sunlight around your house by carrying a light meter (but who has a light meter anymore?). There are phone apps for this, meant to tell you about camera settings. But you can also just look at your garden spaces. Check full sun, check full shade, and see if you can discover levels in between. Make detailed observations during the day (and throughout the growing season), such as: What are the times of day when sunlight hits the place where you hope to have the garden? Is there bright light for most of the day? What is the breeze like and the dominant direction of the wind? Keep track in a note-

OPPOSITE One way to judge the light in a garden is to look at the way plants behave. Simple daylily hybrids will bloom in light shade, but the fanciest new ones need full sun.

ABOVE In filtered light, the stems of smooth hydrangea Annabelle (*Hydrangea arborescens* 'Annabelle') will support their fluffy flowers, but tall lilies will need to be tied to stakes.

book or computer file. And remember, light is cumulative. You may see some sun in one place in the morning, and check back through the day to see if sunlight also streams in again later in the day. Of course, if the sun sets behind a building, it will be blocked. However, if a building across the way is a pale color, light might reflect off that and back to the plants facing that direction.

Or sometimes you can judge the light levels by noting what else grows in one place or another—for instance, fairly thick lawn (which requires quite a bit of sunlight) or moss (which can survive with much less light) or another indicator. Weeds can tell you about the amount of sun or shade in a proposed planting site. Thistles need full sun, clover likes light shade to full sun, violets will grow in the lawn in light shade.

You can also test the sunlight and brightness using garden plants. If you have a fancy-named hybrid daylily in your garden that is blooming in spite of a lack of full sunlight, you probably are looking at the brilliant, most optimistic version of light shade. If you have a fancy daylily that is not flowering, or is small and puts out a couple of flowers at best, you may have a challenging situation for it. However, if you observe the common orange daylily species, which is called tawny or ditch lily (*Hemerocallis fulva*), you might have filtered light or medium shade. This plant and other daylily species are more shade tolerant than most of the modern hybrids.

Another test might be to buy a sun-loving hanging basket of annuals in full flower in the late spring. Suppose you get a planter of ivy-leaved geranium (*Pelargonium peltatum*) and the *Calibrachoa* hybrid 'Million Bells'. If that container continues to blossom for weeks, you've got sun. If the flowers diminish in number over time but still form buds and bloom, you may have light shade or filtered light. If the plant stops blooming, grows spindly, or even dies, you're most likely looking at shade.

Chances are pretty good that you already knew that.

Who Wants Shade?

You can't *always* tell whether a plant wants sunlight or shade just by looking at it, although you often can. The sun-loving plants usually have small leaves arranged in whorls around the tall stems. The leaves are spaced farther apart in spirals and do not overlap each other. The shade lovers tend to have larger leaves that are rarely thick or, like ferns, are lacy and in aggregate cover a large area to absorb light. These plants usually also emerge in spiraling whorls, but that may not be easy to see since quite often the leaf petioles (stems) emerge from basal rosettes nearly at ground level. Not only that, the shade plant leaves may overlap each other and can tolerate shading the ones below.

The tall sun lovers could have evolved in the American prairie. Other plants, like herbs or succulents, might have come from sunbaked hillsides in the Mediterranean region or the drylands of the Southwest. Some of these plants hold moisture in thick leaves or are covered with waxy coatings, powder, or tiny hairs to protect them from the effects of desiccating winds. The shade plants, on the other hand, usually originated in humid, sheltered places and do not need to conserve mois-

ABOVE Leaves that grow in the shade might be either solid and broad (like *Darmera peltata*) to gather as much light as possible, or be finely divided, like ferns, to cover as much territory as they can.

OPPOSITE ABOVE In some cases, gorgeous leaves may attract as much attention as flowers, and they certainly last longer. Umbrella leaf (*Diphylleia cymosa*) even has colorful berries that add to its appeal.

OPPOSITE BELOW Lacecap hydrangeas, such as *H. macrophylla* 'Blue Wave', generally do better in shade than the all-sterile mophead types, but in both cases, there will be fewer, smaller flower clusters in the shade.

ture. Many of these plants often have smooth, shiny leaves. They do not need to be small or thick, or wear coatings. The shiny leaves do not hold dust or debris and wash clean in the rainfalls, which are often more frequent.

Flowers in the Shade and the Glory of Leaves

As you get deeper into sheltered gardening and its plants, you will discover that many shrubs and herbaceous perennials that can live both in sun and shade look different depending on their location. The ones in the shade may have a more open structure, and perhaps fewer leaves than they would in sunnier locations. This is not always bad. The plants may take on some interesting shapes, leaves may grow larger, and the plant will be less dependent on irrigation. Flowering plants that grow in sun, but are tolerant of lower light conditions, may not produce as many blossoms. For example, a mophead hydrangea (*Hydrangea macrophylla*) growing in a shady spot will not look like those dense, plump shrubs covered with giant pom-pom flowers at the seashore. In shade, these plants will have more delicate blossoms, and the shrub's stems may be wispy.

It is hard to generalize about plants—harder still to speak in absolutes, especially when talking about design and personal taste. Flowers are wonderful, but

even in the sunniest positions, colorful blooms rarely last the whole season. In the shade garden, we grow fewer plants for their flowers, more plants for their foliage. Flowers are fleeting, but leaves often last through three seasons and, in the case of evergreens, four. Once you learn to appreciate leaves, you'll discover a world of unlimited diversity, beauty, and yes, color. Even when the leaves are only in shades of green, the palette includes texture, volume, mass, shape, proportion, form, bark, and subtle shadings.

Small leaves may read as a texture, for example, boxwood (*Buxus* spp.) and Japanese holly (*Ilex crenata*). Masses of small foliage can read as solid forms.

OPPOSITE Some favorite shade plants that are famed for their foliage and shade tolerance include the ubiquitous hostas (*H.* 'Chinese Sunrise'), ferns (new growth of *Adiantum felix-femina* 'Lady in Red'), and Siberian bugloss (*Brunnera macrophylla*).

LEFT On sun lovers, it is easy to see leaves growing in whorls around a tall stem. Shade plant leaves grow in compact whorls, which can be seen in the doubly compound bipinnate leaves of *Aralia elata* 'Silver Umbrella'.

ABOVE Some plants have masses of tiny needle-like leaves to cover as much area as possible, as in the case of hardy *Asparagus tenuifolius*.

ABOVE Among the low broad-leaved evergreen and deciduous plants for our shade gardens, are the *Bergenias* (or pigsqueak) like fuzzy *B. ciliata*.

OPPOSITE There are some trees that actually do better in a bit of shade. These are tall woody understory plants like this weeping katsura (*Cercidiphyllum japonicum* 'Morioka Weeping').

Effects can be created with these mounds when they are positioned in the fore-ground or the background.

Medium-sized leaves are large enough to have an impact without dominating: alumroot (*Heuchera*) and hardy geranium, for example, can be used in mass plantings as ground cover or to define the edge of a space.

Large leaves are the province of shady gardens. The potential is in using the giants as specimens, or featured individual plants. Such foliage attracts the eye and holds attention; the leaves are almost like sculpture, and some might be monumental. Plants like *Brunnera*, *Ligularia*, *Bergenia*, and *Hosta* make powerful statements.

Go Ahead, Plant a Tree

Some of us grew up in towns with street names like Maple Drive, Sycamore Avenue, Willow, Ash, Pine, or Redwood. Kids today may not realize that these streets, maybe even the one they live on, are named for trees. Children in the near future may never even know what big old trees *are*. We must try to show the next generations the value in things that are ancient and alive. We have trees that were planted in public and private places toward the end of the nineteenth century, and some even earlier, and many of these venerable mastodons are coming to the end of their lives. We have to plant trees right now for our health and the health of the planet, and also for generations to come.

There aren't many guides about shade that suggest planting trees to make more. Usually, the approach is how to cope. But I am proposing that we add trees for their numerous benefits to the environment and gardens, including filtering the sunlight.

Since we hope to make gardens as well as forests, we might look to deciduous trees that will allow us to plant beneath them. Many of these will have a leafy canopy that is not thick and dense. Compound leaves are made up of small leaflets that diffuse light for plants below, as well as for people who might come to linger in bright, gentle shade on a hot summer day.

Among the trees with compound leaves are those with pinnate and bipinnate forms. Pinnate leaves resemble a feather, with rows of leaflets on either side of a central rib or axis; bipinnate leaves are divided once again, like the fronds of a fern. The delicate leaflets are always moving in the breeze. The shade they create below is moderate and always shifting.

There are large and small trees with pinnate foliage. American mountain ash trees (*Sorbus americana*) grow to about 40 feet. Thornless varieties of native honey locust (*Gleditsia triacanthos* var. *inermis*) grow small or tall. This tree, which produces light shade, is enormously useful for challenging sites and popular on city streets, as it is resistant to damage from pollution, wind, and salt-spray.

One tropical-looking, wide-spreading tree with a very open habit and tiny bipinnate leaves that cast very light shade has an unfortunate reputation. Some people loathe it because it drops its sticky, peach-scented blossoms on cars and tends to self-sow in the warmer climates. What we call mimosa in North America is *Albizia julibrissin*—not to be confused with the tropical genus it resembles, *Acacia*,

which is also known as mimosa. As with many members of the legume or pea family, its leaflets close at night. *Albizia* can be grown in zones 7 through 9, and in a sheltered spot in zone 6 (0 to minus 10 degrees Fahrenheit / minus 18 to minus 23 degrees Celsius). The minute *Albizia* leaflets are green, except for a popular, less hardy variety called 'Summer Chocolate', with foliage that ranges from reddish-green to deep burgundy, perhaps depending on location but possibly due to some mangling of the actual variety in the trade.

The swamp cypress (*Taxodium distichum*) can often be seen in forests, with many of their kind in standing water. The cypress is a deciduous conifer—a tree that drops its delicate needle leaves in the autumn. They have a wonderful prehistoric appearance and look especially natural in a small stand, perhaps of three. Old specimens growing in water often develop what are called "cypress knees"—odd pointed protrusions with rounded tops that grow up from the soil to 3 feet (1 m) tall. It is believed by some that these are adaptations the tree developed to absorb oxygen when growing in soil that stays wet year-round, but that is a mystery that remains unsolved. Despite their affinity for moisture, these trees do fine out of their natural aquatic element and even on streets in northern Midwest cities.

Similarly, the dawn redwood (*Metasequoia glyptostroboides*) is a fast-growing deciduous conifer with a colorful past. It has been found as a fossil in the United States, was thought to be extinct, and then was discovered alive in China in 1948. Is this a native plant? Most likely the American species varied a bit from the single species in the genus that grows here now. The tree can reach up to nearly 100 feet (30 m) in fifty years.

The jacaranda (*Jacaranda mimosifolia*) is a popular street tree in Southern California. This plant is best known for its purple flowers in winter, but it also has tiny compound leaves. Pinnate Chinese pistachio (*Pistacia chinensis*) is hardy to zone 6, and yet I have only seen this tree with its brilliant autumn color in Northern California. The tree might be problematic, so seek out male selections to avoid seeding.

Besides the trees with delicate foliage, we may plant small to medium-sized specimens in our sheltered gardens. These are species that grow in the understory of the woodland, and they, along with cultivars, might make good choices for the shade garden. Some of them, like the redbud (*Cercis canadensis*), have large leaves to gather as much light as possible. If planted on the north side of the garden, they will become handsome spring-flowering features that will not cast too much shade. The flower buds emerge right from the branches and sometimes from the tree trunk as well. There are chartreuse and beet-red-leafed and a few variegated versions of the redbud trees, as well as some with flower colors that range from red to pink to white.

Japanese maples (*Acer palmatum*), of which there are hundreds of varieties, are popular focal points; in fact, they are potential living sculptures for our gardens. Many of them have cut-leaf foliage (the *dissectum* variety and cultivars) and spring, summer, and autumn color. Taller and wider full moon maples (*Acer japonicum*) include selections with small or divided foliage as well, and produce a nice filtered light from above. (For more on trees, see page 141.)

OPPOSITE I look for trees with fine or small leaves that cast a soft shade, like the deciduous conifer, swamp cypress (*Taxodium distichum*).

ABOVE The flowers of the eastern redbud, *Cercis canadensis*, emerge from the twigs and branches of the tree.

BELOW There are many Japanese maples with fine foliage. Look for small versions of *A. japonicum* and *Acer palmatum*, like this diminutive variety.

LIGHTING WITH PLANTS:
FOLIAGE COLOR AND VARIEGATION

Plants selected and arranged for foliage texture, leaf, and flower color can brighten dark spaces. In many cases, contrast is your ally. White flowers stand out against dark green leaves and attract attention. The long wavelengths of red advance toward you, and other warm colors like acid green stand out as well. Blues recede. A planting of shrubs with colorful leaves will make the eye jump from spot to spot, if that is the desired effect.

Today, we are lucky to have so many shrubs with leaves that may be chartreuse and others that are wine red. The list is huge. At one time, when a single plant with odd-colored foliage appeared in a mass sowing of perennials or shrubs, the grower would discard it in the name of quality control. Now these aberrations are sought out—and they are more common than you might imagine. Sometimes, a woody plant might produce a mutation as a branch with colorful foliage. That branch may be propagated and result in a new variety on the market. These mutations are called sports. You might find them yourself when you shop and search at the nursery or garden center: sport fishing.

The customary way to light up the garden with plants is by using variegated foliage. Years ago, many gardeners claimed they hated variegation. I had to laugh. Inevitably, one person or another would see a green-leafed plant splashed with color and fall for it. All of a sudden, he or she would wonder if every treasured green plant in the garden came with stripes and spots of white or cream, pea green or gray.

The days of naysaying are gone. Judging by what I see now, the variegated plants attract the most attention and are the most coveted. They catch the eye, just as they brighten parts of the garden. There are even nurseries that specialize in colorful foliage, and breeders everywhere are selecting for this characteristic.

Variegation refers to a deviation in color, whether in the markings in stone or fur, leaves or flowers. There are several causes for this mottling in leaves. Sometimes, the coloring is caused by physiological or environmental conditions or even a virus—perhaps that is one reason people shied away from variegated plants in the old days. But not that much variegation is caused by active disease, and those plants tend to be less stable, often reverting to green.

When a plant has white along with green on a leaf, there is a lack of chlorophyll in the pale area. Other plants may have nearly metallic, reflective parts to each leaf. The variegation may not be white or silvery but a color, like the red zones on a hothouse geranium.

The plants I'm talking about are from happy accidents that appeared and were selected by plant enthusiasts and growers, propagated, and put into production. When the plants are named and brought to the market they are called cultivars, or cultivated varieties. The cultivar names are usually noted after the genus and species name in single quotes, not in italics. For example: the striped lilyturf, *Liriope muscari* 'Variegata'. Very often, these plants simply have 'Variegata' as the cultivar name, but they may be more specific, like 'Albovariegata' or 'Aureovariegata', which mean white and golden variegation, respectively. 'Marginata' indicates color on the margins. 'Maculata' is marked, or there may be a fancy name that tells you the plant is variegated, for instance, *Podophyllum* 'Spotty Dotty' and even *P.* 'Kaleidoscope'.

Variegated foliage and leaves in bright colors bring light to the shade garden:

1 *Polygonatum × hybridum* 'Grace Barker'—Solomon's seal

2 *Deutzia scabra* 'Variegata'—fuzzy deutzia

3 *Vinca minor* 'Variegata'—variegated periwinkle, vinca (detail)

4 *Aralia cordata* 'Sun King'—Sun King Japanese spikenard

5 *Pieris japonica* 'Flaming Silver'—variegated Japanese andromeda

6 *Podophyllum* 'Spotty Dotty'—Spotty Dotty mayapple

Celebrating Hostas

As hard as it might be to imagine, it wasn't very long ago that gardeners thought little of the hosta. *The Natural Shade Garden*, published in 1992, helped bring both hostas and variegation to light (pardon the pun).

The hostas used to be referred to as funkia or plantain lilies. They were associated with bygone eras, sometimes considered grandma plants, and looked down upon when "new" colorful annuals were all the rage, and before people became nostalgic about gardens. Although you might have found one or two green or variegated ones at the local garden center, the wide world of cultivated varieties remained the domain of the hosta club members. Little did we know these plants would become just about the most popular herbaceous perennial of all.

In the 1990s, when people started to recognize the benefits of shade and the beauty of foliage, they took another look at hostas' leaves, and the plants became stars of the shady world. Today, there are thousands of varieties, including miniatures with leaves barely an inch (2.5 cm) long. There are slender ones with grasslike or spear-shaped foliage. The leaves of some varieties are nearly white, and plenty have multicolor variegation, dark green to yellow to white (*Hosta* 'Striptease', for example). The legions of diverse varieties are nearly irresistible, with new ones coming out every year, including popular new introductions with red leaf stems (called petioles). And of course, there are the giant ones, like golden 'Sum and Substance,' with leaves 16 inches (40 cm) across. A golden hosta likes as much sun as it can get, although it will do well with less. These pale hostas have less chlorophyll and therefore appreciate light as opposed to deep shade.

Some of these hostas emerge from the ground green and turn yellow-gold later. This is due to a genetic trait known as lutescence. The condition of hostas that come up yellow and deepen to green is called viridescence. Gold hostas that turn nearly white are said to be albescent.

Hostas that have a blue cast to their leaves, like the large-leafed species *H. sieboldiana*, usually have a waxy coating that reflects light. As the season progresses, breeze wears and rain washes some of the coating away. The warmer the climate, the more the wax fades. In general, the blue hostas have thicker leaves. In hostas, the thickness of a leaf is referred to as substance.

Slugs and snails love to dine on hosta leaves, and the thicker the leaf—the more substance—the less the plants will be damaged by these voracious critters. Gardeners in California are envious of hosta plants. They cannot grow them easily because European snails, for whom the thickest hosta leaf is just a challenge to

ABOVE   Among my favorite hostas are the ones with upright, vase-like growth habits like this species, *H. nigrescens*, that is growing with the ground cover *Mukdenia rossii*.

OPPOSITE, FROM LEFT TO RIGHT, TOP TO BOTTOM

1 *Hosta* 'Great Expectations'

2 *Hosta* 'Looking Glass'

3 *Hosta* 'Regal Splendor'

4 *Hosta* 'Spilt Milk'

5 *Hosta* 'Strip Tease'

6 *Hosta* 'Frances Williams'

overcome, were imported to the West Coast in an ill-fated effort to start farming the animals for food. They escaped. Fortunately, for those of us in the center of the country and on the East Coast, the "escargot" does not thrive in our climate to dine on our hostas.

I shouldn't say "our" hostas, because these plants originated in Asia. Most come from Japan, and there are some that come from Korea and China as well. It is worth looking into these original species along with the thousands of varieties. There are some with puckered corrugated leaves, cup-shaped leaves, and creeping ground covers, and others that stand straight up on tall, long stems, for example, the species *H. nigrescens*.

FRAGRANT HOSTAS

Some hostas have fragrant flowers, mostly those that have *Hosta plantaginea* in their heritage, like the old rugged plant-'em-and-forget-'em 'August Lily', one of the few species that originated in China, as opposed to Korea or Japan. Cultivated in Chinese gardens for more than 2,000 years, this species is believed to have been the first hosta grown in Europe beginning in 1784.

Large, soft, grass-green leaves typify what was one of the most common hostas in gardens decades ago. I prize the sweet fragrance of its very large trumpet flowers. There are notable hybrids and cultivars, including 'Aphrodite', with double flowers.

Look for hostas with *fragrant* in their names, for example 'Fragrant Blue', 'Fragrant Bouquet', 'Fragrant Dream', and 'Summer Fragrance'.

CULTIVAR NAMES OF NOTABLE FRAGRANT HOSTAS INCLUDE:

'Aphrodite'

'Buckwheat Honey'

'Cathedral Windows'

'Diana Remembered'

'Double Up'

'Fragrant Blue'

'Fragrant Dream'

'Fragrant Queen'

'Fried Green Tomatoes'

'Fried Bananas'

'Frozen Margarita'

'Guacamole'

'Honeybells'

'Iron Gate Delight'

'Ming Treasure'

'Mistress Mabel'

'Old Faithful'

'Royal Standard'

'Stained Glass'

'Sugar and Spice'

OPPOSITE Hostas are grown for their foliage, but they have flowers, too, and some of them are great for color, like the late-summer-blooming creeping rhizomatous species *H. clausa*.

ABOVE Many of the more fragrant hostas are related to the species *H. plantaginea*. This one is blooming in late summer in the Flower Garden at Wave Hill in the Bronx, New York. Photograph by Louis Bauer.

Hostas are rugged winter-hardy plants; they grow in clumps that become larger every year. A few species and varieties have underground runners and spread as ground covers, for example the great rhizomatous species *H. clausa*. They all flower.

Serious hosta collectors often remove the flower spikes. These people are after pristine foliage. But many hostas have wonderful flowers in colors ranging from deep violet to clean white. There are varieties with stems so short they barely peek up above the foliage. Others are bolder, like the vase-shaped *H.* 'Krossa Regal', with 6-foot (2-m) flower spikes that emerge in midsummer. There are also hostas with deliciously fragrant flowers (see the box, Fragrant Hostas, page 81).

Besides being favorites of slugs and snails, hostas are deer candy, and that is a problem (see the box, When a Plan Must Acknowledge Deer, page 116). But take a look at another group of popular shade-loving plants that is resistant to the hoofed marauders: ferns.

Fine, Feathery Friends

Say "fern" and everyone knows what you are talking about, like "leaf" or maybe even "flower." This is probably because ferns are morphologically unique—few other things look like ferns. Most of us grew up seeing ferns in the woods and got to know them as a type of plant with feathery foliage. These ancient plants are among the most popular choices for shade gardens.

The oldest fern fossils are of plants that grew around 360 million years ago during the Carboniferous period. The earliest examples of some of the species we know today are from the Cretaceous epoch, about 145 million years ago—about the same time as the earliest flowering plants. They are vascular plants with leaves and roots, but unlike other plants, ferns do not flower. They reproduce through a complex process involving spores, which is more like mosses (see page 199).

Ferns may be used to fill in around and below the shrubs of the middle layer. Shorter ferns and ones that spread with underground rhizomes can be useful as ground covers. Others may be used as specimens on their own or in clumps and groups.

The cinnamon fern (*Osmundastrum* [syn. *Osmunda*] *cinnamomea*) is so called for its fertile fronds laden with reddish-brown spores. This one looks best in a small grove of several plants. The interrupted fern (*O. claytoniana*) has vertical black-spore-covered clusters that grow at intervals up the stems of the fertile fronds. This fascinating fern can be featured on its own, perhaps next to a rock, or join a stand of its bretheren. Another cousin is so imperial that its names—both common and scientific—reflect this quality: the royal fern (*O. regalis*). This fern is among the loveliest and most useful plants in filtered light to medium shade; it wants more moisture than some and will do best in a damp location.

The fronds of the shield fern species (*Dryopteris*) offer many candidates for shady gardens. Marginal shield fern (*D. marginalis*) has dark evergreen fronds 1 to 2 feet (30 to 60 cm) long and about 6 inches (15 cm) wide. It is native to many parts of the United States, throughout the East, and west to Oklahoma. Goldie's wood fern (*D. goldiana*) can grow to 4 feet (1.2 m). The male fern (*D. filix-mas*) is a crested fern

OPPOSITE Ferns offer a vast array of texture and color:

1 Deer fern (*Blechnum spicant*) here surrounded by botanical companions in Greg Graves and Gary Waller's garden at Old Goat Farm nursery in Graham, Washington.

2 *Adiantum pedatum*—maidenhair fern

3 *Asplenium scolopendrium*—Hart's tongue fern

4 *Athyrium niponicum* 'Burgundy Lace'—Japanese painted fern

5 *Osmundastrum regalis*—royal fern

6 *Pteris dactylina*—ribbon fern (houseplant)

7 *Woodwardia unigemmata*—chain fern

that forms feathery extra growth along the edge of the fronds. This fern can tolerate deeper shade and might be one to try in one of the more challenging places. It is more rare in the wild than many of its relatives. The splashiest of the clan is the autumn fern (*D. erythrosora*) with its orange fronds, and there are selections including 'Brilliance', a low-growing one with pink fiddleheads in spring that turn coppery as they unfurl; it is semievergreen.

Christmas fern (*Polystichum acrostichoides*) is evergreen (hence green for the holiday), and tolerant of light to full shade. It is probably the best evergreen fern for gardens on the East Coast. Western sword fern (*P. munitum*) is indigenous to the western United States from Alaska down to Southern California and east to Montana. The Alaskan fern (*P. setiferum angulare*) looks tropical, but it isn't. The new growth is beautiful with fat brown, shaggy crosiers. With age, this fern becomes a showstopper.

The fern that has arguably become the most popular is the Japanese painted fern (*Athyrium niponicum* 'Pictum'). The first versions of this variety had green fronds overlaid with metallic silver and celadon. More recent selections have brought us shades of beet red to burgundy—also with iridescence. *A. n.* 'Ursula's Red' is what its name says. There is a hybrid of the Japanese painted fern and the North American lady fern (*A. filix-femina*), created by Dr. Nick Nicou of Branford, Connecticut, and named by him for his town: *A.* 'Branford Beauty', which has shiny gray-green fronds. Platinum *A.* 'Ghost' is a tall, rugged hybrid with platinum fronds. Silvery glade fern (*A. thelypteroides*) is also not fussy. The tall, finely divided fronds start out bright green, darken to deep green, and finish the season by turning red-brown in autumn.

One of the most beautiful and delicate ferns is the maidenhair (*Adiantum pedatum*). You may have grown the subtropical version in a pot indoors. The hardy northern one has palmate whorls of tiny leaves on black stems. The maidenhair will grow in average soil, but like many ferns, it prefers a moist location in a loose, humus medium—rich in organic matter.

The list is long, and there are many I have not mentioned that might not make it into our sheltered gardens—for example, those that live on sheer rock cliff faces and ones from the open desert—but such things exist.

(Later, in part 5, page 199, you'll meet some ferns that can be used as ground covers.)

The Blues of the Borage Family

Most plants in the Boraginaceae family have blue flowers, including the culinary herb that gives the family its nickname "borage." One of the most beautiful spring ephemerals in the family is the Virginia bluebell (*Mertensia virginica*). The green leaves emerge early and quickly grow to about 1 foot (30 cm) tall, developing pink flower buds. As the buds open, they turn blue. Bees can see the color blue, so they are especially drawn to it; it is likely that the plants do not reveal the color bees like best until they are ready and ripe for pollination. Soon after the insects visit the flowers, the leaves begin to yellow, and within days, the plants disappear. In just a

month or so, start to finish, the plants have fulfilled their genetic destiny (making seeds) and melted away.

Many gardeners are head over heels in love with blue forget-me-nots (*Myosotis sylvatica*—sylvatica meaning "of the woods") for light shade. These herbaceous perennial plants behave as if they were biennials. They sprout from seeds the first summer, grow a bit, and then explode the following spring to accompany mid-to-late-spring-flowering bulbs with sprays of sky blue flowers. Many gardeners adore this plant and just weed it out where they don't want it. To me it is an unstoppable thug that crowds out the plants I want and seeds everywhere.

Of course, if *Myosotis* weren't such a pesky invader, I would probably like it. But don't judge an entire family by one bad player. Cousin *Brunnera macrophylla*—the *perennial* forget-me-not, also called Siberian bugloss, behaves better. This plant has large, fuzzy heart-shaped leaves and, in midspring, sprays of tiny blue flowers. There are a few wonderful cultivars on the market with leaves that are variegated

OPPOSITE *Symphytum × uplandicum* 'Variegata' is a prized member of the borage family with 10-inch (25-cm) gray-green leaves edged in butter-yellow.

LEFT The ground cover comfrey (*Symphytum grandiflorum*) blooms for a long time in spring with mostly cream-colored flowers.

RIGHT The nectar in the pink buds of many members of the borage family are ready for sampling when the open flowers turn blue, the color that bees are most drawn to.

cream and green or silver splashed. None of them are as rugged as the species. The selection 'Jack Frost' has silver leaves with green veins. I placed that one near my plants of the straight species, and over the years, I have observed more plants with green leaves lightly splashed with silver. *Brunnera* apparently does hybridize and self-sow, but not with the aggression of *Myosotis,* and it is easier to edit.

I would recommend that if you are interested in growing ones like 'Jack Frost', or exquisite 'Looking Glass' and 'Silver Heart' with super-silver leaves, that you keep them apart—especially from the species. If seedlings appear that have all green leaves among the desirable varieties, remove or move them. I've tried white-edged 'Hadspen Cream', which passed away after exhibiting some blackened edges to the foliage. 'Dawson's White' is a similarly variegated version.

Another borage cousin is *Pulmonaria* with its common name, lungwort—*wort,* from Old English, means "plant." The common name may have originated because the silvery spotting on the leaves of some of the species resembled certain lung diseases. Thus, it was imagined to be a cure for lung disease in the ancient practice promoting plants that resembled body parts or the manifestation of diseases as cures. (Other plants prized by those practitioners include the shade plant liverwort, *Hepatica,* named, perhaps, for the shape of its lobed leaf, and bloodroot, *Sanguinaria,* which gets its name from the red sap that drips out when a rhizome is cut.)

There are many species of *Pulmonaria* and even more cultivars. The lungworts do not self-sow with wild abandon. In this easy, well-mannered genus, few fancy varieties have been fussy for me. In general, the plants increase by enlarging their clumps. A clump may be divided into individual plants in early spring to increase the spread for ground covering, or to move some to other parts of the shade garden.

Lungworts produce flowers in midspring that are blue on most of the varieties, but also may be white, pink, or deep coral. The leaves are the main attraction. There are a few species with narrow green leaves. Most cultivars have silver spotted leaves of varying widths. A few have gray-green leaves with creamy-white edges. One challenging variegated variety is *P. rubra* 'David Ward', with coral flowers. A popular older variety is *P. longifolia* 'Bertram Anderson' with magenta buds that open into gentian blue flowers above long, narrow leaves spotted with silver. There are *Pulmonaria* varieties with completely silver leaves. These plants look great in a bit more sun. One that does well for me is 'Majeste'.

Pulmonaria are virtually carefree when grown in a woodland soil with moisture and drainage. However, the plants may look bad after flowering. The faded flowers should be removed. If the leaves on some of the varieties turn black, especially at the center of the plants, simply remove the damaged leaves or cut the whole plant back hard to produce a flush of gorgeous new growth that lasts through the summer.

Not all of the plants in the family Boraginaceae have blue flowers. Large-flowered comfrey (*Symphytum grandiflorum*) has cream-colored blossoms on a low ground-covering plant with fuzzy dark green leaves. One of my favorite herbaceous perennials is *S.* × *uplandicum* 'Axminster Gold'—a variegated hybrid that grows about 18 inches (46 cm) tall. This cross of *Symphytum* species (denoted by the ×) is

OPPOSITE, CLOCKWISE FROM TOP LEFT Members of the borage family, including variegated Siberian bugloss, also called perennial forget-me-not (*Brunnera* 'Dawson's White'); another stunning silvery Siberian bugloss, *Brunnera* 'Looking Glass'; Virginia bluebells—(*Mertensia virginica*); and one of over a dozen of the lungwort (*Pulmonaria*) species and hundreds of cultivars shares space with a speckled violet (*Viola soraria* 'Freckles').

ABOVE Silvery *Pulmonaria* 'Majeste' in a spring planting by Louis Bauer at Greenwood Gardens in Short Hills, New Jersey.

ABOVE Special plants like the latest hellebore hybrids, including *Helleborus × sahinii* 'Winterbells' and 'Pink Frost' can be found at independent nurseries and bought through mail-order suppliers.

OPPOSITE Native and local plants are often available through botanical garden sales like those at Garden in the Woods in Massachusetts, where trillium are produced in nursery beds tended by Dan Jaffe, botanical horticulturist. "Conservation through propagation" provides plants for gardens so people won't take them from the wild.

beautiful, with its large creamy yellow and pale green leaves; however, the flower spike with small white blossoms is unexceptional.

If you love it as I do, and want more, you might be inclined to propagate it as one can with other *Symphytum* species—from root cuttings. But you would be disappointed with the results: lots of plain green plants. Some variegated plants produce the variation in leaf color only in the cells of their meristem, or newest growth. 'Axminster Gold' is an example. The reason it may be expensive to buy is because it must mostly be propagated by dividing the original plant into side shoots with variegated top growth and fleshy roots together. I would advise cutting off the flowering stalk when it emerges; however, another method for propagating this plant that has worked for me has been to take sections of the stalk when it fully emerges to propagate as stem cuttings. These cuttings from above the variegated leaves carry the color to new rooted plants.

Finding Special Plants

A professional garden designer friend of mine once shared an e-mail from an irritated client: "I took your list of ten recommended plants to the nursery, and they only had five!" There are dozens of reasons for this. Not every nursery will have the plants you are hoping to find. Nurseries know that people tend to buy plants when they're in flower, so they try to have as much as possible blooming when the shoppers come, which is usually around Mother's Day. Colorful tags help attract customers, but a shrub that blooms in late winter or summer, for instance, or one that is grown for foliage and not flowers at all, may be harder to find.

To find particular plants, I encourage every gardener to ask the local garden center staff to try to find plants for you, and to support trustworthy mail-order sources, as well. Test a few mail-order nurseries by analyzing their packing, the size of the plants for the money, and the quality and accuracy of identification. Consider connecting with nearby gardening friends and combining orders to help reduce shipping costs.

Other places where plants can be found are at fund-raisers and botanical gardens that propagate them for sale. Most public native plant gardens hold sales at one time or another. The Garden in the Woods (GITW), just outside of Boston, takes the motto "conservation through propagation" seriously. In other words, one way to save threatened plants is to grow more and share them and encourage gardeners to make more, which keeps people from digging them up in semiwild areas and gets more of them into protected places like home gardens. Among the missions of the New England Wild Flower Society, which runs GITW, is education. The group hopes to help people realize how important it is to preserve places where the objects of their passion live, and teach them how to grow wildflowers. GITW has on-site propagation beds, and also an off-site facility dedicated exclusively to propagation. Nasami Farm in Whately, Massachusetts, is their native plant nursery, which focuses on propagation and research into the region's flora.

Find plants we will, and then we will know more about the living ingredients that we want for our garden designs in the shade.

· ·

THREATENED SHADE EPHEMERALS

I am biased in favor of the spring ephemerals, many of which are threatened or endangered or almost extinct. It has been estimated that half of all flowering plants—some 400,000 species—may no longer exist by the end of the twenty-first century. Like all plants, these wildflowers must never be dug from a natural or semiwild area. (It is illegal to take anything out of a State or National Park—even a rock.)

Instead, seek out local and mail-order nurseries that propagate and sell these plants. More and more of these places are popping up around the country to meet the demand for native plants, and the interest in conservation through propagation. Thankfully, there seem to have always been wild plant enthusiasts who specialize in propagating, growing, and selling these stars for our shade gardens.

SOME EXAMPLES OF SPRING EPHEMERALS—EARLY FLOWERING PLANTS THAT MAY GO DORMANT IN SUMMER—IN THE UNITED STATES:

Dicentra cucullaria—Dutchman's breeches
Cardamine (syn. *Dentaria*) *diphylla*—toothwort
Claytonia virginica—spring beauty
Erigenia bulbosa—harbinger of spring, salt-and-pepper plant
Erythronium americanum—trout lily
Hepatica spp.—liverwort

Houstonia caerulea—Quaker-ladies, azure bluet
Jeffersonia diphylla—twinleaf
Mertensia virginica—Virginia bluebells
Podophyllum peltatum—mayapple
Stylophorum diphyllum—wood poppy
Thalictrum thalictroides—rue anemone

RIGHT *Erythronium americanum*, named trout lily for the pattern of its leaves and dogtooth violet, for the shape of the underground corm from which they grow, is so common in some places that it's even mowed down with the lawn, but it's disappearing elsewhere as habitat is lost.

OPPOSITE, CLOCKWISE FROM TOP LEFT Some precious spring wildings: Quaker Ladies (also called bluets, *Houstonia caerulea*); rare Oconee bells (*Shortia galacifolia*); merry bells (*Uvularia grandiflora*); and the ephemeral Dutchman's breeches (*Dicentra cucullaria*), which disappears completely after it blooms and sets seed.

PART 4

A PROGRAM FOR OUR SHADE GARDENS

DREAM BIG

What do you want from your garden in the shade? Before planting anything, professional designers often develop a strategy, or "program," for a landscape, in which the needs of the people who will use it and the realities of the site are reflected. You may even want to write your own program, which is a good idea if you are beginning with a place that has little or no landscape-design history, and you are starting from scratch.

I suppose I did this, at least informally, when I moved to Brooklyn. I started by making a list of what I wanted from the space. Of course, at the top were planting beds for the woodland plants I loved. I also wanted a small entertaining space with sitting areas close to the house. Maybe I would have a small grill for cooking outdoors there too. And I needed a place protected from rain for keeping tools and equipment.

Keeping my wish list in mind, I gradually implemented this simple "program," making both aesthetic and practical changes to the site. I had a paved area by the house made by rearranging bluestone slabs that were already there. These bluestone pavers once lined the perimeter of the backyard when it was used for hanging laundry in the 1870s. More of the paving stones were arranged to make the path that ran from the patio by the house to the back of the garden where there was a raised area I created as a second spot for sitting. I selected the widest pavers for the beginning of the path by the house followed by progressively narrower ones to create an illusion of depth in the 21-by-45-foot (6.5-by-14-m) yard.

The design was casual, inspired by the mid-Atlantic, northeastern woodlands. But even this relaxed space had to function. There had to be access to plants for maintenance, for instance, and I had a list of other desired elements, including a small pond and a little waterfall to create the music in the urban garden that helped to mask the less desirable noise of the neighborhood. I had a stone path cross over the small pond, creating a bridge over urban water.

Most urban gardeners opt for a layout that is more formal, perhaps an entertaining space with a grill, table, and chairs on a patio or deck, and plants in containers. No matter how small or simple, the combination of planting beds, pots, paving, and furniture that form the urban garden needs planning and structure.

A lawn was not on my city-garden wish list, though many other new backyard gardeners in brownstone Brooklyn want lawn, it seems. The only way for them to find out that it is not a realistic option is to plant it and watch it fail. There is usually too much shade, but even if it is sunny, a 10-foot (3-m) square of grass will never stand up to activities like sitting in the same place or kids playing. That abuse would be too much, day after day, in the same spot. And how will the grass be cut? With cuticle scissors?

PREVIOUS SPREAD The view from the sunny second-floor deck of the shaded sitting area in the Brooklyn backyard of the late garden designer Bill Fidelo.

ABOVE We all want plants and gardens wherever we can put them. To make room for a garden in front of my old Brooklyn brownstone, I opted for containers rather than facing the daunting task of taking out the poured concrete.

OPPOSITE Dreaming big, my Clinton Hill, Brooklyn, neighbor, Mary Meyer, opted for breaking up the concrete and creating planting beds and paths in front of her brownstone, which was nearly identical to mine.

However, I do encourage you to dream big at this stage. What if you had a magic wand? It's easier to scale back or edit on paper than when you're shuffling 300-pound pavers.

Next, Get Real

Following the discipline of making a landscape program before any work begins, whether on your own or in consultation with a hired adviser or with more-experienced gardening friends, can help prevent costly mistakes.

Typically, planning a small-space garden is a fairly manageable undertaking. The difficulty tends to be in squeezing all your desires into a limited area. This exercise calls for some clever thinking.

If you move to a much larger garden space from a smaller one, as I did, you may find that some elements of the smaller urban design can be transferred to, say, a corner of the larger property, perhaps right outside the kitchen door of the suburban or exurban home site. The larger landscape can be a more complicated and difficult undertaking. In a home, you might consider renovating one room at a time as opposed to the entire house all at once. Apply that analogy—one room at a time, bit by bit—to your garden. Of course, that remodeled room (or part of your garden) is connected to the house and should hang together with your design for the whole. Planning a greater area requires a lot of thought, observation, and contemplation.

The first thing is to see what might already be there. Note the existing trees, if any, and desirable or undesirable elements—from a handsome rock outcropping to a neighbor's painted pink garage. Just as you observe the patterns of light, direction of seasonal winds, etc., note the permanent features—those to keep, some to hide, and others to remove.

When I moved out to New Jersey, to greater outdoor space, my list of needs for the garden I planned were mostly horticultural. I started out with my wish list for my dream garden, which I then applied to reality. Reality for me included a circle of hundred-plus-year-old trees, a canal and of course the river that splits to run around the island property, and shade.

OPPOSITE
In an outdoor space, many people are looking for a place where children can play, as well as areas set aside for grilling and eating, seating, storage, and the like. Gardeners may want artistic designs with planting beds for favorites, like *Ligularia japonica*.

ABOVE Gardens in the city are challenging: There often isn't any soil, but that can be purchased; space is limited; light can rarely be controlled. Yet, many people still want to try to grow a lawn. Talented designer Jim Golden chose attractive gravel instead—no mowing necessary.

ART IN THE GARDEN

I cannot emphasize enough how challenging it is to place serious art in the garden. If you happen upon a classical sculpture that speaks to you, buy it if you can, or accept your inheritance. But putting a sculpture into an existing garden is difficult. I've found myself moving a small piece around the garden for weeks, trying it here and there. I suggest that if you have a large and heavy work to place, make a cardboard cutout and paint it the color or colors of your piece, attach it to stakes, and shuttle *that* from place to place before the real one arrives.

A better scenario is to acquire the work of art first and build a garden space around it. For example, if you find a sculpture of Priapus, the deity that oversees the garden, give him his own "garden of the gods." If you find four sculptures representing the four seasons, well, you get the picture.

Of course, not all garden art has to be so extravagant. Found objects may also be brought into the garden. The landscape architect W. Gary Smith has some words of advice, taking as an example the popularity of using old garden machines as decorative objects or even planters. He points out that "there's a difference between going down to a junk shop and buying an old rusty wheelbarrow and planting in it, and using one that got rusty while you were gardening with it for ten years." (The latter wheelbarrow would add meaning to your garden.) Smith goes on: "On the other hand, don't be afraid to have fun with incongruous objects."

I once found about a dozen attractive baseball-sized glass paperweights at a decorating store and bought them all on sale for a dollar apiece. They resemble what I imagine dragon eggs might look like. I've placed them on the ground around low plants, and I move them from time to time. Sometimes I come upon one that I had forgotten about and feel happy with that surprise. I am glad to say they have lasted through many winters. I think they look great, and they elicit comments from visitors: "What the heck are those?"

LEFT Placing sculpture in a garden can be difficult, especially a work of fine art, for which you want the perfect spot. Sometimes, it is best to start with the art and create the garden around it.

RIGHT Found objects can become garden art, like these classical early-twentieth-century sink bases, which could be made into pedestals for gazing globes.

OPPOSITE Glass "dragon egg" paperweights (bottom, left) have found their way into a low planting of blue Ajuga, pink *Geranium maculatum* 'Espresso', chartreuse boxwood and lime balm (*Melissa officinalis* 'Lime').

The hope for a sunny flower border had to be amended. I wanted tons of roses—nope, there wasn't enough sun. A high tree-covered ridge shades the garden from the west, and thick woodland casts shadows in the morning. Here in the valley, which friends have nicknamed the "gully," the sunniest spot isn't very sunny but is in shadow for all but about seven hours a day in summer—light shade. The only niche where I could grow tomatoes was on the highest ground: on the driveway up by the road. So I set five big containers for the fruits there.

I do not think of my New Jersey woodland garden beds, which at the time of this writing were still recovering from the effects of the latest flood, as having been designed. My goal was to create something that appeared as wild as possible, and the path that bisected the planting beds was there for utility and to afford the best close-up view of the most precious species. The nearby woods inspired these beds, and I would say the style was definitely informal and naturalistic. Understanding that intention was an important guiding principle of my "program" for that place.

The Factor of Time

I often say that gardening is an art created in the fourth dimension. There are line, plane, and the third dimension of mass and form. And then there is time. It isn't easy to imagine how time will affect your design. Try to anticipate some of the things that will happen in the future. That little sapling from the nursery will grow into a tree, and the shade will change. Plants will need to be pruned to keep your design as planned. Trimming the hedge should not be considered high maintenance, especially in a small space. It's just gardening.

My garden in Brooklyn evolved a lot over time. Yes, the trees I planted grew tall and changed the character of the light and the feeling in the garden. I made mistakes, and some unexpected things happened. For example, one of the five allegedly dwarf trees I bought for the back of the garden when they were dormant was mislabeled. It was not a slow-growing small variety as indicated, and it quickly overwhelmed its neighbors. My plan for a cluster of five trees in that spot became one giant one. I decided to let the big tree stay and sacrifice the smaller ones, which were suffering, anyway.

The next big change in Brooklyn happened when I acquired the New Jersey property. I had to simplify the city garden, and I did that by reducing the wide-ranging assortment of understory plants to a few stalwarts that had proved to be more self-reliant. I hate to kill plants, and luckily for me, many that started out in the urban garden found new homes in the exurban one.

The Layers of an Outdoor Space

Just as we know there is a hierarchy of the woodland from the treetop canopy down to the forest floor, there is another kind of layering going on in the garden. Think of the various areas of your property. Some places are independent and clearly defined, surrounded by lawn or up against the sidewalk or driveway. Other parts gently flow into one another—their perimeters blurred by a consistent surface texture or obscured by dappled shade.

OPPOSITE Among the earliest plantings in my New Jersey garden were the woodland beds beneath the ash, pine, and spruce trees. Local wild plants grew in the bed to the north, and analogous species from Europe and Asia live across the path to the south.

The outer area: The edges of a property are often shady. Simple plantings offer privacy, hide undesirable views, and baffle noise. In conventional designs, a fence or an evergreen hedge might be used to screen the neighbors, but we're not interested in convention. A mix of tree species with varying texture, height, and color—evergreen and deciduous—helps to softly achieve these goals. On the inside of the perimeter, closer to the house, shrubs and smaller trees may be planted near their taller counterparts to naturally introduce and soften the transition from the in-between area to the outer border. Although this place may be left as a low-maintenance zone, spaces beneath and between the woody plants are just right

(*continued on page 107*)

GETTING STARTED: GO SLOW, DO HOMEWORK

Despite it being a pretty good idea, most eager gardeners don't want to hear that they should watch their new garden space for a year before they plant anything. You can guess what the shade may be like in many places and take your chances by just forging ahead. In some spots, you will have to do some diligent observation. But there is plenty to discover before the first plants go in the ground. Begin with research.

Meet other gardeners in your area. Ask about their experiences and their favorite plants. True gardeners have a special empathy for the environment, a need to nurture, and natural or acquired skill. Most of us share knowledge, camaraderie, and often, plants.

Visit public gardens with camera, pencil, and paper. Go to the areas in the shadows and see what is thriving. Try to see private gardens as well. You may be able to join a garden club. You can also check the open days of the Garden Conservancy to find extraordinary private and public gardens nearby that invite visitors or offer guided tours one or two days a year. Whenever possible, attend charity garden tours in your community, which are not uncommon.

Try to visit nature preserves as well. If there are wooded areas for hiking or camping in your area, try to see those too. Notice how the trees grow and what grows in the spaces between them. See what is growing on the forest floor and the shrub layer in between. Try to visit in the spring before the leaves on the trees have emerged, and in the summer and fall as well.

When you go to nurseries, check out the plants in their shade areas. Read the labels to learn what the growers think the plants want. Some plant labels are very thorough and provide useful information, but as mentioned, not all. Some growers tend toward hyperbole and wishful thinking when it comes to shade tolerance or even climate zones. You will discover over time what grows well in your garden.

If you cannot stand passing up shopping opportunities, consider making a nursery for your plants in a spot that suits them. You can grow them until you find a permanent place for them. They will be larger when you hope to move them, and you will get a free pass for being a bit of a shopaholic.

RIGHT Visit nearby public and private gardens on open days for design and plant ideas. Architect Andrea Filippone's Asian Garden is one such place with a vessel and fifteen cultivars of boxwood.

OPPOSITE The summer house and grounds at Greenwood Gardens in New Jersey were designed and built by architect and gardener James Renwick around 1915 and included innovations like poured-in-place concrete pavers. The plantings were renovated ninety years later.

PROGRAM CHECKLIST: EXISTING CONDITIONS

Compiling your program wish list is a fairly straightforward undertaking—and after consulting each member of the family for input, of course you'll be hoping you can design a plan that includes everyone's desires.

You may imagine developing an entire paved outdoor living space with places to sit, cook, and dine. Maybe someone wants views, so a deck to overlook the garden is now on the list too. Your family might be hoping for a child's play area and paths throughout. Other checklist items might include the need to plan for access to utilities like garden hose storage, a spot for the trash cans and easy access to them, and a privacy fence to block an unwanted view. Of course, you dream of beds for growing spring ephemerals in areas under trees.

What's next? You need to determine which items on your wish list can be realized, and if they can be, where they might be situated. The site itself may offer some clues, both constraints and assets. It may be time to take inventory and ask yourself questions such as these:

Where are north, south, east, and west?

Where does the light come from during the day?

Is there a direction that the wind generally comes from?

What are the existing trees like? How large and tall are they and what species? (As I've mentioned, some trees, like maples and beech, tend to have shallow roots; oak roots grow deeper and make planting beneath them less of a challenge.) Evergreen trees present additional challenges.

What is the quality of the existing soil? Is it full of clay, which tends to retain moisture, or is it sandy and thus drains fast? (In part 6, we'll learn how to adjust these circumstances.)

Is the land flat or rolling? Where are the high spots and the low ones?

Is there a place to make a lookout, or a place where water tends to drain that might be right for a rain garden?

Are you lucky enough to have a rock outcropping that could become a landscape feature? Or are there rocks that will force you to scale back your hoped-for schemes?

All of these conditions and situations and more need to be noted for the potential success of the program.

OPPOSITE Rather than blowing up a rock outcropping, plant it, as was done at the New York Botanical Garden in the light shade of the new Azalea Garden.

RIGHT In one area of my garden, a huge Norway spruce presented a challenge both by making shade and competing for moisture. A naturalized ground cover planting of tall rugged ostrich fern (*Matteuccia struthiopteris*) grows well in this environment.

(*continued from page 101*)

for shade plantings, and often for woodland-style gardens with meandering paths among the ephemeral local plants from the forest floor. Spring-flowering bulbs and ferns would also work well there.

The in-between area: This is where you can support your most ambitious plantings. You might choose to create an island bed of herbaceous perennials or of deciduous or evergreen shrubs. You could have a small tree collection—of dwarf Japanese maples, for example—for spring through autumn color. A single tree could become a focal point, and low plants could be placed beneath it. Sculpture and ornament are possible choices for shady gardens.

If this is an area that is constantly wet, you might find that a boardwalk above the plantings could be the best way to experience the garden. If there is a stream, a bridge might be called for, one made of wood or other materials that work with the naturalistic landscape design.

The in-between area might also include some of the sunnier places. These may be where the vegetable garden goes if there is a spot that receives more than eight hours of sunlight per day in the summer. Flower gardens too can go here, even cut-flower gardens. If you want a grass lawn that can stand up to traffic, even

OPPOSITE The in-between area, such as where the edge of the lawn meets trees, is the best place for the most ambitious plantings. Here, light streams down to illuminate a favorite hosta planted at the base of mature trees at the Gardens at Mill Fleurs in southeastern Pennsylvania.

ABOVE The inner area of my patio is for utility, recreation, entertaining, cooking, and in my case, a spot created beneath the sun porch extension (right) where my guests and I, along with the summering houseplants, can find shelter from the sun and heat.

surviving the occasional ball game or a dog, the sunny in-between area is for that as well. A meadow or prairie-style planting could be chosen as a lawn alternative.

The inner area: Consider the inner area as a busy place close to the dwelling. Durable hard-surface materials underfoot make these busy areas easy to maintain. Up against the house, permanent elements may be an alternative to green growth. Color may come from paint. A trellis may serve as home to a vine. Herbaceous plants in narrow beds may bring interest during the growing season.

Plan for access to things like trash receptacles, cable entry, or the filler for the fuel tank. Again, hard-surface, permanent items will help here. You don't want to have to drag the recycling bin down a very narrow path to get to the curb.

Considering Ongoing Garden Care

The media promotes the idea of "get the garden done in no time." We for whom gardening is a passion have no desire to get the garden done—ever. Gardening—making art in the earth—is something we hope to and very well may be able to do for a lifetime. It might seem anathema to discuss "work" when it comes to gardening. I try to avoid that word whenever possible. I try to say "accomplishments," "tasks," "play," fun," or even "dig." But I often find myself saying it out loud: "I have to go work in the garden."

Now, in the planning stages of the program, think about how much time you might want to devote to "playing" outdoors. If you are someone who hates to be outdoors, who doesn't like to kneel or get dirty—well, you're probably not reading this book.

If you like a formal look in the garden, you might find one sort of maintenance, like edging beds and sweeping paved paths. In the informal garden, a looser approach might be acceptable—until the weeds show up.

Gardening does take work. But what the garden gives back to your health, emotional well-being, and satisfaction rewards any amount of time and effort. Time and effort, the size and scale of the plantings, and the dimension of your dream landscape are things to add to your lists for the program.

Playing with Scale

Though your garden has a defined footprint—whether 1,000 square feet or 25 acres—big gardens can be made to feel intimate, and small ones can borrow scenery from outside their borders to give them breathing room. The subject of scale—actual size, and the perceived sense of it in the garden—should also be on your radar as you develop your garden's overall plan.

If your space is small, you could embrace that quality, or you might consider making it seem larger. There are many ways to do this, including playing with perspective, as I did with the path in the Brooklyn garden: The path became narrower as it led away from the main view—making the space appear deeper than it was. That mirror I placed at the back of the garden may not have brightened things substantially, but it accentuated this sense of depth and helped me obscure the actual limit of the boundary.

OPPOSITE An oasis in the city offers a table and chairs for outdoor dining among cooling plants and a privacy fence painted with Spanish Moss Cabot opaque stain, the understated "invisible" color of bark and dirt.

You might have one plant at the entrance to the garden and the same plant, only smaller, in the distance. Space can be made to seem larger with color, as well. Just as the mountains in the distance appear paler, having foliage with darker shades in the foreground and softer colors farther away could have a similar effect.

You can divide a limited space into smaller sections, which, perhaps surprisingly, often makes it seem larger. Seen from above, a little space cut into smaller sections would look pretty tiny. But the entire space is not viewable from the ground, and the experience of walking through this smaller garden becomes much richer and takes longer. In my small garden in Brooklyn, walking over the bridge that spanned the little pond necessitated watching where you stepped, which created a more intricate and therefore longer-lasting trip through the tiny landscape.

A large space can also be divided into what are usually called garden rooms. These more intimate spaces might not make the garden seem larger, but they could make it more sheltered and cozy. The garden "rooms" would also present great opportunities for plantings that attend to detail rather than the grand sweep. On the acre I've developed in New Jersey, I'm happy to present many kinds of experiences. I've set it up so that one type of planting space leads to another, and then the next, with as many surprises as I could produce. Making the experience about looking at points along the way makes the visit richer.

Views and Vistas

We have to look beyond our own space—for better or worse—when making a garden program. When you create areas of special interest, either shrinking the garden or enlarging it, think about what the view of the garden is from your home, as well as views from within the spaces in the garden.

Fortunately, you don't have to own the view to enjoy it. So many gardeners would never think of "borrowing" a view from the surrounding landscape, but why not bring it right into your garden space? If you have a great scene next door, maybe a field or a forest or a rock outcropping, plant something in the foreground, like a low hedge, or even add some low fencing or a nonfunctioning gate to relate it to your space. Another idea is to connect the garden to the borrowed view with something like a path that goes toward it but dissolves when the walk reaches the boundary. Try to imagine the vista in different seasons to be sure that it will serve its purpose year-round.

Your garden may look out toward woodland—or rows of apartment buildings. In any event, you can define, enhance, or obscure these scenes. Create living frames, or make pergolas, archways, even windows in walls, or cut into an outer-area planting to capture the part of the picture you want and block what you don't want. The view may be opened to include the space in the next part of the garden, or be reduced to just a slice, a glimpse of the next something wonderful, which could be a part of a great old tree, or one you've recently planted.

As you plan how you want to stroll through your garden, consider these views and vistas. You'll want to create opportunities that hint at what is to come as you move from one space to the next. Frame the key part of the view you hope to fea-

OPPOSITE The view along the gravel path, from shade to light, at the magnificent Elisabeth C. Miller Botanical Garden in Seattle. In the foreground is a lush Chinese mayapple (*Podophyllum versipelle*).

ABOVE If there is an opportunity to borrow a view from a neighbor, do so, perhaps even to the extent of installing an arch or a path and a working or non-working gate at the property line.

ture. Vary the size and shape of openings, place focal points that catch the eye. Plant for spots where you (or guests) can sit and catch the view, and like all placements of benches and other plans, consider both what is seen from the viewing point as well as what the point itself looks like.

Some of the most important views are from the windows and doors of the house. The main entrance to the garden from the residence should set the tone for the experience to come. The place where you eat breakfast and watch the birds at the feeder may be the spot where you'd like to develop a garden outlook. And there is the main "picture window," if you have one, which might be the dominant view of the outdoor space.

Sometimes, you want to do just the opposite—hide a view or disguise it. If the potential problem can be obscured with plants, or perhaps a lattice screen, all the better.

We all have the utility area where the trash cans are stored. Then there is the gas grill and all that comes with it, or plastic children's play equipment in the neighbor's yard, or just someone else's untidy space. My Brooklyn garden looked toward the back of a neighbor's house—painted red—which contained his entertainment needs, including a giant cola cooler. I planted to obscure that view.

ABOVE I extended the "view" in my former Brooklyn backyard by adding the suggestion of a gate and arranging ever-narrowing pavers along the path to fool the eye with exaggerated perspective. At the far end of the view, I installed a mirror tipped forward to create what appears to be more garden.

When I needed to screen a view in the New Jersey garden, I used shade-tolerant dwarf evergreen southern magnolias (*Magnolia grandiflora*), specifically 'Bracken's Brown Beauty', which are compact and more easily pruned. My friend Tom in Oakland, California, screened his neighbors with a very narrow hedge of podocarpus (*Podocarpus gracilior*) that he prunes annually.

You can also draw attention toward a more arresting view and away from the eyesore. Create something fantastic to look at that necessitates looking away or even turning your back on the difficult subject.

If the problem is a building like a garden shed, it might be possible to bring it into the landscape with color, or potted plants, or maybe even by building a trellis in front of and over it on which a vine could climb. Or make the problem disappear. I've written many times about what I call the invisible paint, a shade of Cabot brand opaque stain in the color Spanish moss that seems to disappear in the landscape. It is the color of bark and dirt, and just recedes from view. I have painted colored plastic with it, and in New Jersey, when a new metal guardrail was installed at eye level on the edge of the garden, I painted the back of it (I am not sure that is legal, but . . .). The shiny galvanized steel barrier disappeared.

LEFT Tom Koster prunes his hedge of *Podocarpus gracilior* about twice a year. It forms the background foil to plantings in his garden in Oakland, California, as well as providing privacy.

RIGHT I've planted dense evergreen southern magnolias (*M. grandiflora* 'Bracken's Brown Beauty') for a screen in medium shade on the north side of taller white pine trees. Another magnolia, *M. g.* 'Edith Bogue', thrives as a cold-hardy buffer despite snow and winter road salt spray.

Make Your Beds

The plantings of the in-between areas require as much planning as the inner area, if not more. Here you don't have the clear need to support the program's functional requirements, the way you do closer in, and you will probably be transforming the lawnscape into planting beds, at least in part.

First, some basic terminology: An **island bed** is one of those large plantings surrounded by lawn or mulch—unlike a **border**, which is a running bed, a strip that may be up against a fence, the outer-area trees and shrubs, a path, or permanent edging for lawn.

Some guidelines for making beds and borders:

Don't go too wide: Do not make garden beds or borders any wider than you have to in order to be able to reach everywhere from the sides, including the center.

In beds that must be wider, install paths: If you make a bed that is very wide, include one or more utility paths to run through it, so every spot can be reached. You will need to get into the beds to deadhead—remove faded flowers—trim away yellow leaves and remove broken branches, weed and clean up in fall, mulch, not to mention install more plants. Stepping-stones may be placed through the beds for the path. Don't be surprised if, as plants develop during the growing season, the stones disappear.

Play around on paper first: If you have a site plan of your property, that's great; you can place some tracing paper over it and draw amorphous island beds and borders. Check out Google Maps to see if your property can be seen in a satellite image.

Take photos of your property from various areas: Print these out and overlay them with a piece of tracing paper to draw what you may hope to create in the literal garden. If you are a Photoshop wiz, you might be able to cut and paste plants right onto your photos of the landscape. If you are handy, or using a digital app, you could create plans on your computer screen and print them out. The plan doesn't have to be drawn to scale, but any kind of sketch will help. You might even care to make some paper cut-outs to lay over your plan and move around to find the best relationships for these permanent elements—as if you were moving furniture in the living room.

OPPOSITE Marco Polo Stufano, the director of horticulture emeritus of Wave Hill in New York, has a small garden on a corner lot with planting beds edged by natural mulch paths and layers of fence walls that delineate areas of interest while screening the traffic.

ABOVE Margaret Roach, who presides over the blog awaytogarden.com, has painted Wave Hill chairs in front of an island bed edged by flagstone. The stone continues on as a pathway with a tantalizing view of garden beds to come.

WHEN A PLAN MUST ACKNOWLEDGE DEER

Often the realities of life, or wildlife—and particularly deer—modify the plans for a dream garden. From Texas to California to Michigan to Connecticut, deer problems press on the minds of gardeners. In the early 1900s, farming and hunting had reduced the population of white-tailed deer to only about 500,000 nationwide. Today, estimates put the number at more than 15 million. Another worry is the Lyme-disease-infected ticks they carry. Seeing populations in fenced parks or preserves starving in the winter—a doe the size of a German shepherd—might be another reason for concern.

The animals we see in the suburbs and semirural areas—deer, raccoons, coyotes, alligators, and even bears—are opportunists that do quite well on what we humans have around us. Why should a bear bother picking tiny berries when it could dine at its leisure from the Dumpster behind a fast-food restaurant or a neighbor's trash can?

Deer don't go for the trash, but they do love the same plants we do. The deer also browse the forest understory, with severe and often overlooked results. In the Everglades, deer browsing has led to erosion. In the woodlands of the Northeast, Midwest, and Northwest, deer have been clearing the forest floor of plants like trillium. Deer also eat young saplings, another reason areas will not be reforested, as their browsing has interrupted succession.

I once visited a several-acre garden in Ohio. It was a collection of rhododendrons amassed over decades. Unfortunately, there wasn't much to see. The plants had been nearly mowed to the ground by deer.

There was a small vegetable garden at the center of this landscape. It was surrounded by a simple picket fence only 2 feet (60 cm) tall, which was really there to stop the bunnies. Deer hadn't touched any of those plants. Why?

The vegetable plants were growing in raised beds with wood plank sides. The paths were narrow. A deer attempting to hop over the fence would not have had a clear place to land. Deer won't jump without a safe spot for a touchdown. The same kind of arrangement can be made with a double fence. Deer hop more than they long jump. One fence 3 to 4 feet (1 to 1.2 m) tall with another one positioned about 4 feet (1.2 m) inside it may keep them out.

I visited another garden where chain-link fencing had been used. But it wasn't installed vertically. It was pegged to the ground. The lawn could be mowed over the fencing, but deer would not walk on it. Deer (like cattle) won't walk where the footing isn't sure. This strategy wouldn't work after a snowstorm, but the fencing I saw was on the West Coast.

RIGHT Spray repellents help deter deer if used unfailingly, but a good fence is the best defense—at least 8 feet (2.4 m) high. Thoughtfully chosen and placed, a fence does not have to be a scene killer.

OPPOSITE Jim Golden's New York City garden is "inside-out." Glass doors lead out to the backyard. A seating area ascends to a gravel "carpet" punctuated by boxwood and flanked by planting beds that frame a tranquil pool.

BRINGING THE GARDEN INDOORS

Considering the views of the garden from the inside of the house, and especially from the place where you tend to spend the most time, should be very high on your list of program requirements. One could say this place will have a kind of intimacy, where a personal connection with the garden is formed, whether it is large or small, grand and loose, or cozy and precise.

Colors and perhaps elements from the interior could be repeated outside. I can't imagine copying chintz-covered couch colors with flowers in a shade garden. I would be more inclined to have a bird feeder or a water feature there. My hummingbird feeders are part of my view from the living room, and a slice of the gravel garden with a red-leafed beech trimmed into a column is seen from the kitchen window. If you are building or remodeling a house, consider the windows on the garden and where you want the view to be. With modern insulated glass, windows can be large without letting cold or heat into the home.

Jim Golden has a rambling, naturalistic garden in New Jersey across the river from the charming Pennsylvania town of New Hope. He also has a town garden in New York City behind a brownstone in Brooklyn. Most of that house is rented to tenants. The part of the house he shares with his husband is what could be called an English basement, what we in Brooklyn often refer to as the "garden level."

The planted space behind the house is 20 feet by 47 feet (6 by 14.3 m), similar to most brownstone backyards. Jim made an open area of gravel at the center with a 4-by-7.5-foot (1.2-by-2.3-m) rectangular water feature. There is a deep bed at the back and narrower beds on the south and north sides. The back wall of Jim's home has glass windows and doors designed to bring the outdoors in, with a year-round view of the garden.

Use a garden hose: Another way to "draw" beds out in the garden is to use a hose or two and lay those on an area of lawn or open ground to see what the bed might look like. Climb a ladder to get a bird's-eye view. Sprinkle some dolomite lime over the hose and when you remove it, you will have a drawn outline of the bed.

Visual Inspiration: Looking for Clues

So now we've prepared our program's wish lists and thought about the reality of the site we are working with. Yet we have barely addressed what may be the reason you started this whole thing in the first place—the art of the landscape, or making aesthetic choices. What do you want the scene to look like? Many of the descriptions above suggest a naturalistic style with soft edges that mimic woodland, but that's only one of many directions you could take. The sky's the limit—or rather, the land is.

My New Jersey woodland planting beds are not near the house, which I suspect was once a mill store built in the early 1800s. If it has a style, it might be hodgepodge Colonial farmhouse. If the shady woodland garden were closer to the house, I might have designed it to fit in with the style of the building.

A critical visual question you need to ask yourself is: What is the context? How will the elements you hope to create relate to existing factors, including the immediate architecture and perhaps the neighborhood or even the region? (Not only will some extremes of garden style not "match" certain homes, but also you won't have much success making an alpine-style rock garden where summers are hot and humid and the objective is to find refuge from the sun.) If my shady plantings were next to the house, I would have arranged the paths to logically relate to the traffic pattern with entrances and exits to the building. I might have made a dry stone wall like the ones that bound the borders of the farms nearby; in fact, that is pretty much what I did for the gravel garden behind the house.

Your next steps, then: Consider the character of your home's design and in addition, think about what else attracts you. Is there an inspiring famous garden from another part of the world that has elements you wish to borrow? Or perhaps there is a painting of a garden you are attracted to? Look through books with photographs and artwork of gardens. A Japanese style would go well with a mid-century-modern home. An informal cottage-style garden might be right for an American country house. An English country house is what we in the United States would call a mansion. Scaling down the country-house look for light shade might mean featuring a boxwood hedge; a mass planting of a local wild plant could stand in for a sunny perennial border.

The exteriors of many houses built in the United States in the first decade of the twenty-first century were designed to have a kind of neo-Spanish appearance, for instance—clad in stucco with arched doorways. The look of the garden might conform to that design, in an Islamic style. In southern Spain, the Moorish influence is familiar, and homes are often built around a courtyard. The walls of the house cast shade on a sheltered court that often includes a cooling central water feature, a bubbling fountain or runnel—a narrow channel or course for water.

Site-Specific Inspirations: Coastal California

The inspiration for my woodland beds was the land around my property in a temperate mixed hardwood forest region of the world that is cold in the winter and hot in the summer. The rainfall is an average of 50 inches (127 cm) a year. In much of the United States, nature creates a logical shade garden prototype when there is adequate rainfall.

What if I lived in the parts of Sonoma County, California, where the annual rainfall can be less than 30 inches (76 cm) each year (even as low as 20 in some spots)? There, the garden would be made out of necessity and regional appropriateness. There is rarely a frost near the coast north of San Francisco, but occasional freezes occur at the higher elevations. In the summer months, the sky is clear and the sun is blazing hot. Temperatures can exceed 100 degrees Fahrenheit (38 degrees Celsius). Shade would be welcome.

A native shade garden there could be based on the coast live oak (*Quercus agrifolia*) savanna. A savanna is a grassland habitat with only a few trees, often oaks in North America, growing alone or in clusters. Limited rainfall keeps the area from developing into a thick woodland.

Huge coast live oaks dot the savannas, a plant community that ranges from Mexico north through California. The plants that grow beneath a solitary live oak

might include broadleaf shrubs like toyon (*Heteromeles arbutifolia*) and manzani-
tas (*Arctostaphylos* spp.) with grasses and herbaceous flowering plants (California
fescue, *Festuca californica,* and the Douglas iris, *Iris douglasiana,* for example) and
bulbs (like Mariposa lilies, *Calochortus* spp.). The land around residences in these
areas could be cleared for fire protection, and a savanna-style shade garden could
be developed with extra water for irrigation collected in a cistern.

In the moister areas heading north along the West Coast, there are many native
trees adapted to seasonal rainfall and wet air: Alaska cedar (*Callitropsis nootkaten-
sis*), paper birch (*Betula papyrifera*), western hemlock (*Tsuga heterophylla*), Mon-
terey pine (*Pinus radiata*), or Sitka spruce (*Picea sitchensis*). The widest and tallest
trees in the country are in California—the redwoods (*Sequoia sempervirens*) and
giant redwoods (*Sequoiadendron giganteum*). Ferns and redwood sorrel grow on
the floor beneath these titans.

Another version of savanna used to be common in the tall grass prairies in
parts of the Midwest where forests don't always succeed. Unlike the slightly acidic
and moist soils common in eastern forests, soils in the Midwest are likely to be
neutral to alkaline and described as "mesic"—normally having a moderate supply
of moisture, neither too moist nor too dry. The canopy is often open enough for the
dominant understory of grasses and forbs to be continuous below. Savanna may
also be found as an edge community between a forest and grassland, scrub, or
desert.

In the Great Plains, a lack of rain and the presence of grazing animals keep
trees from getting a foothold. In some places, lightning may touch off prairie fires
that burn tree seedlings and saplings but do not kill the herbaceous plants. At one
time, Native Americans did controlled burns to clear land for hunting, which also
limited tree growth.

The Rocky Mountains do not have trees above the timberline. In areas lower
down, however, there are woodlands. The southern Rockies have ponderosa pine,
piñon pine, aspens, and one-seed juniper in Colorado. The northern Rocky Mountain
forests up in Canada have a wide variety of species, for example western larch, Douglas fir, ponderosa pine, lodgepole pine, western red cedar, and western hemlock.

All of these regional plant communities could be drawn upon for shade garden
inspiration.

Adding Water to the Garden Program

Nothing brings life to a garden like a water feature—both figuratively and literally. A
body of water captures a bit of the sky and reflects it back to the rest of the garden.
Moving water, whether the gentle sound of a fountain or an exuberant waterfall,
brings sparkle. The water also attracts animals, especially birds.

Of course not everyone has a natural body of water in his or her garden (and
frankly, you may not want one). But human-made aquatic elements of some kind
should be included in every garden.

Bear in mind that water features—even simple ones—require maintenance.
The small pond in Brooklyn was the most demanding part of that garden. Every

OPPOSITE A Japanese-style gate adds
to an eclectic design in a cold-climate
Massachusetts garden that also
includes a red Japanese maple, brick
path, and stone ornaments.

ABOVE On the West Coast, nature is
an inspiration, for example, in big-tree
country where summers are dry and
winters are cold, where moss, inside-
out flower (*Vancouveria hexandra*)
and California huckleberry (*Vaccinum
ovatum*) cover the ground below a
western red cedar (*Thuja plicata*).

ABOVE Water takes on many forms in gardens. It runs in a stream under a bridge at Hay Honey Farm, a garden in northern New Jersey cared for by horticulturists Hilary and Michael Clayton.

RIGHT An overflowing urn becomes a fountain as water trickles over the edge, down the sides, and into a reservoir hidden beneath a gravel bed, and then is piped back up through a hole in the vessel to repeat the process.

OPPOSITE Water captures a bit of the sky and brings it down to earth. The pond at Rocky Hills, the New York garden of Henriette Suhr, adds light and sound to a backdrop of hybrid deciduous and evergreen azaleas.

week, I had to check the intake of the pump for debris. I had to clean the mechanical filter, which isn't hard, but then there are the unexpected (but frequent) emergencies: All of a sudden, the water level drops; a fish gets sick (you must have fish to limit the mosquito population); the pump quits; roots from a nearby tree find their way over the liner and into the water; the valve on the timer that trickles extra water gets stuck open; the fish are exposed to too much chlorine; the list of problems goes on. Aside from the water feature, my Brooklyn garden was quietly self-reliant.

Many references on how to make a small garden pond start with "choose a sunny site" or "you can't make a pond in the shade." I understand these warnings. If your goal is to grow flowering water lilies, you won't have a lot of success without full sun. The other reason to avoid a shady spot is that, in autumn, fallen leaves make a mess in the water. These tips are worth paying attention to, but they do not mean that a pond in the shade cannot be successful.

In a shady garden, you will have to cover the pond in the autumn to keep leaves from fouling the water. Some people use bird netting for this purpose, but I found that leaves get intractably caught in the net. I used an enormous sheet of window screen, which can be bought on a roll; it allows rainwater to drip into the pond and air to circulate. I laid the screen over the pond, on top of bamboo sticks positioned to cross from side to side and keep the screen from sagging, then attached it with those inexpensive spring clamps that are like oversized clothespins to vertical stakes driven into the ground. I removed the screen after the leaves fell, so it was only covered for a month or so.

In shade, the pond won't turn green from an explosion of algae, which often happens in a sunny location. There is also more oxygen in the water, since it won't heat up as much as it would in the sun. Oxygenated water is necessary for the kinds of fish that can live in an outdoor pond year-round. Those species and varieties are mostly carp, like goldfish, and for the more adventurous and devoted water gar-

OPPOSITE Nothing adds life to a garden like moving water. A small waterfall makes music in a rural garden, or a pleasant sound in an urban garden to temper the clamoring city.

ABOVE A constructed stream leads to a pond in a shaded Brooklyn garden that is home to the fish that help to control mosquitoes. Water isn't a place where bugs proliferate when it is stocked with the right kind of fish to catch and eat bothersome insects.

dener, there are koi—ornamental Japanese carp bred for extraordinary beauty. Let me tell you, koi require more maintenance, because they grow quite large and like to eat, making it necessary to clean the filter system even more often.

Koi can grow to a yard long or more, and it is not unheard of for them to live up to fifty years. You might consider putting the koi in your will, because if you keep them happy and healthy, they may outlive you. As with many pets, it will be harder to spend time away, and don't expect not to worry (is there an app for that?), especially if you have fish you have known since they were as long as your index finger, or that were born in the pond and could by now be graduating from med school.

The good news (yes, there is some) is that since there is so much interest in water gardens, technology keeps improving. There are new products coming out all the time that make caring for an outdoor pond more efficient and easier. When I first made my pond, I designed and built a skimmer out of a plastic trash container to keep debris off the surface of the water. The receptacle was buried in the soil and also housed the pump for the waterfall. About a decade later, one could buy complete ready-made skimmer, pump, filter, and waterfall units.

Of course, you don't need to have a pond to have water and the life it attracts, or movement and the sound that accompanies that. Birdbaths are practically necessary, and they do reflect the sky down to the shade garden. Small fountains that spray and overflowing urns that trickle will keep things moving. All of these do require, at the very least, cleaning and a replenishment of fresh water.

Is it all worth it? Yes. Just be ready to watch the lively fish in the pond at play and to welcome the birds that come to your garden for a drink—and plan to take more vacations in your own backyard.

OPPOSITE The pool built by Karl Garlid for the town garden planted by his wife, Mary Meyer, is quintessentially naturalistic. A lava rock was drilled and piped to have water constantly flowing over it and into the pond.

ABOVE A pond must be stocked with fish such as simple goldfish from the pet store or precious Japanese koi, which have vivid colors, can grow up to 2 feet (60 cm) long, and can live for fifty years.

CONTAINER GARDENS AND DRY SHADE IN THE GARDEN

When people describe to me the problem of shallow-rooted trees or incredibly dry shade due to tree-root competition, I recommend using containers for any plants they want to grow beneath those trees. This often comes as a surprise. Having containers requires some watering, but so would a planting in that same location. The plants you hope to grow will not be starved for moisture. The containers should be elevated on three bricks that are not placed directly on tree roots, if possible. The trees will not be harmed, and there will be air circulation for its shallow roots beneath the surface.

For permanent containers, select pots that are frost-proof and plants that are at least one USDA zone hardier than your garden. Hardy hostas are terrific in containers, for example. Woody plants tend to become a bit miniaturized, and at some point, they may either have to be planted in larger containers or have their roots trimmed bonsai-style.

As with all things garden, there are surprises. One year, I had an opportunity to buy some columnar box-wood, *Buxus sempervirens* 'Graham Blandy'. I didn't get around to planting all of them in the ground, so some stayed in the containers I bought them in. Well, after ten years, these plants are still alive—they're much hardier than I suspected. They have remained quite compact in their containers, which is an advantage in a shady spot. The growth, rather than splaying or becoming shaggy, is quite dense.

The containers I use are usually large—the larger the better. But that means I need a great deal of planting medium to fill them. If I am planting herbaceous perennials or annuals for temporary effects, I like to place something in the bottom of the planters to take up space. I have used inverted large nursery pots, packing peanuts or chunks of recycled blocks of Styrofoam packaging or rigid insulation. With these fillers the containers are lighter and easier to move. The technique is useful unless the containers are going to have tall plants and be placed in a windy site, for example a rooftop garden, in which case, they might blow over. Plastic containers can be bolted in place to wooden pallets or decking—with wooden spacers between the bottom and the deck surface. (For more on containers and planting, see page 226.)

RIGHT Styrofoam "peanuts" or blocks of expanded polystyrene foam from packing containers can be used in the bottom of a large pot to take up space and lighten the load by reducing the planting medium.

OPPOSITE Containers elevated on bricks allow plantings in an area above tree roots where they would otherwise be damaged by digging. The plants could be temporary tender species or permanent hardy ones like this collection of small hostas.

WANT A VEGETABLE GARDEN, TOO?

Can a home be found in your shade-garden program for growing food? No vegetables will grow or deliver fruit or even useable leaves in dense shade. Most fruiting plants, such as tomatoes, eggplants, and summer squash, need more than six hours of direct sunlight per day.

As with all vegetable gardens, soil is very important. Soil for most crops can be topped with compost and a mulch to retain moisture and suppress weeds. Soil for root crops such as carrots should be loosened up for the roots to grow straight and long. If you want to grow root vegetables but also want to avoid disturbing the ground, you can make raised beds—a garden bed that is built up above the existing ground level and contained by wood boards, stones, bricks, or other edging. New amended soil is brought in for planting.

There are some edibles that will produce in as few as three hours of sunlight. Like some of the spring ephemerals, early edibles such as radishes, leafy greens, and a few cool-season crops could deliver with the extra sunlight early and late in the season (woodland shade, filtered light, and light shade). Some people have more success when they use a mulch of reflective material to augment the light. Aluminum foil will work, or reflective silver Mylar (metallic, coated polyester film) on rolls. You can cover the soil between the plants too. Red plastic mulch, which is available from many sources, will help plants by reflecting the spectrum of light they use. However, I am not sure the aesthetic drawbacks make these extreme undertakings worthwhile.

I have grown winter squash in a half day of sun (filtered light) in New Jersey, but I have never had high yields. Root vegetables and leafy greens have the best chances for success in less than full-day sunlight. Vegetables such as potatoes, carrots, sweet potatoes, turnips, and rutabagas will grow in a bit of shade, but the harvest will be later than it would be in sun, the yields will be much smaller.

Greens such as leaf lettuce, endive, mesclun, arugula, Asian greens, Swiss chard, watercress, spinach, kale, and mustard and collard greens may be the best to try. Cardoon is an artichoke relative that is gorgeous in light shade and is also edible. Spinach will bolt in heat, and might prefer a bit of shade, especially in the middle of the day. You might not get big beets without full sun, but you will get beet greens. Some people have even had success with rhubarb. And, of course, there are the crosiers of the ostrich fern (page 199).

There are leafy herbs you can grow in shade. In light shade, feverfew, thyme, hyssop, tarragon, parsley, chamomile, chervil, sage, and chives will do well. You can try basil, especially the large-leaf varieties that gather more light. And although there are not all that many uses for it, lemon balm and a wonderful yellow-leaved variety commonly called lime balm do quite well even in light to medium shade. Lemon balm—*Melissa officinalis*—is a member of the mint family, and besides having typical square stems, it also has a habit of running, or invading surrounding areas. Most true mints, from the genus *Mentha*, will tolerate filtered light to medium shade; however, these plants will all do more than run—they'll gallop—and should be grown in containers.

Another tale of a galloping plant: I wanted to grow watercress in a very shady spot in the Brooklyn garden. I started with a bunch of watercress from the grocery store and tossed it into the reservoir of moving water in the waterfall at the top of the pond. It worked. So well, in fact, that the watercress began to steal gallons of water from the pond. I thought the liner had sprung a leak, but it was the plants. Out went the watercress.

There are a few ornamental plants that have edible shoots, but cutting them, of course, means no pretty plants. Ostrich fern crosiers are popular with foragers. The emerging shoots, which are shaped like bishop's crooks, are cut and sautéed in butter or olive oil. I've read warnings suggesting that eating too many of these could lead to a stomachache, so as with all things, enjoy in moderation. In any event, leave plenty of new growth for the fronds that will develop (page 199). As with anything from the ornamental garden, be sure you know well what you are eating.

A few perennial fruits will produce in varying amounts of sunlight. Pawpaws are small understory trees that bear fruit and are quite shade tolerant. Currants and gooseberries bear fruit in light shade. Alpine strawberry plants are not like their sun-loving cultivated counterparts. They do not put out runners, but stay in tidy clumps in light shade and bear continuously. You won't get tons of these small, fragrant, and intensely flavorful fruits, perhaps a tablespoonful at a time to top the morning cereal.

ABOVE It is challenging to grow human food in a shaded garden. However, leafy vegetables with large foliage like biennial kale (left) and perennial rhubarb (right) are good for light shade. You may have to experiment to find what works best in your shade.

RIGHT Among the handful of fruits that will bear in filtered light to medium shade are alpine strawberries. This one is *Fragaria vesca* 'Golden Alexandria', a handsome plant with chartreuse leaves that bears sweet aromatic berries.

PART 5

PLANTS WITH PURPOSE

THE RIGHT PLANT? YES, WITHIN REASON

TOP The yellow lady slipper orchid (*Cypripedium parviflorum* var. *pubescens*) likes acidic soil. Once stolen from the wild for sale, terrestrial slipper orchids are now being propagated by nurseries.

LEFT The right place for tiny liverwort (*Hepatica* spp.), with its ground-hugging lobed leaves and flower stems about 4 inches (10 cm) tall, is found nearly anywhere from deep to light shade and, surprisingly for a woodlander, neutral to slightly alkaline soil.

RIGHT Reddish foliage is usually a sign of cold resistance, but the new growth of plants like rodgersia (*R. pinnata* 'Chocolate Wings') is often damaged by a late frost. In our new climate, there are more warmer days in late winter that encourage new growth and flower buds at a time when there is still the danger of a freeze that could kill them.

In this section, we'll cover the primary plant groups of the shade garden, from trees on down to ground level.

That often-quoted gardening instruction advocating planting "the right plant in the right place" is excellent advice to enhance success and reduce garden maintenance, providing you have good places for plants, and your soil wasn't stripped away during the construction of your house.

"Right plant" means suitable for the conditions you have and the garden you want to create. An obvious example: It is better to plant a naturally low-growing shrub in front of a window than one that will grow large and require endless pruning to keep it from obscuring the view. Or when you have bright sunlight and clay soil, plant something that loves those conditions, rather than trying a plant that wants fast drainage and shelter from the sun. The rule has its applications and some exceptions. We'll discuss when it's best to follow such suggestions strictly and when there is wiggle room.

The more familiar we are with the natural growth habit of our plants, the more successful we can be in getting them to accommodate our needs. If you dream of creating formality, and your need is to express yourself by pruning shrubs into perfect balls and slabs, learn which ones will survive this extreme approach. If you insist on forcing a deciduous shrub like a deutzia (*Deutzia* spp.), which naturally produces long, arching stems, into a hedge or topiary shape, know that you will be disappointed.

On the other hand, shade-tolerant yews (*Taxus* spp.) can be pruned for years, even centuries, by you and your descendants. Near my property in New Jersey, a thick planting of yew hedge grows next to the road around the sign of a nearby pharmaceutical company. Every winter, deer venture out from the adjacent forest and browse these plants back to bare wood, and every spring, the yews replace the loss with lush new growth, in time to be eaten again the following winter. While the yews grow beautifully in the soil, moisture, and light in this spot, they are a deer favorite and not the best choice for this location.

Besides working to cultivate an awareness of their intended growth habits and sites, we can also look to nature for assistance when it comes to figuring out how to grow a plant or create a specific garden bed. The most logical way to determine a plant's needs is to learn about the place where it originated. If it grows in the local woodlands, chances are that it will succeed in your patch of woods as well. If a species originated in a part of the world with cold winters and very hot summers, it might do well in a similar climate in the United States.

Now, what if I want to grow a plant that does not come from a place that matches my conditions? Should I reject it as a "wrong" plant? In some cases, the right place can be created. We're going to be adding moisture-retaining organic matter whenever we can. So, although we might not have a woodsy soil from the get-go for a plant that likes that condition, we'll be creating it when possible. I met one gardener who grew acid-loving orchids. He placed large granite rocks around his plants at angles so the rain would wash down the stones toward the soil. He believed the acidic stone contributed to lowering the pH. I do not think this kind of manipulation should be a general approach, but this is horticulture, and here again, I am not against bending the rules to give a special plant what it likes.

We can also capitalize on the natural niches and microconditions that exist in any garden, no matter how small. For instance, if you know a plant doesn't like heat, don't plant it in a breeze-free location up against an obstruction. If you have a plant that needs a few more hours of sunlight than your garden receives, try it where it will enjoy a bit of extra heat radiating off a structure.

Right plant/right place would mean that you could try a plant that is said to be only marginally hardy in your climate. It might like the spot against the building or near rocks that absorb the heat by day and return it to the soil at night. However, an early flowering plant such as a weigela—say, *Weigela subsessilis* 'Canary'—would be encouraged to open its buds too soon in a warm spot, and those buds could be damaged by cold nights or a late frost. The same plant placed near the north side of a building, where the sunlight will not warm the buds until later in the season, may not suffer the same damage.

Damage can happen to herbaceous new growth as well. Kirengeshomas and rodgersias (*Kirengeshoma* spp. and *Rodgersia* spp.) often lose their first flush of leaves if planted in a low area. It might be warm during the day, but cold air could settle there at night and ruin the foliage (believe me). Most plants, thankfully, will survive such events once or even twice, but not forever. Take care where you place certain plants by carefully considering all conditions, and if necessary, move others to more hospitable settings.

PREVIOUS SPREAD A shaded path in Margaret Roach's garden leads under a large shrub willow to a flowering oakleaf hydrangea in late summer, but arguably, the most useful plant is the *Geranium macrorrhizum*, a weed-smothering ground cover with spice-scented foliage.

ABOVE Two drought-tolerant choices, variegated fairy bells (*Disporum sessile* 'Variegatum') above the ground covering dwarf Solomon's seal (*Polygonatum humile*).

Other Factors to Figure In

Along with light and the high and low summer and winter temperatures, there are matters such as moisture and drainage to consider when evaluating a location. Nearly all garden plants, excluding aquatic species, want air around their roots. In most temperate zones, a guaranteed snow cover in winter and excellent drainage year-round are the ideal. Most of the woodlanders, those that are our shade plants, like an evenly moist soil that neither dries out completely nor becomes water-logged. Too much moisture might lead to suffocation or rot. Too little water, and a plant that is not from an arid region might wilt, wither, shrink, and die.

In gardening, we probably discover the most from trial and error. You will learn by your successes, but also by your failures. I like to think that I never killed a plant without learning something. And that is especially true if, like I do, you try to coax certain plants to push the envelope. Tony Avent of Plant Delights Nursery says, "I believe every plant to be hardy until I have killed it myself . . . at least three times." I can't say that I go along totally with that notion, but you get the message. Some-times, whether it is me, climate, light, whatever, a plant I want to grow just won't make it in the garden. Before I give up on it, I'll move it around. If a plant is not doing well in a certain spot, I am more apt to move it than to watch it suffer a long, linger-ing death, and I've succeeded more often than I have failed. Put on your Sherlock Holmes hat and puzzle out what might be the cause and cure.

Everybody loses plants, even professionals, and more often than you might imagine. Please do not believe you should only have no-maintenance plants that grow without care. That is an impossible dream for a living garden. The best plant for a place might be the one that gives you the most pleasure, whether it is a local species or not, and whether or not it needs some TLC—especially in the beginning. It is comforting to remember that plants are on your side. They want to live.

A Sample Shade Garden

Let's look at a couple of actual shade plantings. An Eastern woodland could begin with the lowest level: a ground cover from the Appalachian Piedmont, mountain stonecrop (*Sedum ternatum*), which blooms with tiny white flowers. Here and there, a few wake-robin (*Trillium grandiflorum*) could pop up through the sedum. Just behind the stonecrop in a slightly brighter spot could be an early herbaceous perennial that spreads into a narrow stream of nearly blue flowers: wild sweet Wil-liam (*Phlox divaricata*). Among these plants might be few that are slightly taller and bloom later, such as wild columbine (*Aquilegia canadensis*) and bleeding heart (*Dicentra eximia*). These spring plants could bask in the shadows of a flowering dogwood tree (*Cornus florida*).

In light shade, a foreground plant could be the incredibly useful lady's mantle (*Alchemilla mollis*), flanked by a boxwood with chartreuse new growth that lasts for months before it turns dark green splashed with yellow or with yellow margins (for example, *Buxus microphylla* 'Wanford Page'). Behind the lady's mantle, there could be a mass of Japanese Solomon's seal (*Polygonatum odoratum* 'Variegatum' syn.

P. o. var. *pluriflorum* 'Variegatum') and, on the edge of this dense colony, a few self-sown violet columbine flowers and white allium (*Allium stipitatum*) from bulbs.

In another area, the ground cover might also be ephemeral, perhaps a late-winter blanket of blue-flowered glory-of-the-snow (*Chionodoxa sardensis*) bulbs. As those flowers fade, you could have a creeping ground cover of Jacob's ladder (*Polemonium reptans*). Soon, pale green points will appear in small clumps through the Jacob's ladder, and when its blue flowers have faded, the newly arrived leaves will unfurl from the pointed growth, and the plant will become a hosta in medium

ABOVE A typical woodland shade garden has low, spring-flowering perennials beneath high-limbed trees along a path, like here in Michigan. The path allows for close up viewing of flowers and easy maintenance. Inhabitants of the forest floor, like blue wild sweet Wiliam phlox, yellow slipper orchid, white foamflower, and trillium, are welcome in this environment.

SITING PLANTS FOR BEST EFFECT

Remember the garden "hierarchy:" As you consider a planting in your garden, you might try picturing it in your mind's eye as layers from the ground up, or from front to back. We talked about the forest hierarchy in part 3 (page 49) and how it can provide inspiration. When imagining your garden, think about low plants knitting together in the foreground, taller herbaceous plants in the mid-ground, and larger, more full plants, as well as shrubs, as a background foil. Or perhaps a fence or wall will mark the boundary of your property and form a background for a planting bed. Small trees come next, and all of these are in the shadows of tall existing trees, or whatever is the source of garden shade.

Follow the light: Another practical consideration: If possible, try to have plantings face south, or the direction from which the brightest light is coming in shady areas. In that way, the low plants will be in front and the taller ones behind them so as not to cast additional shade.

Repeat and repeat: There are aesthetic tactics to call upon, too, in visualizing the garden-to-be: the use of repetition, for instance, and also the shapes of each plant in a design. Repeating can bring a planting together. Echoing color can create cohesion. One lime-green hosta here, another one that is the same farther along, and another could become a motif that ties the spaces together.

Capitalize on shapes: Variety makes for a rich and active experience, but having what might be considered a less-distinctive sameness, with less contrast in shapes and heights, and perhaps a ground cover of one plant in a large swath, actually can make for a very soothing spot to stop and relax. In some places, though, you will want a bit more energy and impact in what is usually a reserved and quiet space.

I like to think of the shapes of plants as similar to punctuation in a sentence. Vertical plants always seem like exciting exclamation points and encourage me to move through a space. Repeating these fastigiate or columnar plants carries me along. Round objects, mounding shrubs, or floral globes held above foliage are like commas, telling me I may stop and linger for a moment to take in the scene. You can easily imagine one large spherical mound of boxwood in one spot, perhaps where paths come together, telling the viewer to stop: period.

OPPOSITE A variety of textures combined with shapes can be as rich and effective as arrangements of color. Here, globes of allium float above the small leaves of a boxwood, the arching stems of variegated Solomon's seal, and the tiny chartreuse flowers and water-beaded leaves of lady's mantle.

RIGHT Some arrangements of plant shapes and forms can act like punctuation marks. Vertical plants might be exclamation points, adding excitement to a planting; floating balls of the orange Exbury hybrid azalea 'Gibraltar' are the commas or periods that may add a pause to a stroll through the garden.

shade. Around the hosta could be selections of ferns like the Japanese painted fern (*Athyrium niponicum* 'Pictum') and alumroot, *Heuchera* species, for instance *H. americana* and *H. villosa*.

Behind the herbaceous perennials are a few azaleas that have just finished blooming. All of these plants grow below a mature oak tree with deep roots that do not compete with the perennials for moisture, and which has had some of its lower limbs removed.

The emerging pointed shoots of the hostas are an exciting sign of spring, and new or pubescent growth in some other perennials could be considered part of the show. Just as autumn color is amazing, as well as tree bark in winter, midspring could be a time to acknowledge some plants that display unusual forms and colors for weeks before they spread their leaves or form flower buds—for instance, blue cohosh (*Caulophyllum thalictroides*). This perennial emerges from the ground early in spring with smoky charcoal gray stems bent like a cobra head. The stems quickly climb to about 1 foot (30 cm) tall, then three-part, purple compound leaves emerge. The leaves turn green, and small clusters of buds open to unassuming greenish-yellow blossoms. In the summer, those pollinated flowers become perfectly round inedible blue berries.

Berries such as those also contribute to the aesthetics of a planting. I like to include local plants with autumn fruit to provide color through the winter and for wildlife to eat. Fruit is the way many plants disperse their seeds with the help of animals. I do not want to spread exotic plants, so I lean toward local fruiting plants.

Of course, seasonal interest from berries is just one point of interest, and these might form on herbaceous perennials, shrubs, or trees. Let's get to know some of the different types of plants that will live in our gardens.

Trees

You can't move your house, so the shadows it casts are a fixed factor in your garden-making puzzle. Sure, you can add a pergola (or take one down), but most of the addition or subtraction in a shade garden will center around trees, whether adding more, or editing existing ones.

No group of trees has more impact on shade than the tallest ones of the canopy, but none are more relevant to shade garden making than the ones that grow beneath them in the understory. We've learned about staging plantings from the ground covers in the foreground, the taller herbaceous perennials and then shade-tolerant shrubs in the middle areas, and behind those, small woodland trees. Depending on where you live, these understory trees are often spring-flowering species with open habits—space between their spreading branches.

The same trees are often seen on the lawns of suburbia—for example, white-flowering dogwood (*Cornus florida*). Out in the open, the small trees grow thick with branches and cover themselves with dense blankets of flowers in spring. In their forest origins, these same trees have sparse growth and, in the case of the dogwood, delicate blossoms spaced apart; they look more like fluttering butterflies than white clouds.

The understory trees native to your location could be the ones to learn about first when choosing species and varieties to grow behind and above the shrubs and in front of the tall trees.

Shrubs

Some of the best shrubs for light to medium shade are found in nature in the transitional edge between the open meadow and the woodland. Depending on the soil conditions, and pH (see page 209), these shrubs could range from acid loving, like North American native rhododendrons, to plants tolerant of alkaline soil, like arrowwood viburnum (*Viburnum dentatum*). Shrubs provide a good background foil for many shade plantings.

When integrating shrubs into a planting, arrange them by size and shade tolerance. Ideally, the largest plants would be close to the source of the shade, for example, near the trunk of the tall trees, a wall, or a fence. There may be competition for moisture from the tree, however. In all cases, you will want to leave space between the shrub and its neighbor.

And planting up against a house wall might be asking a lot of a shrub, or any plant. Depending on the material used for the wall, there could be alkalinity from

OPPOSITE LEFT In the timeline of the shade garden, some herbaceous perennials provide three-season interest. Blue cohosh (*Caulophyllum thalictroides*), native to eastern North America, begins in spring with charcoal gray shoots, then frothy flowers in summer, and later, turquoise berries.

OPPOSITE RIGHT Most shade gardens reach their colorful peak in spring before the trees of the canopy leaf out, when shrubs like azaleas, trees, bulbs, and herbaceous woodlanders explode with colorful flowers to attract pollinators.

ABOVE Understory trees like the eastern redbud (*Cercis canadensis*) can be found in colorful variety, such as the purple-leafed cultivar 'Forest Pansy'. In its shade are charteuse Japanese shrub mint (*Leucosceptrum japonicum* 'Gold Angel') and the wild Indian pink (*Spigelia marilandica*).

concrete, and the space below the roof's overhang can be dry (or being at the edge of a roof that has no gutters might mean there will be constant pounding during rainstorms).

I planted *Kerria japonica* close to a tree, because this shrub can be divided into individual wandlike stems with just a bit of root for planting in shallow spaces, as opposed to digging a large hole for a good-sized, balled-and-burlapped shrub that could disturb tree roots. Kerria is a member of the rose family that blooms in light to medium shade in midspring with single, inch-wide (2.5-cm) yellow flowers. I like the off-white variety, *K. j.* 'Albiflora', for its subtlety. Then there is the bright double pom-pom one, *K. j.* 'Pleniflora', which I thought might be too bright and ostentatious, but when it blooms early in spring, I am always glad to see its cheerful flowers.

New kerria canes emerge from the ground, like a nonaggressive clumping bamboo, and flower for a few years before they become old and woody, like mop-head hydrangeas. Those oldest stems should be pruned away to make room for young vigorous stems that are always coming up to replace them. In general, three-year-old stems should be removed at the ground right after the plant blossoms.

Shrubs in the shade will most likely lean in the direction of the brightest light. There may have to be some permanent stakes on which to tie the stems, and the branches will most likely need pruning as they begin to cover plants in front of them. Plants that have more permanent growth, unlike the triennial shoots of the kerria, may be pruned back to buds that face away from the center of the shrub, and also in the opposite direction of the brightest light. In general, you hope to make a vase shape with most deciduous shrubs, avoid crossed branches, and create an open center to allow in the most light. Never trim these shrubs as if they were hedges in full sunlight. That could make them produce a dense umbrella of foliage that would shade parts of the plant below and would lead to an unsightly mess, naked stems, and, in the worst case, death.

OPPOSITE Steps down to the creek-side walk at the Gardens at Mill Fleurs pass by every category of plant from trees and shrubs to perennials and annuals. White dogwood blossoms, perennial corydalis (*C. ochreleuca*) bloom with the airy, tender perennial *Euphorbia* 'Diamond Frost' in the foreground.

ABOVE The easy and reliable white-flowered shrub Japanese kerria (*Kerria japonica* 'Albiflora') pushes slender canes up as it creeps along the ground. As with *Hydrangea macrophylla*, the oldest stems can be pruned away at the ground.

· ·

SMALL NORTH AMERICAN TREES (UNDER 30 FEET/9M) FOR LIGHT SHADE AND FILTERED LIGHT

Acer pensylvanicum—snake-bark maple, moosewood

Aesculus pavia—red buckeye

Alnus incana subsp. *rugosa*—speckled alder

Amelanchier spp. and hybrids—shadblow, serviceberry

Asimina triloba—pawpaw

Carpinus caroliniana—hornbeam, ironwood

Celtis occidentalis—hackberry

Cercis canadensis—redbud

Chamaecyparis thyoides—Atlantic white cypress or Atlantic white cedar

Chionanthus virginicus—fringe tree

Cornus alternifolia—pagoda dogwood

Cornus florida—flowering dogwood, eastern dogwood

Corylus americana—American filbert, American hazelnut

Hamamelis virginiana—American witch hazel

Ilex opaca—American holly, and other *Ilex* spp.

Malus coronaria—sweet crabapple

Prunus americana—American plum

Prunus virginiana—chokecherry

Ptelea trifoliata—hop tree

Rhus typhina—staghorn sumac

Staphylea trifolia—American bladdernut

Stewartia spp.—stewartia, mountain camellia (American)

Styrax spp.—snowbell (American)

RIGHT A variegated selection of the eastern redbud, *Cercis canadensis* 'Silver Cloud', brightens an area in filtered light.

OPPOSITE, CLOCKWISE FROM TOP The flowering dogwood is famous for the white bracts (leaves) that surround its inconspicuous tiny flowers. It is a familiar understory tree that grows to 30 feet (9 m).

The fringe tree (*Chionanthus virginicus*) was aptly named.

One of the earliest signs of spring is when the serviceberry or shadblow (*Amelanchier arborea*) blooms. The flowers resemble flights of butterflies against the naked stems of the winter woodland.

Red buckeye (*Aesculus pavia*) is a small tree for light shade.

A FEW EXOTIC TREES FOR LIGHT SHADE AND FILTERED LIGHT

Acer japonicum varieties (not all)—full moon maples

Acer palmatum varieties (not all)—Japanese maple

Albizia julibrissin—mimosa (small leaves)

Cercidiphyllum japonicum and varieties—katsura

Chionanthus retusus—Chinese fringe tree

Cornus kousa and varieties—kousa dogwood

Heptacodium miconioides—seven-son flower

Pseudocydonia sinensis—Chinese quince

Stewartia pseudocamellia—Japanese stewartia

Styrax spp.—snowbell (Japanese, etc.)

ABOVE There were some unusual trees on my New Jersey property when I first arrived there in 1995. The multi-stemmed Japanese maple might be more than a hundred years old.

OPPOSITE One of the most beautiful small trees I added was the variegated Asian dogwood (*Cornus kousa* 'Wolf Eyes'). I planted it when it was only 3 feet (1 m) tall.

. . . .

A CASE FOR TREES

Scientists warn of an alarming increase in death rates among trees 100 to 300 years old in many of the world's forests, woodlands, savannas, farming areas, and even in cities. These are among the oldest living organisms on earth.

According to Professor David Lindenmayer of the ARC Centre of Excellence for Environmental Decisions (CEED) and Australian National University, this is a worldwide problem that affects most types of forests. And it is not only the trees; the loss will impact the wildlife that depends on them for survival.

A thirty-year study of eucalyptus forest in Australia showed that old trees were dying at ten times the normal rate in years without fires—apparently due to drought, high temperatures, logging, and other causes. According to their findings, similar trends were appearing in places like California and Brazil and in forests at all latitudes, from the savannas of Africa to the far-north European woodlands. The environmental consequences may be dire.

Consider Haiti and the Dominican Republic. They share the island of Hispaniola, but the Haitians have deforested their half of the island from the earliest times, especially when they paid for their independence from France in 1804, in part with timber. And, of course, that means the loss of species of birds and countless other animals that depend on the habitat. Now, when hurricanes hit the island, Haiti suffers terrible floods and erosion. The Dominican Republic, which has not been completely deforested, does not. The Dominican Republic is now cutting its forests, but fortunately, there are some protected areas, so around 40 percent of that part of the island is still covered with trees.

RIGHT Forests of eucalyptus in Australia, the tallest flowering plants on earth, are threatened with destruction.

OPPOSITE The empress tree (*Paulownia tomentosa*) has become a weed in recent times, as it favors a warming climate. I cut mine back to 4 inches (10 cm) every spring in order to produce huge leaves on a shoot up to 15 feet (4.5 m) in one season, and to prevent invasive seed production.

SOME TREES, PERHAPS, TO AVOID

Not all trees are created equal, and there are some trees to avoid. Norway maples (*Acer platanoides*) should never be planted in the United States, for example. For one thing, they are moisture-guzzling invasive aliens that leaf out earlier and drop their leaves later than local species. They put an allelopathic chemical in the soil that inhibits the growth of other plants, and they produce blackish-green shingle-like leaves creating some of the densest shade of any deciduous tree. Planting beneath them is next to impossible. This species is commonly sold at nurseries and is also available from mail-order sources.

Thankfully, most (but not all) real pest trees will not be found in nurseries. Tree of heaven (*Ailanthus altissima*) was originally brought to the United States in a failed attempt to establish a silkworm industry. The caterpillars didn't eat it, but the tree escaped to invade woodlands, tree farms, and cities all over America. The princess or empress tree (*Paulownia tomentosa*) below makes an interesting "cutback" specimen that produces huge leaves on new growth when sawed at ground level each spring. But if not cut, its handsome flowers lead to millions of seeds that drift on the wind to become weeds wherever they can.

There are trees that are notorious for dropping branches, or those that have pest issues. The silver maple (*Acer saccharinum*) is a brittle tree not commonly chosen for landscapes, but found in them, nonetheless. A dead branch falling on the shade garden with all its weight and velocity could wipe out any plant in its path. Smaller trees can be planted below taller trees to break the fall of branches, pinecones, and other debris from above. But of course, be aware that damage could happen to the understory tree.

In Brooklyn, the European little-leaf linden (*Tilia cordata*) is a common street tree, and it's a pretty good one, but for much of the summer, it is attacked by aphids that secrete a sticky "honeydew," the bane of people who park beneath them. In Washington, DC, the Osage orange (*Maclura pomifera*) is a familiar street tree. In the autumn, its beautiful fruits, which are the size of softballs—and somewhat heavier—fall and dent the parked cars below.

We're dealing with nature here, so there will be surprises. I'm not thrilled when a fallen tree presents an "opportunity" for new plantings, but it happens. As in other calamitous situations, pitch in, get involved, and become part of the process of cleaning up and planning for the future.

· ×

SHOP FOR GREAT BARK

Bark is a tree's first line of defense, its armor—and like our skin, bark is mostly made of dead cells. Some trees, like the common juniper, slough off strips of outer tissue every year. Others keep adding to their bark, building it into a thick, hard shell over time.

Choosing a tree for its bark might be rather low on your list. But down in the shade, the trunk of a tree can be a focal point. However overlooked, bark may be one of the best things to consider for year-round, and especially winter, interest. While most of us know the birch, with its white bark and black dashes, other trees may be considered, such as the kousa dogwood's patchy camouflage, much like the Japanese stewartia's, and the vivid crape myrtle, or the peeling amber curls of the paperbark maple. Tall trees with interesting bark at ground level include the sycamore, lacebark pine, and even the smooth gray hide of the beech.

Some trees with wonderful bark

Acer buergerianum—trident maple (1)

Acer griseum—paperbark maple (2)

Betula spp.—birch (various) (3, 4, 12)

Fagus spp.—beech (various) (5)

Heptacodium miconioides—seven-son flower (6)

Lagerstroemia indica—crape myrtle (7)

Metasequoia glyptostroboides—dawn redwood (8)

Phellodendron lavallei—lavalle's cork tree (and others) (9)

Pinus bungeana—lacebark pine (10)

Platanus occidentalis—sycamore (11)

Platanus × acerifolia—London plane

Populus tremuloides—quaking aspen (and others)

RIGHT The paperbark maple (*Acer griseum*) is renowned for its cinnamon colored exfoliating bark. Plant it where the low rays of the afternoon sun in winter can ignite the peeling bark.

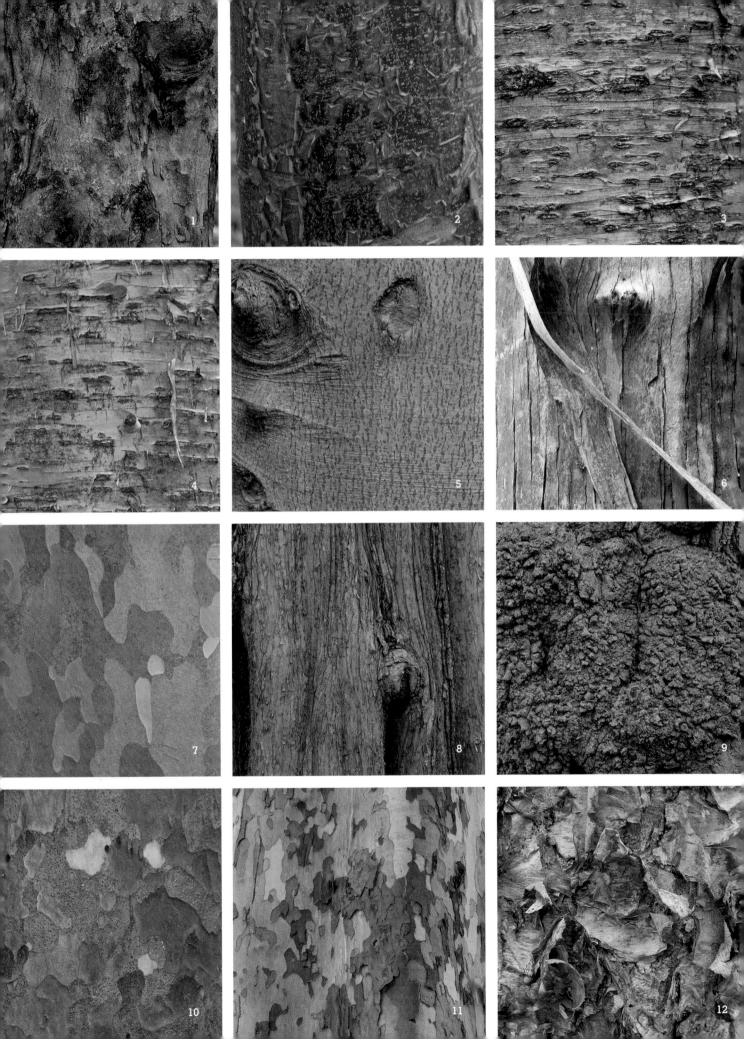

SHRUBS FOR SHADE

EVERGREEN SHRUBS

Andromeda glaucophylla—bog rosemary

Aucuba japonica—Japanese aucuba, spotted laurel

Berberis darwinii—Darwin's barberry

Brahea armata—Mexican blue palm

Buxus spp. and varieties—boxwood

Camellia spp.—camellia

Cephalotaxus harringtonia—Japanese plum yew

Choisya ternata—Mexican orange

Coprosma repens and varieties—looking-glass bush

Cycas revoluta—sago palm

Daphniphyllum macropodum—daphnaphyllum

Euonymus fortunei—wintercreeper

Euonymus japonicus—Japanese spindle

Euonymus kilautschovicus 'Manhattan'—Manhattan euonymus

Fatsia japonica—fatsia, glossy-leaved paper plant

Fargesia nitida—fargesia, fountain bamboo

Gardenia jasminoides—gardenia

Gaultheria procumbens—American wintergreen

Ilex spp.—holly

Ilex crenata—Japanese holly

Illicium spp.—Florida anise, star-anise

Jasminum nudiflorum—winter jasmine (variegated)

Kalmia latifolia—mountain laurel

Leucothoe spp.—leucothoe

Loropetalum chinense—Chinese fringe

× *Mahoberberis* hybrids—mahoberberis

Mahonia spp.—holly grape

Michelia (syn. *Magnolia*) *figo*—banana shrub

Microbiota decussata—Siberian cypress

Nandina domestica—heavenly bamboo

Osmanthus spp.—osmanthus, tea olive

Pieris japonica—Japanese pieris, andromeda

Pittosporum tobira—Japanese pittosporum, Japanese mock-orange

Podocarpus spp.—podocarpus

Prunus laurocerasus—cherry laurel

Rhododendron spp.—azalea

Rhododendron spp.—rhododendron

Ruscus aculeatus—butcher's broom

Sabal minor—dwarf palmetto

Sarcococca spp.—sweet box

Schefflera brevipedunculata—hardy schefflera

Skimmia japonica—Japanese skimmia

Ternstroemia gymnanthera—cleyera

Trochodendron aralioides—wheel tree

Viburnum rhytidophyllum—leatherleaf viburnum

Vaccinium spp.—huckleberry

Viburnum spp.—viburnum

Viburnum tinus—laurustinus

NEEDLE-LEAFED EVERGREEN SHRUBS

Cephalotaxus harringtonii—Japanese plum yew

Chamaecyparis obtusa and varieties—hinoki cypress

Cryptomeria japonica—Japanese cedar

Microbiota decussata—Siberian cypress

Podocarpus spp. and varieties—yew pine, podocarpus

Sequoia sempervirens 'Prostrata'—prostrate coast redwood

Taxus spp. and cultivars—yew

Thuja plicata—western red cedar

Tsuga canadensis—Canadian hemlock

DECIDUOUS SHRUBS

Abelia × *grandiflora*—glossy abelia

Abelia mosanesis—fragrant abelia

Abutilon spp. and varieties—flowering mallow

Aesculus parviflora—bottlebrush buckeye

Aesculus californica—California buckeye

Aronia arbutifolia—red chokeberry

Callicarpa spp.—beautyberry

Calycanthus floridus—Carolina sweetshrub

Cardiandra alternifolia—herbal hydrangea

Ceanothus americanus—New Jersey tea

Chaenomeles speciosa—flowering quince

Chimonanthus praecox—wintersweet

Clerodendrum trichotomum—harlequin glorybower (potentially invasive)

Clethra alnifolia—summersweet

Corylopsis spp.—fragrant winter hazel

Daphne spp.—daphne

Deutzia spp. and varieties—deutzia

Edgeworthia chrysantha—paperbush

Eleutherococcus sieboldianus—fiveleaf aralia

Enkianthus campanulatus—redvein enkianthus

Exochorda × *macrantha*—pearlbush

Fothergilla spp.—fothergilla, witch-alder

Garrya spp. and varieties—silk-tassel shrub

Hamamelis spp.—witch hazel

Hibiscus syriacus—rose of Sharon

Hydrangea arborescens—smooth hydrangea

Hydrangea aspera—bigleaf hydrangea

Hydrangea macrophylla—mophead hydrangea

Hydrangea paniculata varieties—panicle hydrangea

Hydrangea quercifolia spp. and varieties—oakleaf hydrangea

Hypericum spp.—St. John's wort

Itea virginica—Virginia sweetspire

Kerria japonica—Japanese kerria

Lindera spp.—spicebush

(*photos of evergreen shrubs continue on page 155*)

Lonicera nitida—boxleaf honeysuckle

Paeonia woody species and varieties—tree peony

Poncirus (syn. *Citrus*) *trifoliata*—hardy trifoliate orange

Rhododendron spp.—native azaleas

Rhodotypos scandens—jetbead

Rubus odoratus—purple-flowering raspberry, thimbleberry

Salix integra 'Hakuro Nishiki'—Nishiki willow, Japanese variegated willow

Spiraea × vanhouttei—Vanhoutte spiraea

Spiraea prunifolia 'Plena'—bridal wreath spiraea

Spiraea thunbergii 'Ogon'—Thunberg's meadowsweet

Stachyurus praecox—stachyurus

Symphoricarpos albus—snowberry

Tetrapanax papyifera—rice paper plant

Vaccinium arboreum—farkleberry

Vaccinium ashei—rabbit eye blueberry

Viburnum acerifolium—maple leaf viburnum

Viburnum dentatum—arrowwood

Viburnum lentago—nannyberry

Viburnum macrocephalum—Chinese snowball

Viburnum nudum var. *nudum*—possumhaw, smooth witherod

Viburnum nudum var. *Cassinoides*—witherod

Viburnum opulus var. *americanum*—American cranberry bush

Viburnum rafinesquianum—downy arrowwood

Viburnum sargentii 'Onondaga'—Sargent viburnum

Weigela subsesselis 'Canary'—weigela

Xanthorhiza simplicissima—yellowroot

PREVIOUS SPREAD
Evergreen shrubs:

1 *Choiysa ternata* 'Sundance'—gold Mexican orange

2 *Daphniphyllum macropodom*—Daphniphyllum, false daphne

3 *Euonymus kiautschovicus* 'Manhattan'—Manhattan euonymus

4 *Kalmia latifolia*—mountain laurel

5 *Mahonia hybrid*—holly grape

6 *Microbiota decussata*—Siberian cypress

7 *Pieris japonica*—Japanese pieris, andromeda

8 *Pittosporum tobira* 'Variegata'—variegated pittosporum, variegated Japanese mock-orange

9 *Camellia japonica*—camellia

10 *Prunus laurocerasus*—cherry laurel

11 *Buxus sempervirens* 'Rotundifolia'—round-leaved boxwood

12 *Viburnum rhytidophyllum*—leatherleaf viburnum

OPPOSITE
Evergreen shrubs (continued):

13 *Sarcococca hookeriana* var. *humilis*—sweet box

14 *Skimmia japonica*—Japanese skimmia

15 *Taxus baccata* 'Fastigiata'—Irish yew

16 *Ilex glabra*—inkberry

17 *Leucothoe fontanesiana* 'Rainbow'—Variegated doghobble

18 *Loropetalum chinensis* var. *rubrum*—Chinese fringe

Deciduous shrubs:

1 *Calycanthus floridus*—Carolina sweetshrub (detail)

2 *Kerria japonica* 'Pleniflora'—Japanese kerria

3 *Clethra alnifolia*—summersweet

4 *Corylopsis* 'Winterthur'—Winterthur winter hazel

5 *Clerodendron trichotomum*—harlequin glorybower

6 *Poncirus trifoliata* (syn. *Citrus trifoliata*)—trifoliate orange (detail)

Deciduous shrubs (continued):

7 *Deutzia scabra* 'Codsall Pink'—deutzia

8 *Edgeworthia chrysantha*—paper bush (detail)

9 *Enkianthus campanulatus*—redvein enkianthus (fall color)

10 *Hibiscus syriacus* 'Diana'—Rose-of-Sharon

11 *Fothergilla major*—fothergilla (detail)

12 *Viburnum macrocephalum*—Chinese snowball (detail)

13 *Symphoricarpos albus*—snowberry

14 *Lindera glauca*—narrow-leaf spicebush (fall color)

15 *Cardiandra alternifolia*—herbal hydrangea

16 *Callicarpa americana*—American beautyberry

17 *Rubus odoratus*—thimbleberry, purple flowered raspberry

18 *Stachyurus praecox* 'Rubriflora'—stachyurus, early spiketail

19 *Hydrangea quercifolia* 'Snowflake'—snowflake oakleaf hydrangea

....

HARDY PALMS

In climate zones 8 and warmer, gardeners might consider shrubby palms, many of which have pinnate fronds that pass light through to the ground below. Select a spot for a palm where it will be out of direct winter winds, which may not kill the plant, but could result in unsightly burning of evergreen foliage.

The best time to transplant palms is in spring to early summer, after the soil has warmed. Be careful not to overly disturb the roots. If the palm has arrived bare-root (washed clean of soil) from a mail-order source, soak it in water for an hour or so and plant it as soon as possible (as with all bare-root plants), and if you can't, wrap the roots with damp burlap and place the plant out of any direct sunlight.

Some palms can tolerate moist soil; others cannot, but in general, avoid a site that remains wet through the growing season. Still, you'll want to keep the planting area moist for the first growing season to help establish the young plant. Do not fertilize in the first year.

In time, and in frost-free climates, some of the shrubby palms will grow into trees. Those that form trunks over the years with scars from faded fronds have the potential to outgrow their selected sites in the shade garden. Palms grow up or out from the center of the plant—they only put on growth from terminal sites. Unlike other branching woody plants, pruning a palm to keep it short will kill it.

There are some hardier species for the adventurous "tropical-style" gardener in somewhat colder zone 7 in light to medium shade. Here are some examples of the cold-hardier palms and a palm-like cycad, along with the probable minimum temperatures they should be expected to withstand:

Allagoptera arenaria—seashore palm (25°F / -4°C)

Arenga engleri—dwarf sugar palm (25°F / -4°C)

Brahea armata—blue hesper palm (10°F / -12°C)

Butia capitata—jelly palm (15°F / -9.5°C)

Chamaedorea microspadix—hardy bamboo palm (20°F / -6°C)

Chamaerops humilis—Mediterranean fan palm (10°F / -12°C)

Cycas revoluta—sago palm (a cycad, not a palm; 20°F / -6°C)

Rhapidophyllum hystrix—needle palm (0°F / -18°C or below)

Rhapis excelsa—lady palm (20°F / -6°C)

Sabal minor—dwarf palmetto (-5°F / -20°C)

Serenoa repens (syn. *Sabal serrulatum*)—saw palmetto (15°F / -9.5°C)

Trachycarpus fortunei—windmill palm (5°F / -15°C)

Washingtonia filifera—California fan palm (15°F / -9.5°C)

OPPOSITE The windmill palm (*Trachycarpus fortunei*), which can grow over 10 feet (3 m), is among the cold-hardiest palms, as it can withstand temperatures reported as low as 5°F (-15°C).

Vines

Vines climb toward the treetops to capture as much light as possible. They can add a lot to the garden scene, and even in some shade—since many vines love to have their roots where it is cool and moist. But as with other types of plants, we must choose carefully, with eyes open. Leaning on a friend is often a good idea, but it can also be a bit of a drag, and in the garden, vines can be difficult. Scampering plants can damage trees if they grow on them, or twist a trellis into a contorted mess.

But don't dismiss an entire genus if one of the members is a dangerous thug. The deliciously fragrant Hall's honeysuckle (*Lonicera japonica* 'Halliana') is an invasive monster that has caused horrible destruction to natural woodland areas in just about every place where it has been planted. On the other hand, one of the nicest vine choices is an eastern North American cousin, the evergreen or trumpet honeysuckle (*Lonicera sempervirens*) and its varieties, which grow naturally from Texas north through Quebec. The tubular blossoms of the species are usually red, but a very nice selection is the creamy-yellow flowered 'John Clayton'. These nonaggressive vines are favorites of hummingbirds. They will not produce heavy shade and therefore could be a good choice to grow over a pergola to cast medium shade. Unfortunately, unlike their evil cousin, these honeysuckles do not have fragrant flowers.

Perhaps the deepest living-shade producer is another North American climber, the pipe vine or Dutchman's pipe (*Aristolochia macrophylla*), named for the shape of its tiny flowers. The vine is the specific host for the larva of the pipevine swallowtail butterfly. The plant's heart-shaped leaves overlap like shingles and provide a good deal of unbroken shade at the height of summer. The vine itself is also shade-tolerant, in case you are building a pergola that does not get full sun all day. There is a less hardy variant from the West Coast, *A. californica*, which does not have showy flowers, either, but there are several tropical species with spectacular blossoms for seasonal plantings or the greenhouse.

Another choice for warmer climates might be Armand's clematis (*Clematis armandii*), with lance-shaped evergreen leaves and slightly fragrant white flowers in late winter to early spring, depending on where you live. This is just one of many clematis species and varieties, a good number of which are tolerant of filtered light. You won't get as many flowers on vines in the shade, but some of the large-flowered hybrids could be worth trying. These plants also prefer to have their roots in cool well-drained soil that does not dry out.

Vines generally work on making roots when first planted. It is said of them that "first year they sleep; second year they creep; third year they leap." The point is that it takes vines a while to get established, and that seems to be especially true of the deciduous climbing hydrangea (*Hydrangea anomala* subsp. *petiolaris*) and its cousins, the *Schizophragma* species and varieties, the best known of which is the Japanese climbing hydrangea (*S. hydrangeoides*). Both of these deciduous vines will tolerate some shade, and both have little rootlets, like the trumpet vine, that will grow into wood and are best kept to the pergola and off the house.

Vines can be tricky, though, and aggressive. A North American native with lovely flowers, the trumpet creeper (*Campsis radicans* and varieties) can become

a monster. The vine climbs in various ways—with holdfasts (little rootlets along the stem that can grow into and damage wood siding), and with the vine itself, which can slip behind a trellis that might be attached to a dwelling, and as it grows, break the support or pull it right off the house. The vine also produces runners that sprout new plants in unwanted places, like garden beds or between the stepping-stones of the path. Just because a plant is native, or even local, does not mean it should be welcome in every garden.

There are hundreds of cultivars of English ivy (*Hedera helix*), and most are as hardy as the species and fairly well-behaved. The original species is not, and quite simply does not, belong in any garden. If you find a nice cultivated variety with blue leaves, or gold ones, variegation in white, gray, or yellow, ruffled miniature leaves, and more, keep your eye on it and have pruners ready at all times to cut off any foliage that does not resemble the selected variety but looks like the species—this is what is called a reversion. That said, I wouldn't be without 'Buttercup', which is bright yellow the first year and turns very dark green the second. This one is good ground cover for use away from tree trunks, but can also climb over and soften a stone wall. 'Goldheart' has a yellow splotch in the center of its green leaves and brightens a shady spot. Neither of these has reverted for me, and they are demure in shade, but I still do not let them out of my sight.

ABOVE Vines can fill in the layers between the plants of the forest floor and the treetops above them. Keep your eye on vines growing on trees. If variegated Miranda climbing hydrangea (*H. anomala petiolaris* 'Miranda') grows too tall, it will have to be pruned.

Vines for Filtered Light to Light Shade

Actinidia kolomikta—kiwi vine (the showy male form) and its hardy cultivar, 'Arctic Beauty'

Aristolochia macrophylla—Dutchman's pipe

Bignonia capreolata—cross vine

Clematis spp. and varieties, such as evergreen Armand's clematis (*C. armandii*) and *C. montana*

Gelsemium sempervirens—Carolina jessamine, Carolina jasmine, evening trumpet flower

Holboellia coriacea 'China Blue'— evergreen holboellia (tender)

Jasminum nudiflorum—winter jasmine

Lonicera periclymenum and varieties— woodbine

Lonicera sempervirens and varieties— trumpet honeysuckle

Wisteria frutescens—American wisteria

Vines for Medium Shade

Hedera canariensis varieties—Algerian ivy (for warm climates; watch this one)

Hedera colchica varieties—Persian ivy (another to keep an eye on)

Hedera helix—English ivy, varieties like 'Glacier', 'Goldheart', and 'Buttercup'

Hydrangea anomala subsp. *petiolaris*— climbing hydrangea

Parthenocissus tricuspidata and cultivars—Boston ivy

Parthenocissus quinquefolia and cultivars—Virginia creeper

Schizophragma hydrangeoides— Japanese climbing hydrangea

1 *Aristolochia macrophylla*— Dutchman's pipe

2 *Clematis armandii*—Armand's clematis

3 *Clematis* 'Betty Corning'—clematis (detail)

4 *Clematis rehderiana*—nodding virgin's bower

5 *Clematis*, large-flowered hybrid— clematis

6 *Hedera helix* 'Buttercup'—gold English ivy

7 *Jasminum nudiflorum*—winter jasmine

8 *Lonicera sempervirens*—trumpet honeysuckle

9 *Parthenocissus henryana*—silver vein creeper

10 *Hedera colchica* 'Sulphur Heart'— variegated Persian ivy

In Between—the Herbaceous Perennials

As we have discussed, the woodland is composed of layers based on height: the canopy of the tall trees, the understory of smaller trees, the shrub layer in the middle, and spring ephemerals on the forest floor. This is the inspiration for the shade garden as well, where the lowest plants are in front, and the tallest at the rear. In between are the plants of the middle layer, mostly the herbaceous perennials that are the subject of this section. Unlike the woody plants (shrubs, trees, and most vines) these plants appear to die after the killing frost but will return with new growth in the spring.

The herbaceous perennials for shade may be short or tall, and are useful for their size, foliage form and texture, and time of bloom. Some of the plants may be local to your area; others may have originated in different regions of the temperate world. Some are spring ephemerals, but most begin to bloom just after, are taller, and do not always become dormant in the summer. We want some of them to carry on right through the fall, perhaps producing berries like a few of the *Actaea* species.

It's the job of taxonomists to keep relationships of plants up to date as science discovers more and more ways (including DNA analysis) to classify plants, and there have been many name changes in the recent past. (I've heard that some taxonomists may want to change the name of those who practice this discipline to "systematists.") The number of members of the *Actaea* genus grew; the *Dicentra* genus shrank. I'll try to help with a few examples of good plants (and some new terms as of this writing).

Many people are familiar with the woodland species of *Dicentra* that are ephemeral, like Dutchman's breeches (*Dicentra cucullaria*) and squirrel corn (*D. canadensis*). A few other species do not fade away, and may even continue to bloom in a cool shady spot for months, for example, the foot-tall (30-cm) wild bleeding heart or fringed bleeding heart from the eastern United States that is common in the Appalachian mountain range (*D. eximia*). Even if this one quits blooming when the days get hot, it often produces a flush of new blossoms in late summer when the weather cools off again. The flowers are heart-shaped, and the inner petals seem to drip from the outer petals, giving it its common name. Plants in the wild have variably colored flowers, most often a dull lavender-pink, but one that I grew in my garden before the floods had deep ruby red blossoms. *D. formosa* is a very similar plant from the West Coast with common names such as western bleeding heart, Pacific bleeding heart, and usually, just bleeding heart.

The best-known plant with this common name is a showy perennial growing 2 to 3 feet (60 cm to 1 m) tall. This one begins to blossom as the ephemerals fade, and continues for several weeks, but the flowers and foliage melt away by midsummer. Formerly *Dicentra spectabilis*, this Asian cousin is now known by the genus and species names *Lamprocapnos spectabilis*. The foliage is lovely, kind of like Italian parsley, but the flowers steal the show, and really do suggest the familiar name. There is an exquisite white-flowered cultivar, *L. s.* 'Alba', and an over-the-top version with golden foliage called 'Gold Heart'.

(continued on page 173)

OPPOSITE

1 *Acanthus hungaricus*—bear's breeches

2 *Aconitum* spp.—monkshood

3 *Alchemilla mollis*—lady's mantle

4 *Amsonia elliptica*—blue star

5 *Astrantia major* 'Alba'—masterwort

6 *Begonia grandis* subsp. *evansiana* 'Alba'—hardy begonia

HERBACEOUS PERENNIALS

Unlike trees and shrubs, which are woody perennials, herbaceous perennials have soft tissues. The ones we are interested in here will bloom with or after spring ephemerals, or will have berries for later interest or colorful foliage or both. Some are tall and slender; others have low basal growth—most famously, of course, the hostas. The list on page 168 includes some of the best perennials for gardens, along with flower color, height, season of bloom, and estimated light requirements.

Herbaceous perennials (cont.):

7 *Heuchera americana* 'Sterling Silver'—sterling silver alum root, coral bells

8 *Heuchera villosa* 'Caramel'—caramel alum root, coral bells

9 *Iris foetidissima*—stinking iris

10 *Iris fulva*—copper iris

11 *Symphyotrichum* spp.—aster

12 *Lamium orvala*—balm-leaved archangel, red dead nettle

13 *Paeonia obovata*—species peony

14 *Pycnanthemum muticum*—mountain mint

15 *Rohdea japonica* (variegated)—sacred lily (semievergreen)

16 *Sedum spectabile* 'Brilliant'—stonecrop (detail)

17 *Syneilesis aconitifolia*—syneilesis

18 *Tricyrtis* spp.—toad lily

19 *Aruncus dioicus*—goatsbeard

20 *Boehmeria nipononivea* 'Kogane Mushi'—Japanese false nettle

21 *Geum rivale*—water avens (detail)

22 *Lamprocapnos spectabilis* 'Gold Heart'—gold heart old-fashioned bleeding heart

23 *Disporum flavens*—fairy bells

24 *Ligularia dentata* 'Britt Marie Crawford'—ligularia

25 *Polygonatum humile*—dwarf Solomon's seal

26 *Lamprocapnos spectabilis* 'Alba'—white old-fashioned bleeding heart

. . . .

Herbaceous Perennials

Key: LS—light shade; FL—filtered light; MS—medium shade; SH—full or dense shade; WS—woodland shade. For more about the degrees of light, see page 46.

Acanthus hungaricus—bear's breeches; zones 5–10; LS, FL, MS; purple and white; 3' (1 m); summer

Acanthus mollis—bear's breeches; zones 7–10; LS, FL, MS; white with maroon bracts; 3–5' (1–1.5 m); summer

Acanthus spinosus—bear's breeches; zones 5–10; LS, FL, MS; purple, pink; 3–4' (1–1.2 m); summer

Aconitum spp.—monkshood; zones 2–9; LS; most have blue flowers; 2'+ (60 cm+) by variety; summer to fall

Actaea pachypoda—doll's eyes, white baneberry; zones 3–8; WS, LS, FL, MS, SH; white with charming (toxic) white berries; 1.5–2.5' (45–75 cm); mid- to late spring

Actaea rubra—red baneberry; zones 3–8; WS, LS, FL, MS, SH; white with (toxic) red berries; 1.5–2.5' (45–75 cm); mid- to late spring

Actaea species with tall flower spikes formerly classified as *Cimicifuga*—bugbane; zones 3–9; LS, FL, MS; white; 4–5' (1.2–1.5 m); late spring to fall by species

Adenophora spp. and varieties—ladybells; zones 3–9; LS, FL, MS; purple/blue; 1.5–3' (45 cm–1 m); midspring to summer

Adonis spp.—adonis; zones 4–8; WS, FL, LS; yellow; 1' (30 cm); early spring

Alchemilla mollis—lady's mantle; zones 3–8; LS, FL; acid green flowers; 1–1.5' (30–45 cm); early summer

Amsonia spp.—blue star; zones 3–9 depending on species; LS, FL; blue flowers; 2'+ (60 cm+); spring

Anaphalis margaritacea var. *cinnamomea*—common pearly everlasting; zones 3–9; LS; white; 2' (60 cm); late summer to fall

Anaphalis triplinervis—three-veined pearly everlasting; zones 3–9; LS; white; 2' (60 cm); summer to early fall

Anemone (fall) hybrids—Japanese anemone; zones 4, 5–8; LS, FL; white, pink; 2.5–4' (75 cm–1.2 m); late summer to fall

Anemone (woodland, spring-blooming) spp.—windflower; zones 4–8; WS, LS, FL, MS by species; white, yellow; 4–15" (10–38 cm) by species; midspring to summer; a few are aggressive spreaders

Angelica archangelica—garden angelica; zones 4–9; LS, FL; white; 5–7' (1.5–2 m); summer

Aquilegia spp.—columbine; zones 3–10; LS, FL; all colors; 1–3' (30 cm–1 m) by variety; spring through summer by variety

Aralia (herbaceous) species—spikenard, aralia; zones 3–8; LS, FL, MS, SH; white and green; 3–7' (1–2 m); summer

Arisaema spp.—jack-in-the-pulpit, cobra lily; zones 4–9; FL, MS, SH; brown; 1–2.5' (30–76 cm); spring to early summer by species

Arum italicum—Italian arum; zones 6–10; LS, FL, MS; white; 1.5' (45 cm); late spring (red berries in fall, invasive in some areas)

Aruncus dioicus—goatsbeard; zones 3–9; LS, FL, MS; white; 5' (1.5 m); summer

Asarum spp.—wild ginger; zones 5–9 by species; LS, FL, MS, SH; brown; 3" (7.5 cm); early to midspring

Aster (syn. *Eurybia*) spp. (woodland species)—aster; zones 3–8; LS, FL, MS; white with yellow and red; 1.5–2.5' (45–75 cm); late summer

Astilbe spp. and varieties—astilbe, false spiraea; LS, FL, MS; white, pink, lavender, red; 1–4' (30 cm–1.2 m); summer

Astrantia major—masterwort; zones 4–9; LS, FL; white; 2.5–3' (75 cm–1 m); midspring to early summer (look for cultivars)

Begonia grandis subsp. *evansiana*—hardy begonia; zones 6, 7–10; LS, FL, MS, SH; pink, white; 2' (60 cm); late summer

Boehmeria spp.—Japanese false nettle; zones 6–9; LS, FL; white; variable 1–6' (30 cm–2 m); summer

Brunnera macrophylla and cultivars—perennial forget-me-not, Siberian bugloss; zones 3–8; LS, FL, MS, SH (except for variegated forms); blue; 1–1.5' (30–45 cm); mid- to late spring

Campanula selected species and varieties—bellflower; zones variable; LS, FL,MS (by variety); white, blue, pink; 3"+ (7.5 cm+) by species and variety

Cardamine spp.—bitter cress; zones 3–9; LS, FL, MS; white, violet; 6"–1' (15–30 cm); mid- to late spring

Chasmanthium latifolium—northern sea oats; zones 5–9; LS, FL; brown; 3' (1 m); late summer (dried in winter)

Chelone lyonii—turtlehead; zones 3–8; LS, FL; pink; 2–4' (60 cm–1.2 m); summer

Chloranthus spp.—chloranthus; zones 6–8; LS, FL, WS; white; 2–3' (60 cm–1 m); midspring

Codonopsis spp.—bonnet bellflower; zones 5–9; LS, FL; blue and white flowers; herbaceous climber to 5'+ (1.5 m+); summer

Corydalis lutea—yellow corydalis; zones 5–10; LS, FL, MS; yellow; 6"–1' (15–30 cm); midspring to fall

Corydalis ochroleuca—white corydalis; zones 4–8; LS, FL, MS; cream; 6"–1' (15–30 cm); midspring to fall

Darmera peltatum—umbrella plant; zones 5–9; LS, FL, MS; pink; 3' (1 m); early spring before the leaves emerge

Deinanthe bifida—false hydrangea; zones 4–8; LS, FL, MS; violet and white; 1.5–2' (45cm–60cm); early to midsummer

Lamprocapnos (syn. *Dicentra*) *spectabilis*—Asian or old-fashioned bleeding heart; zones 3–9; LS, FL, MS; dark pink, pink, white; 2–3' (60 cm–1 m); early through midspring

Dicentra eximia, D. formosa—eastern and western bleeding heart; zones 3–9; LS, FL, MS, SH; 1–1.5' (30–45 cm); red, pink, white; early spring through midsummer

Digitalis grandiflora—perennial foxglove; zones 3–8; LS, FL, MS; yellow; 2–3' (60 cm–1 m); late spring

Digitalis purpurea varieties—common foxglove; zones 4–9; LS; white, tan, pink; 2–6' (60 cm–2 m); spring to summer by variety (some are biennials)

Diphylleia cymosa—umbrella leaf; zones 6–8; LS, FL, MS; 3' (1 m); late spring (colorful berries)

Disporum spp.—fairy bells; zones 5–8 (10); LS, FL, MS; white, yellow, cream; 8" to 2' (20–60 cm) by species; spring

Doronicum cordatum—leopard's bane; zones 4–9; LS, FL; yellow; 1–2' (30–60 cm); spring

Eomecon chionantha—snow poppy; zones 6–10; LS, FL, MS, SH; white; 1–1.5' (30–45 cm); spring

Epimedium spp.—barrenwort, bishop's hat; zones 4–9; LS, FL, MS, SH; all colors but blue; 8–15" (20–38 cm); early to late spring

Eupatorium coelestinum—hardy ageratum; zones 5–9; LS, FL, MS; blue; 1.5–3' (45 cm– 1 m); summer to fall

Eupatorium rugosum—white snakeroot; zones 4–9; LS, FL, MS; white; 3' (1 m); late summer to fall (potentially invasive from seed)

Euphorbia spp. and varieties—euphorbia, spurge; zones variable; LS–SH depending on species; yellow, green, white, brown; 3" (7.5 cm) creeping to 4' (1.2 m); spring through summer

Filipendula spp.—meadowsweet; zones 3, 6–9; LS, FL, MS; white, pink; 4"–6' (10 cm–2 m) depending on species; late spring through summer

Galax urceolata—galax; zones 3–8; white; 1.5' (45 cm); late spring to early summer

Gentiana spp.—gentian; zones variable; LS to SH depending on species; usually blue; 2"+ (5 cm+); spring through fall by species

Geranium shade-tolerant spp.— geranium, cranesbill; zones 4–9 depending on species; LS to MS by species; white, pink, brown; 1–2.5' (30–75 cm); late spring into summer

Geum coccineum and hybrids—avens, geum; zones 5–7; LS, FL; orange, red; 1–1.5' (30–45 cm); midspring to summer

Geum triflorum and *G. rivale*—water avens, prairie smoke, geum; zones 3–7; LS, FL, MS; tan/red and buff; 1–1.5' (30–45 cm); midspring

Helleborus argutifolius—Corsican hellebore; zones 6–9; LS, FL; pale green; 2–3' (60 cm–1 m); late winter to early spring

Helleborus foetidus—stinking hellebore; zones 5–8; LS, FL, MS, SH; pale green; 1.5–2' (45–60 cm); late winter to midspring

Helleborus orientalis (syn. *H. × hybridus*)—Lenten rose; zones 5–9; LS, FL, MS, SH; white, pink, dark gray, yellow, spotted; 1–1.5' (30–45 cm); late winter to early summer

Hemerocallis (species, not fancy hybrids)—daylily; zones 3–9; LS; yellow, orange; 1.5–4' (45 cm–1.2 m); midspring through late summer by species

Hesperis matronalis—dame's rocket; zones 4–8; LS, FL, MS; white, lavender; 3' (1 m); late spring to summer (biennial, self-sows, weed plants in the wrong place)

Heuchera spp.—heuchera, alumroot, coral bells; zones 4–9; LS, FL, MS; white to dark pink; 1–2' (30–60 cm); early to mid- to late summer

× Heucherella—heucherella, foamy bells; zones 4–9; LS, FL, MS, SH; white; 1.5" (4 cm); late spring to early summer

Hosta spp. and varieties—hosta; zones 3–9 by species; LS, FL, MS, SH; dark to pale lilac, white; 1–6' (30 cm–2 m) by species and varieties; early summer to fall

Hylomecon japonicum—hylomecon; zones 5–9; LS, FL, MS, SH; yellow; 1' (30 cm); spring

Hylotelephium (syn. *Sedum*) *telephium* and *H. spectabile* and cultivars—stonecrop, sedum, live forever; zones 3–9; LS, FL; light pink, dark pink, rust, white; 1.5–2.5' (45–75 cm); late summer to fall

Hylotelephium (syn. *Sedum*) 'Vera Jameson'—Vera Jameson sedum; zones 4–9; LS; dark pink; 9"–1' (23–30 cm); mid- to late summer

Iris foetidissima—stinking iris; zones 6–9; LS, FL; lilac; 1–2' (30–60 cm); spring (summer berries)

Iris fulva—copper iris; zones 5–9; LS, FL; rust; 1' (30 cm); spring

Kirengeshoma palmata—kirengeshoma, yellow wax bells; zones 5–8; LS, FL, MS; yellow; 3–4' (1–1.2 m); late summer into fall

Lamiastrum galeobdolon 'Herman's Pride'—yellow archangel; zones 3–9; LS, FL, MS; yellow; late spring (the species is an aggressive spreader, but good in a container on a paved surface)

Lamium spp.—dead nettle; zones 3–8; LS, SH; white, pink, dark pink; 6"–1' (15–30 cm); midspring variable

Lathyrus vernus—spring vetch, vernal pea; zones 5–9; LS, FL, MS; blue/magenta, pink, white; 1' (30 cm); midspring

Ligularia spp.—ligularia; zones 4–10; LS, FL (species vary, larger-leaved ones may tolerate MS); yellow; 2–5' (60 cm–1.5 m); summer

Liriope spp. and varieties—lilyturf; zones

5–10; LS, FL, MS; light to dark lavender; 1–1.5' (30 cm–45 cm); mid- to late summer

Lobelia cardinalis—cardinal flower; zones 2–9; LS, FL, MS; red, purple; 2–3' (60 cm–1 m); summer (in moist soil)

Lunaria rediviva—perennial honesty; zones 5–8; LS, FL, MS; lavender; 2'–3' (60 cm–1 m); late spring

Meconopsis cambrica—Welsh poppy; zones 6–9; LS, FL, MS; yellow, orange; 1.5' (45 cm); late spring to summer

Mentha spp. and varieties—mint; zones 5–10; LS; lavender; 1.5–2' (45–60 cm); summer (aggressive spreader, grow in containers only)

Mertensia virginica—Virginia bluebells; zones 3–10; WS, LS, FL, MS; blue; 1.5' (45 cm); spring; summer dormant

Maianthemum (syn. *Smilacina*) *racemosum*—false Solomon's seal; zones 3–9; LS, FL, MS, SH; cream; 2' (60 cm); spring

Mimulus spp.—monkey flower; zones 6–9; LS; yellow, orange, red; height and season of bloom vary by species

Monarda didyma and varieties—bee balm, bergamot; zones 4–9; LS; white, pink, lavender, red; 2–4' (60 cm–1.2 m); summer

Monarda fistulosa—bee balm, wild bergamot; zones 4–9; LS; lavender-pink; 3' (1 m); summer

Monarda punctata—horsemint, dotted bee balm; zones 3–8; LS; yellow w/ purple spots; 1.5–2.5' (45–75 cm); early to midsummer

Omphalodes cappadocica—blue-eyed Mary; zones 6–9; LS, FL, MS, SH; vivid blue flowers; 6–9" (15–23 cm); midspring into summer

Ophiopogon spp.—mondo grass; zones 6, 7–10; LS, FL, MS, SH; light to dark

lavender (blue-black berries too); 6"–1' (15–30 cm); summer

Paeonia (deciduous shrubs)—tree peony; zones 4–8; LS, FL; white, pink, lavender, yellow; 3–5' (1–1.5 m); early spring to midspring

Paeonia (herbaceous species)—peony; zones 3, 4–8; LS, FL, WS; white, pink, red, yellow, coral; 1–5' (30 cm–1.5 m); early spring to early summer, varieties with single flowers may not flop in some shade—double flowers need staking

Paris polyphylla—Paris; zones 5–9; LS, FL, MS, SH; green; 1.5–2' (45–60 cm); midspring (variable)

Persicaria (syn. *Tovara*) *virginiana* (variegated group)—knotweed, tovara; zones 4, 5–8; LS, FL; red, 1.5–8' (45 cm–2.4 m) by variety, mid- to late summer (may spread aggressively)

Phlox carolina—Carolina phlox, wedding phlox; zones 4–9; LS, FL; white, pale lilac; 2–2.5' (60–75 cm); early summer

Phlox divaricata—wild sweet William; zones 4–9; LS, FL, MS; lilac, lavender-blue, white; 1–1.5' (30–45 cm); spring

Physostegia virginiana—obedient plant, false dragonhead; zones 3–9; LS, FL; MS; pink, white; 3–4' (1–1.2 m); early to late summer

Podophyllum peltatum—mayapple; zones 3–9; LS, FL, MS, SH; white; spring

Polemonium caeruleum—Jacob's ladder; zones 4–8; LS, FL, MS, SH; pale blue, blue, or white; 1.5–2' (45–60 cm); late spring to midsummer

Polemonium reptans—Jacob's ladder, Greek valerian; zones 3–8; LS, FL, MS; pale blue; 1–1.5' (30–45 cm);

Polygonatum spp.—Solomon's seal; zones 4–9; LS, FL, MS; white; 8"–4' (20 cm–1.2 m) by species; spring

Primula japonica—Japanese primula; zones 3–9; LS, FL, MS; red, white, pink; 1.5–2' (45–60 cm); midspring to early summer

Pulmonaria spp., hybrids and cultivars—lungwort; zones 4–8; LS, FL, MS, SH; blue, dark pink, white; mid- to early summer

Pycnanthemum spp.—mountain mint; zones 4–8; LS, FL; white; 1–3' (30–90 cm); summer

Rodgersia spp.—rodgersia; zones 4–9; LS, FL, MS; white, pink, dark pink; 3'+ (1 m+); early summer

Rohdea japonica—sacred lily; zones 6–10; LS, SH; white, red berries; 1' (30 cm); spring (summer berries)

Saxifraga stolonifera—strawberry begonia; zones 6–10; LS, FL, MS, SH; white; 1.5' (45 cm) above low foliage; late spring to early summer

Sedum (selected shade-tolerant, taller species)—sedum, stonecrop, live forever; zones 4–10, variable; LS, FL; pink, red, white; 1.5' (45 cm); summer to fall

Stachys byzantina 'Countess Helene von Stein' (syn. 'Big Ears')—lamb's ears; zones 4–9; LS, FL; white/lavender; 6"–1' (15–30 cm); rarely flowers

Stylophorum diphyllum—celandine poppy, wood poppy; zones 4–8; LS, FL, MS; yellow; 1.5' (45 cm); early spring to summer

Symphyotrichum (syn. *Aster*) *novi-belgii*—New York aster; zones 4–8; LS, FL, MS; purple with yellow eye; 1–3' (30 cm–1 m); late summer to fall

Syneilesis aconitifolia—syneilesis; zones 4–8; LS, MS; insignificant; 1.5–3' (45–90 cm); summer

Tellima grandiflora—false alumroot, fringe cup; zones 4–9; LS, FL, MS, SH; white; 1.5' (45 cm); late spring to early summer

Thalictrum aquilegifolium—columbine meadow rue; zones 5–8; LS, FL; lilac-purple; 2–3' (60 cm–1 m); late spring to summer

Thalictrum kiusianum—dwarf meadow rue; zones 5–8; LS, FL, MS; lavender; 6" (15 cm); early summer

Thalictrum rochebrunianum—lavender mist meadow rue; zones 4–7; LS, FL; purple and yellow; 6' (2 m); summer

Thalictrum thalictroides—rue anemone, windflower; zones 5–8; LS, FL; white to pink; 4–8" (10–20 cm); midspring to summer

Tiarella spp. and varieties—foamflower; zones 4–9; LS, FL, MS, SH; white, pink; 8–14" (20–35 cm); spring

Trachystemon orientalis—trachystemon, Abraham-Isaac-Jacob; zones 7–9; LS, FL, MS, SH; blue; 1.5' (45 cm); spring

Tradescantia × *andersoniana* varieties—spiderwort; zones 4–9; LS, FL, MS; purple, white; 1–2' (30–60 cm); midspring to early summer

Tricyrtis spp.—toad lily; zones 5–9; LS, FL, MS, SH; violet, yellow, white; 1–2.5' (30–75 cm); late spring to early fall by variety

Trollius spp.—globe flower; zones 3–10; LS, FL; yellow, orange; 2' (60 cm); spring (various)

Uvularia grandiflora—merry bells; zones 3–9; LS, FL, MS; yellow; 2.5' (75 cm); spring

Veratrum spp.—false hellebore; zones 3–9; LS, FL, MS; white and green to dark brown by species; 3'+ (1 m+); summer

Veronica spp.—veronica, speedwell; zones variable; light varies depending on species; blue, pink, or white; 2"+ (5 cm+); spring through summer by species

Yucca filamentosa (variegated varieties)—Adam's needle; zones 4–10; LS, FL, MS; white; 4' (1.2 m); summer

(continued from page 164)

I grow relatives of the dicentras in the genus *Corydalis*. Some of those plants are ephemeral; others are tough to cultivate where springs are warm, and a few are pretty much carefree. *Corydalis lutea*, a small plant with yellow flowers, can be a bit too happy in some gardens, self-sowing in the shade. When I first came to New Jersey, I found white corydalis (*C. ochroleuca*) growing between the cracks in the arched stone bridge. This one, similar to *C. lutea,* has ivory flowers but is not aggressive for me. Best of all, it blooms from May until November.

Flowers are wonderful, but foliage is king in the shade. When the old-fashioned bleeding heart fades away, we might look to other plants with more lasting leaves, and there are many. All of the Solomon's seal species bloom for a short time, but their foliage stays around for the long haul. There are short ground-covering ones, like *Polygonatum humile*, and giants like *P. biflorum* var. *commutatum* that grow up to 5 feet (1.5 m) tall.

Once in the lily family, the Solomon's seals are now in Asparagaceae, along with edible asparagus. There are many species that resemble the Solomon's seal, and they too have been split into bits. False Solomon's seal has gotten a genus shift: from *Smilacena racemosa* to *Maianthemum racemosum*—the mayflower genus. Similar genera include the Asian fairy bells (*Disporum* spp.) and North American merry bells (*Uvularia* spp.). *Uvularia perfoliata* and *U. grandiflora* have perfoliate leaves, which makes it appear as if the stem pierces straight through the leaves and, in this case, as if they have been sown together with a zig-zag stitch. The nodding flowers are cream or yellow respectively.

Herbaceous plants with bold foliage effects include American spikenard (*Aralia racemosa*) and Japanese *Aralia cordata,* with compound leaves, and its gold-leafed cultivar 'Sun King'. Ligularia have varied leaves by species and variety. Some are finely divided; others have colorful, near-black leaves. Both *Ligularia japonica,* and *L. stenocephala* 'The Rocket' have jagged-edged leaves, but *L. dentata* 'Desdemona' and 'Britt Marie Crawford' have large, round dark maroon foliage. Most of these plants like moist soil and the most light you can provide.

A list of more herbaceous perennials, along with suggestions for their light requirements, height, and time of bloom, can be found on page 168.

OPPOSITE There are many hardy geraniums for conditions that range from light to medium shade. The spotted, wild, or wood geranium (*G. maculatum*) blooms for a long time in spring, and the foliage lasts to fall.

ABOVE The longest blooming plant in my garden is *Corydalis ochroleuca* (corydalis). It begins to bloom in May and continues until November. A potential thug, I suppose, if planted in the wrong spot, it has been perfectly well-behaved for me.

ABOVE *Tricyrtis* is a genus with orchid-like flowers that do well in medium to deep shade. A few have yellow blossoms in early summer, but most, like *T. hirta*, appear in late summer to fall, in jewel tones like amethyst.

OPPOSITE ABOVE LEFT Kirengeshoma (*Kirengeshoma palmata*) is another tall late-summer-flowering perennial. However, the buds, which are as ornamental as the blossoms, form earlier and last for weeks.

OPPOSITE ABOVE RIGHT Late summer Japanese anemone blooms in light shade with delicate white to dark pink flowers on long arching wands 2 to 3 feet (60 cm to 1 m) above leafy basal growth.

OPPOSITE BELOW Next to chrysanthemum, the genus that might be best known for late summer to autumn flowers is one formerly known as *Aster* and now called *Symphyotrichum*. This one is calico aster, *S. lateriflorum* 'Lady in Black'.

Later-Season Stars

I once heard a famous garden designer say "anyone can do spring." I get that. Spring-flowering bulbs have their flowers inside them when you buy them, and they will blossom, at least for one year. The deciduous and semievergreen early shrubs like azaleas will put on a show with little care. The spring ephemerals blossom with ease—and the garden center is all decked out with irresistible flowering plants.

Things get quieter as summer proceeds and during the months of high heat. With planning, however, some perennials will make a comeback after being dead-headed or cut back for late summer, and there are plenty that do not even begin to bloom until the cooler weather returns.

The stars of the late shady garden include the Japanese and hybrid anemones (*Anemone hupehensis* var. *japonica* and *A.* × *hybrida*). Long wiry wands shoot 24 to 48 inches (60 cm to 1.2 m) tall, depending on the variety, light, and moisture, and end in little round buds of pink or white that open to handsome flat flowers. Do not expect the stems to be straight, regardless of the amount of light. They will arch in the direction of the brightest light, and the heavy flowers will make the stems dip.

Although hostas are mostly known for their foliage, a few could be grown for their flowers, for example that rhizomatous species, *H. clausa,* which produces dark violet blossoms late in the season. *Hosta* 'August Moon' also blooms late, with pale lavender flowers. Others that bloom as the season comes to an end include *H. cathayana*, narrow-leafed *H. lancifolia*, grassy *H. longissima*, *H. rupifraga*, and *H. ventricosa*. The August lily, *H. plantaginea*, bears long tubular fragrant white trumpet flowers in late summer to early fall, and there are even double-flower varieties. All of these hostas can be reliably grown in zones 4 through 8 and are worth trying in zones 3 and 9.

Another stalwart of the shade garden in late summer to autumn interests me as much for its flower buds as the blossoms. The plant is *Kirengeshoma palmata*, hardy in zones 5 through 8, and suitable for light to medium shade. It grows up to 4 feet (1.2 m) tall. The butter-yellow flower buds form as early as late June (in my zone) but do not open until August or September. The green leaves are attractive and somewhat maple-like. *K. koreana* is virtually identical, though its flowers may be more upright, as opposed to the nodding ones of the former species.

Asters have small daisy flowers in colors from white through pink, red, and even dark blue. They used to be in a genus called *Aster*, but nearly all of them have had their names changed. The woodland asters bloom late in the season, and are now in the genus *Eurybia* (*E. divaricata* and *E. macrophylla*, for example). The New York aster is now *Symphyotrichum novi-belgii*. But I have seen this plant listed in the genera *Eurybia* and *Aster*. This is one case where the common name might be best: aster.

Toad lilies (*Tricyrtis* spp. and varieties), which bear orchid-like flowers, are among the most wonderful plants for the late woodland shade garden. There are many species and varieties, including variegated forms. A few bloom early with yellow flowers, and another blooms yellow and late, but most have spotted purple

(*continued on page 183*)

THE ACTAEAS WE USED TO CALL CIMICIFUGAS

A host of popular perennial species for shade gardens used to be known by the generic name *Cimicifuga,* but taxonomists moved them to the genus *Actaea.* These newly joined species bear bottlebrush flowers on long wands above divided astilbe-like foliage.

The formerly named *Cimicifuga* species includes American and Asian plants (more examples of plants that grew together before the breakup of Pangaea). The common names include snakeroot, black cohosh, or bugbanes. One with a nicer name, *A. matsumurae* 'White Pearl' (syn. *Cimicifuga simplex* 'White Pearl', below left), which fits, for the buds do look like the gem. A few smell unpleasant when they open, others are sweetly fragrant, and they bloom by species from late spring right up until fall. There are cultivars with black stems. Others have wonderful maroon to near-black foliage, for example those in the *Atropurpurea* group, such as 'Brunette' and 'Hillside Black Beauty' (below right). All of these plants will lean toward the light.

The one that comes from North America is *A. racemosa,* black cohosh. This plant bears typical white fragrant flowers on racemes that are like long tails on tall, 4- to 6-foot (1.2- to 2-m) wands in early summer. This *Actaea* will grow in light to full shade in humusy, organically rich, moisture-retentive soil. The plants should not be sited where there are strong winds and where sunlight might burn the foliage.

Other *Actaea* species with bottlebrush-like blossoms have attractive fruits, such as *Actaea pachypoda* and *A. rubra.* These plants bloom early, and their starry flowers are followed by fruits, which in the case of *A. pachypoda* are perfectly described by their common name: doll's eyes. The fruits appear on magenta stems and are snow-white with a little black dot at the ends. *A. rubra* has red fruits (*rubra* means "red" in Latin). Another common name for them is baneberry.

These plants are members of the buttercup or Ranunculus family, and like many cousins, they are poisonous, so the berries must be left alone. Young children especially might be attracted to them. Some parents try to banish all potentially dangerous plants from their gardens. Unfortunately, many, many plants can be toxic if consumed in large quantities. Often, plants that have important medicinal value in controlled circumstances and correct dosages are toxic in unsupervised situations. Just tell children not to put any plant in their mouths unless a parent says it is okay.

RIGHT The genus *Cimicifuga* has been lumped into *Actaea.* These species are known for tall wands of white flowers, for example, *A. matsumurae* 'White Pearl' (left) named for its flower buds. Several varieties have deep burgundy foliage and pink-tinged flowers, like *A. simplex* 'Hillside Black Beauty' (right).

OPPOSITE LEFT *Astilbe chinensis* 'Superba' is a rugged cultivar with stout scapes of lavender-pink flowers.

OPPOSITE RIGHT The extremely shade tolerant *Astilbe* × *andresii* 'Color Flash' is grown for its red-tinged foliage.

DEPENDABLE ASTILBES

Astilbe species and hybrids are favorite shade plants, and I have found that although many references suggest deep shade, the plants look better in more light. It might be worth experimenting in various situations. All astilbe like moisture and are mostly resistant to deer browsing.

Astilbe, sometimes called false spiraea, is a clump-forming perennial producing feathery mounds of often low compound leaves with toothed leaflets. The most commonly seen are the *arendsii* hybrids, which are often compact and come in colors from white to dark red. Here's a tip: the flowers turn brown after they bloom. If you do not feel like deadheading them or do not like the look of faded flowers, avoid the pure white versions that fade to dirty brown. The deep red ones, like *A. × arendsii* 'Fanal', turn a darker reddish brown and still look acceptable after the tiny florets have passed their prime.

There are other hybrids to look for with the species names *A. simplicifolia*, *A. japonica*, and *A. thunbergii*. One of the nicest is the informal, beautiful *A.* 'Ostrich Plume' (syn. *A. thunbergii* 'Ostrich Plume', *A. simplicifolia* 'Straussenfeder') with large mauve-pink arching panicles. The larger species and varieties may have a tolerance for shadier locations than the *arendsii* hybrids.

I talk about a short, thick ground cover, *Astilbe chinensis* 'Pumila', later, but here, I'm thinking of the larger, taller plants for the middle layer, such as *A. chinensis* 'Superba', below left. Look for the tall North American *Astilbe biternata*. Another giant is Asian *A. grandis*. And there is even an intergeneric hybrid between an *Astilbe* and an *Aruncus* (goatsbeard)—another big feathery-flowered choice for the shade garden.

A few new entries to the astilbe group come from the Color Flash series, which have colorful foliage in addition to flowers. One has chartreuse leaves (*Astilbe × arendsii* 'Color Flash Lime') and the other, more striking one, has a red tinge to the leaves and keeps the color, even in full shade (*Astilbe × arendsii* 'Color Flash Beauty of Ernst', below right). Flowers? Yes, but the leaves are the attraction.

FOXGLOVES FOR FILTERED LIGHT AND LIGHT SHADE

Consider the foxglove, or *Digitalis*. These plants are the source of an important cardiac medication (and play a role in a few English mystery novels). Most foxgloves are biennials, or short-lived perennials, and do well in filtered light to light shade. Many gardeners grow *Digitalis purpurea*, but for some reason, that plant doesn't like me. I am on good terms with *Digitalis lanata*, however. The first year from seed, they make some small to large (depending on species) basal growth, and they bolt, sending up spires with flowers the following year. These two species are listed as invasive in some states. The only one that self-sows reliably for me is *D. lutea* with tiny pale yellow flowers. A half dozen of these plants sprout here and there and they are welcome.

After the biennials bloom, they do not return, but very often, there is a young plant nearby that sprouted from a seed of the original to take its place. *D. lanata* grows up to about 4 feet (1.2 m), with half of that height being a stalk covered with small buff, brown, and yellow flowers that are just the right size to hold a bumblebee. This species has always been an easy one for me, in my sandy soil and light to medium shade. In medium shade, beware that the plant will lean way out of the garden bed and toward the light.

Digitalis ferruginea is the rusty foxglove. Though often called a perennial, it is another biennial that often drops seeds in place to replace the fading ones. The plants have 3- to 5-foot- (1- to 1.5-m-) tall spires bearing tiny rusty-brown and gold flowers on the top 2 feet (60 cm) of the stem. One reliably perennial foxglove is *D. grandiflora* (syn. *D. ambigua*) with spikes of creamy-yellow blossoms in late spring on a plant about 2 feet (60 cm) tall. This one comes back and forms a larger clump every year. These two plants bloom for me from late spring through early summer.

OPPOSITE In shade, the flowers on a spike of *Digitalis lanata* are spaced far apart. Perhaps they are more curious looking than beautiful, but I love curious, and so do the bumblebees that slip inside the flowers for nectar and pollen.

RIGHT A creamy white form of the best-known foxglove, the biennial *Digitalis purpurea* 'Alba', prefers light shade to filtered light.

STAKING IN THE SHADE GARDEN

In the semishady garden, foxgloves and other tall summer-flowering plants will lean toward the source of the brightest light, but usually do not flop over. However, some perennials do—especially hybrids and cultivars bred for large or double flowers. When you visit a public planting of perennials, you may not be able to see the support system, but believe me, it is usually there. Individual stakes, with a plant's flowering stalks tied to them, may be pushed into the ground. Or wire rings may have been put in place before the plants emerged, allowing them to grow up through the open hoop, which provides support.

In summer, we gardeners sometimes "brush up" our plants using what some people refer to as "pea stakes." This material is cut from twiggy deciduous shrubs when they are pruned. Plants with many stems that have flopped to the ground are lifted with one arm, while the dry twiggy support is pushed into the soil, and then the collapsed plant is allowed to lean on the dead shrubby branch.

When you are at the garden center, look at the various means of support offered, from green-painted bamboo stakes (who came up with that color?) to wire that has an open loop at the top for individual stalks to rings, and even double rings, for taller plants. Think about putting the stakes in before growth takes off in areas where you know a plant has flopped over in the previous growing seasons. The hoops are sometimes called peony rings and are made to support big, double-flowered hybrids that cannot support their blossoms, although we won't be growing those peonies in shade. We might, however, try a woodland peony species in light to medium shade or a hybrid with single flowers in a bit more sun that might not need staking.

As for ties, I do not like wire, because it may cut the plant's stems. I prefer to use green-colored jute, hemp, or cotton string, depending on the situation. These materials degrade after about a year and the ties have to be replaced (not an issue with herbaceous perennials). Ties that degrade won't choke expanding growth on a woody plant like permanent materials can or end up stuck in the garden forever even if they do not kill a tree.

RIGHT Many plants require a bit of help standing up. Vines like the tropical rex begonia vine (*Cissus discolor*) need support and appreciate a simple tripod of bamboo stakes pushed into the pot and tied at the top.

OPPOSITE Naturally columnar and fastigiate shrubs may need a bit of help staying upright—their tendency is to splay apart in a shady location. For *Ilex crenata* 'Sky Pencil', tie biodegradable twine at the bottom, spiral it up to the top, and tie.

(continued from page 174)

spidery jewel-like blossoms that often appear at the leaf axils up and down the stems. The plants are hardy in zones 5 through 9, and blossom by species and variety from June through to a killing frost. Like hostas, toad lilies are favorites of gardeners, slugs, and snails.

Amsonia species are called blue stars for their flowers in late spring to early summer. They are without a doubt charming herbaceous plants. But one species for light shade stands out, not for its clear blue flowers but for its autumn color: *A. hubrichtii*. The threadlike willowy leaves begin to change color before the frost: the green turns to pink and orange and finally to burnt-orange-brown.

The Low Down

Some people think of ground covers as filler to be plopped down like linoleum. The tendency is to smother the soil with low-growing, spreading creepers like periwinkle (*Vinca minor*), army-green Japanese spurge (*Pachysandra terminalis*), and species ivies. All of these are invasive and should never be planted where they can climb up and smother a tree, fence, or house, for example, or any wild-like land. To me, "spreading" is a red flag, along with "quick," "fast," and "easy." But an open mind will find a compendium of well-behaved plants that hug the forest floors of the temperate world. There are a multitude of choices for every region, and they do not have to be matlike plants you order by the yard.

I like to think of drifts of plants, gentle ponds of green, or streams of flowering plants. There may be yin-and-yang interlocking swaths of texture and form, but don't be rigid; mix it up for visual interest. Look for things like dwarf hostas, *Epimedium*, or the new, more unusual alternative pachysandra species. There is even an eastern North American pachysandra, *P. procumbens,* the Allegheny spurge. These plants are often well-behaved and, as with so much of gardening, a bit of patience is required, but the reward makes it all worthwhile. The plants do not always increase their territory on their own; you may have to divide and transplant some to areas where they are needed.

Plants to use as ground covers do not have to be low-growing. Anything that is used in a mass planting, which grows horizontally as well as vertically, could be a cover in just the right place. There could even be a colony of 3-foot- (1-m-) tall native deciduous azaleas. In general, however, we are looking for low-growing plants for the front of a planting, as an edging for a path, and to introduce the beds beyond them.

Herbaceous Perennial Ground Covers

There are also quite a few flowering herbaceous plants that make good ground covers in varying amounts of shade. *Astilbe chinensis* 'Pumila' is a dwarf creeping plant that grows to about 6 inches (15 cm) before it adds its taller flower spikes. It formed a dense, weedproof mat for me up against a wall that faces west but is shaded by the building in the morning, by evergreens a little later on, and by deciduous flowering trees and shrubs throughout the rest of the day. The plants are in bright light but hardly any direct sunlight. This astilbe is a reminder of how important

OPPOSITE An area of ground covers does not have to consist of one kind of plant. In my garden there is a varied collection of low herbaceous, woody, and bulbous plants in a color scheme highlighted by blue ajuga, pink dead nettle, and the chartreuse new growth from low-growing shrubs.

ABOVE Punctuate ground covers with surprises like tall airy plants or slender flowering bulbs like *Lilium martagon* 'Album' that push up through the low-growing plants.

it is to experiment; the patch was planted before the trees grew up to shade it, and so, I suppose, the discovery was made by the plant and then shared with me.

In other places, some tall, slender plants may be planted to pepper the cover and shoot up through it, and these, sometimes called see-through plants, have flowers on top of wiry stems. One favorite is lavender mist meadow rue (*Thalictrum rochebrunianum*). The plant produces columbine-like foliage up to 3 or 4 feet (1 to 1.2 m), and then continues to grow stems 6 or more feet (2 m) high that are topped by clusters of purple, white, and yellow flowers that flutter like butterflies. Another plant I like to use in this way is martagon lily (*Lilium martagon*). I grow my martagons from seeds and select those seeds from plants that have bloomed with white flowers (*L. m.* var. *album*), which generally bloom true to color. The lilies push up through a low mass planting of ground cover to bear their small transparent flowers that do not block the background plantings, but introduce them.

Patience

I grow the martagon lilies from seeds indoors, which is a lot of fun, for transplanting later. People say that you have to have patience to garden, and that's not one of my virtues. But it is not as if I stand and stare at the soil, tapping my foot, waiting for a new shoot to germinate from a planted seed. There are many rewarding things to see and enjoy all over the place, and many projects too. Then one day, you happen to notice that the plant you were impatient about *has* grown. Celebrate the progress and successes along the way and keep going.

Filling in at Ground Level

Some of the most beautiful woodland covers come and go all too soon, so they are not conventional ground covers, but I would not be without them in my shade garden. Ephemeral lovers such as myself accept that some of these plants disappear.

I think there are few things lovelier than the lily-pad-like foliage of the mayapple (*Podophyllum peltatum*), with its umbrella leaves on rigid stems all growing at the same height. But after they bloom with dangling white flowers and quickly form juicy fruits, the plants melt away.

Bloodroot (*Sanguinaria canadensis*) is similar to the mayapple, with fleeting flowers, but its leaves do not vanish. One day, snow-white daisy-like blossoms will appear flowing across the ground, and a few days later, they will be gone, but they are nearly instantly replaced by lobed, dark matte green leaves that last the season.

If you were going to create a cover using either of these plants, you would need a lot of them. In a way, it is like the spring-flowering bulbs; there never seem to be enough. I suggest installing at least one plant on 1-foot- (30-cm-) wide center, and wait for it to get happy. If you can find a source and have the funds, plant as many as you can. There are nurseries and even some mail-order sources that sell what are called "liners" or "plugs." These are baby plants sold by the dozens and not very expensive. Most of the growers of plugs are only wholesale, but it is worth investigating. If your order is large enough, you could go in with a few friends; you might be able to meet a minimum.

Some plants increase the size of their clumps in more than one way, generally by self-sowing and, for example in the case of the bloodroot, with a slowly elongating underground stem or rhizome. If this thick stem breaks, it bleeds, and that is exactly how one would propagate it. Dig up the dormant rhizome after the leaves have faded in fall or late winter; cut it into sections, making sure each segment includes a small growing point, or eye; and replant the pieces.

Now, I've said *spreading* is a bad word, but I think *fast-spreading* could be worse. Our best ground covers get around, just not at lightning speed, and if they threaten to escape, they can easily be corralled. The mechanisms by which they increase are varied. Some have rhizomes like bloodroot, while others have wiry stems—runners or stolons—that travel just under or on the surface of the soil, root in, and sprout along the way. Bugleweeds, for instance, in the *Ajuga* genus of non-native perennials, have short runners that crawl across the soil, root, and make more leafy top growth as well as flowers in the spring.

Not all *Ajuga* grow low or spread as fast as others. Among those that do, perhaps the most common and successful is the bronze-colored upright variety, *A. pyramidalis* 'Metallica Crispa'. Many other selected varieties are of the semiever-green species *Ajuga reptans*. Other gardeners and I have found that if we put a delicate unusual variegated ajuga cultivar near a more vigorous one, we lose the precious new one. This is not due to interbreeding, I don't think, just a space invasion. One like 'Metallica Crispa' will push out less-vigorous varieties. I have found

WOODY GROUND COVERS

Some shrubs and subshrubs will never grow tall. Certain woody plants, not just some soft-tissue herbaceous ones, make great long-lasting and often evergreen covers. A few twiggy creepers are American wintergreen (*Gaultheria procumbens*, below right), bearberry (*Arctostaphylos uva-ursi*) in acidic soil, and wintercreeper (*Euonymus fortunei* 'Wolong Ghost', for example, and other varieties). There are a few shade-tolerant evergreen conifers like plum yew (*Cephalotaxus harringtonia* 'Prostrata', below left), spreading yew (*Taxus baccata* 'Repandens'), and other low-growing selections. Names like *procumbens* and *prostrata* mean lying down; *repens* and *reptans* mean creeping—a good hint to keep in mind when looking for plants that will cover the ground.

A SEMIEVERGREEN COVER

There may be no better low-growing plant for shade than the hellebores, and certainly none that bloom better in winter. I remember when the toughest, the so-called Oriental hybrids, were enormously expensive. I began to realize that a single plant became four in a few years and could be divided in the early spring (only) to fill in an area. These plants might be thought of as evergreen. They produce new growth in the spring that lasts all the way through to the end of winter, when the leaves look tattered and most crisp up and turn brown. By then, lush new growth pushes up to replace the dead leaves. I carefully cut off the old foliage just as the new growth is beginning to show.

To divide the plants, I dig them up at that time, shake the soil off the roots, and cut the woody crowns into sections with a serrated bread knife dedicated to that purpose. The sections are replanted at once about 1 foot (30 cm) apart. They begin to grow together and fill in.

The semievergreen hellebores in the garden, mostly the so-called Oriental hybrids, seemed to be somewhat promiscuous and effortlessly bore seed-filled fruit. I used to collect the seeds for propagation. After sowing and growing these plants for years, I discovered that there were seedlings beneath the leaves of the adult plants. In fact, there was a carpet of them. So these plants are not as difficult to propagate as their reputation suggested; it just took time.

Oriental hellebore seedlings left alone seem to stay small and barely grow. I suppose in time, they would duke it out, and a few would survive to mature into blossoming plants. The seedlings transplant easily, however, and grow larger right away. I gave some seedlings away and, unfortunately, had to weed some out.

The hellebores that bloomed from self-sown seed were not all that special, mostly single pink or white. In the recent past, hybridizers have produced some smashing introductions. There are many other *Helleborus* species and varieties to try for foliage and winter flowers, and if you live in a climate warmer than mine, even more. Look through catalogs for these and also some of the fancy new Oriental hybrids. Adventurous gardeners could begin to make their own crosses choosing parents with special attributes, for instance double blossoms and vivid colors like daffodil yellow and slate gray, and cultivate some of their own stunning new varieties.

OPPOSITE ABOVE A naturalized colony of hybrid Oriental hellebore hybrids mixes with spring-flowering bulbs in a hillside planting.

OPPOSITE BELOW There are scores of *Helleborus × hybridus* varieties on the market, and many look-alikes. I've done my best to identify the varieties below.

1 Winter Jewels 'Harlequin Gem' hybridized by Marietta O'Byrne

2 Yellow with Red Spots mix

3 Ashwood Garden "slatey grey" hybrid

4 'White Spotted Lady'

5 Glenn Withey and Charles Price's yellow selection 'Ya Self'

6 Winter Jewels 'Sparkling Diamond'

that the miniature variety 'Chocolate Chip,' with small, slender coffee-brown leaves and the typical pretty blue flowers on spikes up to 6 inches (15 cm) tall in midspring, can compete with the best of them. After blooming, the flower spikes should be trimmed with garden shears and gently raked away.

My local wild ginger (*Asarum canadense*) has short stems that creep along the soil's surface. The popular evergreen European ginger (*A. europaeum*) has congested growth. I have found that if you buy a pot of that plant and plop it in the ground, it will sit in a pot-sized clump forever. Both of these plants and other wild gingers want—and *need*—to be divided. Once you separate the individual leaves, stems, and roots, which slip apart easily, and replant them, they will catch on, truly. You could have a decent patch the following year. Dividing to conquer is one way to get the most for your initial investment.

Lawn Alternatives—Some for Light Traffic

When professionals use the popular buzz-phrase "lawn alternatives," they are talking about replacing an area covered by grass lawn with ornamental or edible plants or even gravel and paving—rarely planting other things one can walk on. Mown grass is the most familiar ground cover, and a bit of turfgrass is useful for paths or for when recreation is part of the program. I do not know of a plant besides grass that can, for example, be planted and mowed for the path often taken. That said, there is a lot you can do to lower the carbon footprint of conventional mowed grass. Ignore the advice of the lawn-care product industry, for one, which calls for frequent feeding and weeding with herbicides.

ABOVE Wild ginger (*Asarum* spp.) from Europe, Asia, and North America are great ground covers. *A. caudatum* from the western United States lines this path with *Hosta* 'June' and the Asian maidenhair fern (*Adiantum venustum*) below *Paris polyphylla* and a flowering hybrid of *Trillium albidum*.

OPPOSITE The specific epithet of the grassy ground cover variegated lilyturf, *Liriope muscari* 'Variegata', refers to the *muscari*, or grape, hyacinth-like flowers.

There has been quite a bit of investigation into native grasses for lawns, including buffalo grass (*Buchloe dactyloides*), selections of which have been made for various parts of the country. These do not require as much water or fertilizer as traditional lawn varieties (few of which are native), but they also cannot stand up to foot traffic or shade. Like sedge (page 196), it might be a good choice for lawn next to a gravel path, and in that situation it would not need to be mowed at all.

Fescue is a more environmentally friendly grass, some species of which are native to the United States. Fine fescues, such as red, Chewings, sheep, and hard (*Festuca rubra*, *F. rubra* subsp. *fallax*, *F. ovina*, *F. longifolia*) are among the most shade-tolerant grass lawn varieties. Blending fescues produces turf that prefers low nitrogen fertility and reduced water requirements, making them low-input and low-maintenance choices. They are cool-season plants and may brown in summer heat.

My so-called lawn is a mix of grass and low broad-leaved plants that can be mowed. It can be walked on and will recover when crushed and worn (think garden tour). As far as other plants that one *can* step on without killing, there are a few that will survive, but they will be damaged. With hope, they, too, will recover with new growth to take the place of the old. Moss is the option for places that may be too shady and too acidic for grass lawn. Moss is a gorgeous cover, but does require some preparation and maintenance for the greatest success (as does grass lawn, for that matter). (See page 199.)

Ajuga, as mentioned above, is one choice that can be stepped on occasionally. Another flowering cover is *Mazus reptans* (*reptans* means "creeping"). Mazus has either white or purple-blue flowers. Moneywort (*Lysimachia nummularia*) will take a little traffic, and the green species is vigorous in moist shade. The popular brilliant golden variety, *L. n.* 'Aurea' is well-behaved, and perhaps not as satisfying as a lawn

alternative on its own, but mixed with other ground covers, it will bring light to a shaded spot, and it keeps its color fairly well through the season. This moneywort likes moisture, as well.

A nongrass grasslike genus for moist places is *Acorus,* or sweet flag, with foliage that is a bit like iris plants, and there are species that range from tall (about 2 feet / 60 cm) to very small (a few inches), with many narrow-leaved variegated varieties. These are plants for wet spots, even the shallow water at the edge of the pond. Large plants are often versions of *A. calamus.* The species *A. gramineus* has varieties that are golden, variegated, dwarfs, and miniatures shorter than 6 inches (15 cm) and can grow in water.

If you want the look of grass as an "alternative" for your lawn, but not for walking on, there are grasses and nongrass plants with bladelike foliage. Lilyturf (*Liriope* spp. and varieties), for example, has strappy foliage, along with blue flowers and berries, and there are variegated versions. Mondo grass, or *Ophiopogon,* is another genus with fine foliage, and many species are shade tolerant. These plants also have berries, including blue and black ones; there are a few with stylish black foliage as well.

If you are thinking of a grasslike alternative for shade, something that might produce the wispy texture of grass to move in the breeze, although it won't necessarily be mowed or have to stand up to heavy traffic, consider sedge: the *Carex* species. Pennsylvania or oak sedge (*Carex pensylvanica*), for example, is found on the East Coast through to the Dakotas, south to Mississippi, and north through Quebec. It can be used as a ground cover in varying degrees of shade. I have talked to gardeners who have tried mowing sedge, and it can be done, and even walked on, but not as much as true grass or turf.

My Alternative Lawn

I do not water, feed, or weed my lawn in New Jersey. As mentioned previously, the low green cover is a mixture of several grasses and plenty of weeds, the kind that weed killers are supposed to annihilate. I jokingly call it the "cropped meadow." This lawn is in shade for part of the day, which helps with moisture loss. I do not cut the grass shorter than 3 inches (7.5 cm) in the summer, which also conserves moisture. Unless I need to collect the clippings to add nitrogen to the compost pile, I use a mulching mower so the cuttings remain on the lawn to degrade and return nutrients to the grass. In spring, I spread about an inch (2.5 cm) of sieved compost over the areas that get the most traffic, like the arched stone sod-covered bridge over the canal.

I have sandy soil, but the compost works its way down to the roots, feeding the grass and improving the soil's ability to retain moisture. If you do irrigate, water less often and more deeply to encourage deep, drought-tolerant roots. Shallow watering, a short spray from the hose, for example, just brings roots to the surface, where they are vulnerable to dry weather. Deep watering requires a device like a sprinkler left in place until it delivers about an inch (2.5 cm) of water over the surface. You can test this in an unscientific way by setting a shallow baking pan in the path of the

OPPOSITE ABOVE Pennsylvania sedge (*Carex pensylvanica*) is a ground cover that waves in the breeze.

OPPOSITE BELOW Creeping mazus (*Mazus reptans*) is a flowering ground cover barely 3 inches (7.5 cm) tall.

ABOVE There are many varieties of ajuga, or bugleweed, for shade, including the crinkled oddity *Ajuga pyrimadalis* 'Purple Crispa'.

BELOW Two golden variegated grassy-leaved sweet flags—*Acorus gramineus* 'Ogon', and in the lower right, dwarf *Acorus gramineus* 'Minimus'—love moist soil.

sprinkler to serve as a water gauge. The general idea is that when the water in the pan is 1 inch (2.5 cm) deep, you've done the job.

Ornamental Grasses

Most true grasses evolved in the open plains in full sun, where they colonized huge areas in their natural habitats. In horticulture, ornamental grasses are famed for their fountain-like growth—tall blades topped by feather plumes late in the summer, and after a killing frost, tawny foliage that persists through fall and into winter. Fortunately, or unfortunately depending on your point of view since some of these grasses seed and escape into nearby meadows, there are few shade-tolerant ornamental grass species. There are a couple that will do okay in some shade and generally won't become overly aggressive there.

For autumn interest, northern sea oats (*Chasmanthium latifolium*) stands out. I have read of complaints that this North American native can be invasive, but that has not been my experience, which may be due to my growing it in light shade instead of full sun. The grass grows just over 2 feet (60 cm) and has dangling flowers shaped like chevrons, celadon green through the growing season and coppery tan as they age; the entire plant turns color in autumn.

Prairie dropseed (*Sporobolus heterolepis*) is a delicate-looking native grass that makes a beautiful cover in light shade. When it flowers, the air is filled with the smell of buttered popcorn.

Most of the other ornamental grasses for shade are short, like the blue fescues. Besides those used for lawns, ornamental *Festuca* species are low, clump-forming plants for relatively dry soil in filtered light, light to medium shade. The hemispheric clumps of fine foliage grow to about 10 inches (25 cm) tall before they flower. Some plants may die off in the center, a sign that they need to be divided and replanted, which is best done in late winter to early spring. The evergreen *F. muelleri*, or Mueller's fescue, is one for West Coast gardeners.

Milium effusum is American millet grass. The green species from North America isn't seen very often, but the familiar golden cultivar, *M. e.* 'Aureum' is a striking choice for filtered light, light to medium shade. The common name is Bowles's golden grass, named for E. A. Bowles, a revered British horticulturist noted for his ability to find unusual but worthwhile variations among plants in the wild. As the season passes, the grass changes color from canary yellow to lime green. Then flowers appear as tiny golden beads on hair-thin stems. In some gardens, this grass behaves as an annual and will need to be propagated or purchased and replanted.

Perhaps the best and prettiest grass for light shade and filtered light is Japanese forest grass, *Hakonechloa macra* species and varieties. The most popular cultivar is *H. m.* 'Aureola', which is gold and green striped. This beautiful arching plant is slow growing, depending on soil moisture or lack of it. Another cultivar has the descriptive name 'All Gold'; it is a much faster-growing selection. Others include variegated green and white varieties such as 'Albovariegata' and 'Albo-Striata,'; one with red coloring to the ends of the blades, 'Beni-kaze'; and *H. m.* 'Nicolas', with reddish-orange blades.

OPPOSITE Most of the true grasses are sun lovers, like wheat and ornamental varieties. But there are a few, like those listed below, for light shade to filtered light.

1 *Hakonechloa macra* 'All Gold'—golden Japanese forest grass

2 *Chasmanthium latifolium*—northern sea oats

3 *Fargesia nitida*—blue fountain clumping bamboo

4 *Hakonechloa macra* 'Aureola'—variegated Japanese forest grass, Hakone grass

5 *Millium effusum* 'Aureum'— Bowles's golden grass

6 *Hakonechloa macra* 'Albovariegata'—white striped Hakone grass

7 *Sporobolus heterolepis*—prairie dropseed (their fragrant flowers smell like popcorn to me, others describe it as cilantro)

SOME RECOMMENDED SEDGES

If you are wondering about those *Carex* species and cultivars mentioned previously, many thrive in shade. Sedges are not grasses, although they are grasslike plants, and yes, they are wonderful. For a large area in shade, *Carex pensylvanica* stands out. There are species with plain green leaves and others that have chartreuse, bluish gray-green, orange, or brass-brown blades.

Some of the species and varieties for light to medium shade include:

C. buchananii—brown leatherleaf sedge (3)

C. caryophyllea 'The Beatles'

C. comans 'Bronze'

C. dipsacea—autumn sedge, green sedge

C. dolichostachya 'Kaga-nishiki'—Gold Fountains sedge

C. elata—tufted sedge

C. flacca—blue-green sedge

C. flagellifera—weeping brown sedge

C. glauca 'Blue Zinger'—blue sedge

C. laxiculmis 'Hobb'—Bunny Blue sedge

C. morrowii 'Ice Dance' (green edged in white)

C. morrowii 'Silver Scepter' (narrow variegated blades)

C. morrowii var. *temnolepis* 'Silk Tassel'

C. muskingumensis 'Oehme' palm sedge (pale green yellow margins)

C. oshimensis 'Evergold'

C. pensylvanica—Pennsylvania sedge

C. phyllocephala—palm sedge

C. plantaginea—plantainleaf sedge, seersucker sedge

C. platyphylla—silver sedge (wide leaves; tolerates dry once established)

C. siderosticha 'Variegata'—creeping broadleaf sedge (1)

C. stricta—tussock sedge

C. testacea—orange New Zealand sedge

Low Plants for Ground Cover

Aruncus aethusifolius—dwarf goat's beard *Bergenia* (selected semievergreen species and varieties)—bergenia, pig squeak

Carex spp. and varieties—sedge

Cerastium tomentosum—snow-in-summer

Epimedium spp. and varieties—barrenwort, epimedium

Erigeron karvinskianus—Santa Barbara daisy, fleabane

Galium odoratum—sweet woodruff (may be invasive in some areas)

Geranium spp. and varieties—hardy geranium, cranesbill

Hedera varieties only—ivy (potentially invasive)

Heuchera spp. and varieties—coral bells, alum root

Hypericum calycinum—creeping St.-John's-wort, Aaron's beard St.-John's-wort

Lamium spp. and varieties—dead nettle

Liriope spp. and varieties—lilyturf

Ophiopogon and varieties—mondo grass

Pachysandra procumbens spp. and varieties—Allegheny spurge

Pachysandra terminalis spp. and varieties—pachysandra (potentially invasive)—Japanese spurge

Rubus calycinoides (syn. *R. pentalobus*)—creeping raspberry

Stachys byzantina—'Countess Helene von Stein' lamb's ears, big ears

Symphytum grandiflorum—comfrey (choose short, spreading types)

Trachystemon orientalis—trachystemon; Abraham-Isaac-Joseph (may be a thug in some places, a wimp in others)

Vinca minor varieties only—vinca, periwinkle (definitely invasive: showier varieties only in areas contained by paving; do not plant near wild areas)

Viola hybrids—viola

Viola labradorica—Labrador violet

Viola odorata—sweet violet

Viola sororia—common violet

Waldsteinia fragarioides—barren strawberry

OPPOSITE, FROM LEFT TO RIGHT Nurseryman Dan Hinkley calls his selection of the broad-leaf sedge (*Carex siderosticha*) "a good variegated form"; *Carex elata* 'Aurea'—Bowles' golden sedge; *Carex buchanii*—brown leatherleaf sedge.

ABOVE In midspring, the petals of the saucer magnolia (*Magnolia × soulangeana*) fall to the ground upon a mostly white form of the common violet (*Viola sororia*).

Ferns as Ground Covers

There are several ferns that spread below the surface and are good candidates for ground covering. I won't even mention invasive bracken and the handful of others that are noted for their tenacity. Some of the good ones include the following: Hay-scented fern (*Dennstaedtia punctilobula*), named for the fragrance of its leaves when crushed, can even grow in full sun and likes clay soil, but will tolerate light shade. New York fern (*Thelypteris noveboreacensis*) likes moist soil and acidity, but will grow in average soil. Lady fern (*Athyrium filix-femina*) will even grow in dry shade, but it spreads more vigorously in a moist situation. The fronds are longer than 2 feet (60 cm) and lime green.

Sensitive fern (*Onoclea sensibilis*) is not a typical-looking fern. The fronds are not feathery; the leaves are deeply lobed, but not finely divided. These plants make a good ground cover, and will grow 12 to 18 inches (30 to 46 cm) tall in light shade, and even in sun if there is abundant moisture. The fern is sensitive because it is vulnerable to, and may be devastated by, the first frost. The fertile "fronds," however, which look like espresso-colored beads on a stalk, persist through the winter. If the fern is happy, it will spread. If it is growing in overly dry, dark conditions, it may be able to survive, just limping along.

Ostrich fern (*Matteuccia struthiopteris*), like many ferns, takes a while to become established, but once it is—STAND BACK. The individual plants produce an annual rhizome, or stem, just below the surface of the soil, and each new plant grows up from that. This fern may grow 3 feet (1 m) tall or more and colonizes areas as large as it is allowed to. You will be weeding it out. If you have a spot in deep shade where you need an unbroken cover, with no other plants planned for that area, ostrich fern will fill it up. The ostrich fern is also the source of edible fiddleheads, but don't overdo it. There is some question as to how healthful these emerging crosiers are for us, and you will lose the year's growth if too many are harvested.

A Carpet of Moss

Moss? Hallelujah! What could be more beautiful than a moss lawn that you can even walk on? Yet I've often seen the question in the mainstream garden media: "How can I kill the moss that grows in a shady spot where I want to have grass lawn? I've sown grass seed over and over, and the moss keeps killing it." To me, this question misses the point entirely. Besides, the moss isn't even killing the grass, it simply grows better in those particular conditions than grass lawn, perhaps because the soil is infertile, compacted, acidic, in too much shade, or all of the above.

In general, moss grows where moss likes to grow. You can encourage these plants to thrive, especially if you have the right location, moisture-retentive acidic soil, and filtered light to shade.

There are scores of species that, because of their appearance, are collectively called moss. But some of them aren't actually mosses. While a moss is considered a plant, it does not have true leaves, branches, or even roots. True moss also does not have flowers or make seeds like other plants; instead it spreads by spores, creeps, or with the help of division.

OPPOSITE, CLOCKWISE FROM TOP LEFT The delicate foliage of Himalayan maidenhair fern, *Adiantum venustum*; the evergreen Christmas fern, *Polystichum acrostichoides*, a native of the East Coast west to Minnesota; the popular painted fern, *Athyrium niponicum* 'Pictum', in colors that range from red to green to silver; plumes of ostrich fern (*Matteuccia struthiopteris*) flank timber and gravel steps.

ABOVE The sensitive fern, *Onoclea sensibilis*, is a handsome companion to the flowering *Astilbe chinensis* 'Superba' until frost ends its season.

There are two basic kinds of mosses: clumpers and spreaders. The clumpers are what you might grow between stepping-stones, or nestling among rocks. The spreaders are for "lawns" and paths that do not get too much foot traffic; for ground cover, the goal is to encourage the moss to spread over the desired area.

If you have an area where there is a bit of moss or the grass is losing the turf war, you can probably encourage it to grow and plant more moss. If you are starting from scratch, read on.

These primitive green plants, in the division Bryophyta, lack roots and absorb water from rain or dew, or by wicking moisture from the soil, but they still do photosynthesize. So choose an area that is shaded but not completely dark. The competition from any other plants must be reduced, especially if lawn grass is hanging on in a spot where there is moss already established. One way to chase away any remaining grass and promote the moss is by altering the acidity of the soil. Moss wants a pH range between 5 and 6, so you want to lower the pH to the bottom of that range (see page 209). Here is a right plant/right place situation. But I will provide some thoughts on developing a moss lawn when your soil is neutral.

Aluminum sulfate is often the recommended acidifier, but this can backfire. It can be dangerous to soil and plants (resulting in death). The safer alternative is sulfur. Once the soil has been acidified, sulfur can be used from time to time to maintain the acidity. Aluminum sulfate might damage established moss; sulfur won't.

Sulfur is available in several types of preparations, including a wettable powder for spraying or using with a watering can, and a pelletized version that is easier to control for use over a large area with a spreader. To change neutral soil (pH 7) to very acidic (pH 5), one would have to spread 4 pounds (1.8 kg) of sulfur per 100 square feet (9 m^2). The transformation may take up to a year. (Do not use the wettable powder unless mixed with water—be sure to follow the package directions to achieve the changes you're after.)

In general, you will be propagating the moss vegetatively—that is, from little bits of existing moss. There are retail propagators/suppliers, a relatively new development in the United States, who will have plenty of ideas and knowledge on ways to grow your moss lawn. Avoid sources that wild collect. The slow-growing moss might be decades old.

Discover whether the moss nursery collects their plants from the wild or propagates them for sale. Of course, like any wild plants, moss should not be harvested from the woods or public parks and preserves, which in many cases is illegal.

It is best to "inoculate" your newly acidic area in the late fall or early spring when cool weather is guaranteed, and better still, on a cloudy day or even when it's sprinkling. If the moss you've harvested from elsewhere on your own land is dry, saturate it before planting. The soil is best when it is compressed either from foot traffic or tools, such as a roller. This solid soil then has to be scuffed with a garden rake so the surface will make good contact with the pieces or sheets of moss.

One method of planting calls for taking postage-stamp-sized pieces of moss and placing them on an imaginary grid about 4 inches (10 cm) apart. The little pieces

should then be stepped on to make sure that the bottom, the brown part below the green living moss, makes very good contact with the disturbed soil.

Moss can also be shredded and sprinkled over the entire area. I've read about a method of harvesting bits of the plants by using a wire brush and lightly scrubbing it over a patch of existing moss and into a dustpan. The feathery bits can be sprinkled over the area for planting. Moss may also be "sown" by dusting a prepared area with purchased moss spores. This is a much slower process.

The fastest and most expensive way is to buy and place sheets of moss, like putting down sod, over the prepared area. (I would question the supplier's method of production or harvest to be sure the sheets of moss are nursery-grown and not collected from the wild. Wild moss may take years to grow, even decades. It would be a shame to take it from the places where it belongs. It is possible to cultivate moss and grow it faster and in more convenient ways for harvest.)

After the spores, moss squares, feathery fragments, or sheets are laid and pressed into the soil, water the area with a sprinkler every day for at least two weeks. Moss only grows when it is wet, and it wants to be moist pretty much all the time. But once established, the plants will live through periods between rainfalls, even dry spells. They may turn brown, but they will green up with the next rain.

There will be some ongoing maintenance. It is important to prevent the moss from getting covered. That is especially the case in the autumn when the leaves fall. Rake the moss lawn or sweep it gently and frequently to keep the leaves at bay. Some people spread netting over the mossy area in the fall until the leaves are off the trees, and then roll up the net with the leaves inside and take it to a place where the leaves can be spread out and collected. Shred the leaves for mulching beds or making leaf mold and compost.

OPPOSITE ABOVE Moss likes to grow where moss likes to grow. Moisture and humidity at the Bloedel Reserve in Washington State give these plants the places they love, including on the stump of an old tree that is also home to seedlings, insects, and microorganisms.

OPPOSITE BELOW The original moss steps designed by Fletcher Steele (shown here) were destroyed. But a copy is being cultivated at the Tower Hill Botanic Garden in Boylston, Massachusetts.

ABOVE A pool of moss is nearly as prized as any specimen in the extensive collection of rare plant connoisseur, Barbara Tiffany.

···

BULBS AMONG THE GROUND COVERS

Many spring-flowering bulbs can grow in deciduous shade with ground covers or low woodland plants. Depending on the circumstances, the early bulbs that want sunlight will get enough to ripen their foliage and nourish them before the trees fully leaf out in midspring. Some bulbs, such as tulips, may or may not be able to get enough light, and although they will blossom the first year after planting, because they had been raised in fields in full sun, they may not bloom again in shade. These plants can be considered decorative annuals. Therefore, if tulips and most other bulbs are used in dense shade, they can be left in the ground, or dug up and discarded, and new bulbs may be purchased for temporary color.

That said, there are many other bulbs that will return year after year in various amounts of shade. Look for early blooming daffodils. The early ones may ripen sooner, as well, and tolerate a woodland shade situation. Blue glory-of-the-snow (*Chionodoxa forbesii*) is one of the earliest bloomers (but will spread from self-sown seed). Siberian squill (*Scilla siberica*) produces its little flowers just as the late-winter crocus are ending. Super-short winter aconite (*Eranthis hyemalis*) blooms even earlier.

The fall-blooming crocus and *Colchicum* send large leaves in spring, become dormant and blossom at the end of the growing season. On the other hand, some bulblike plants get most of their nutrition after the leaves on the trees fall. Several cyclamen species bloom in early spring or late summer, then produce striking leaves that may last the entire winter. These plants want excellent drainage. Nurseries and private individuals are now propagating hardy cyclamen (once endangered) like summer-blooming *Cyclamen hederifolium*. Cyclamen is also being grown under the trees in orchards in Turkey, for example, which gives local farmers an extra source of income and stops tubers from being wild collected—scraped off the nearby hillsides.

···

Early Bulbs Among the Ground Covers

Anemone blanda—windflower; zones 5–8; LS, MS

Chionodoxa forbesii (syn. *C. luciliae*)—glory-of-the-snow; zones 3–8; WS, LS, MS

Colchicum autumnale—autumn crocus; zones 5–8; WS, FL, LS

Crocus spp.—crocus; zones 4–8; WS, LS, MS

Cyclamen spp.—hardy cyclamen, spring and fall blooming; zones by species; LS, WS

Eranthis spp.—winter aconite; zones 4–8; WS, LS, MS

Erythronium spp. and varieties—dogtooth violet, trout lily; zones 3–8; MS

Fritillaria meleagris—checkered lily, guinea-hen flower; zones 3–8; LS

Galanthus spp. and varieties—snowdrops; zones 3–9; WS, MS

Hyacinthoides spp. and varieties—bluebell, Spanish bluebell; zones 3–8; LS, MS

Ipheion uniflorum—spring starflower; zones 5–9; WS, LS

Iris reticulata—netted or reticulated iris; zones 4–9; WS, LS

Leucojum vernum—spring snowflake; zones 3–9; WS, LS, MS

Muscari spp.—grape hyacinth; zones 5–10; LS

Puschkinia scilloides—puschkinia; zones 4–8; LS, MS

Scilla siberica—Siberian squill, scilla; zones 2–8; WS, LS, MS

Many small bulbs can grow up through evergreen and herbaceous ground covers before they appear:

1 The foliage of the autumn crocus (*Colchicum autumnale*) emerges in spring, but the flowers arrive in fall.

2 *Cyclamen coum* with 4-inch- (10-cm-) tall late winter flowers and mottled foliage is a good choice for dry shade.

3 *Cyclamen hederifolium* is prized for its silver to green leaves that follows the late-summer

flowers and persist until late spring.

4 Snowdrop varieties (*Galanthus nivalis*, here), the earliest sign of spring, have spawned a trend of collectors in the United Kingdom that is spreading to the United States.

5 Just under 1 foot (30 cm), *Fritillaria meleagris*, the guinea flower or checkered lily, pops up through a low ground cover.

6 English bluebells (*Hyacinthoides non-scripta*) will gently naturalize in an area they like.

∙∙

NONLIVING COVER FOR PATHS AND OTHER USES

Materials for pathways range from those made of organic sources to manufactured products and stone. There are also recycled resources like chopped car tires. Of course, one might opt for something hard, easily cleaned, and long lasting surrounding the house. In any event, do not set pavers—from brick to block—in concrete with mortared joints. You want water to percolate down to the soil, and air to move up through the joints and spaces.

I saw a product called Superhumus used on trails at the Coastal Maine Botanical Gardens. This mixture was a combination of finely chopped bark and sand. Nothing seemed to be coming up through it or seeding down into it, and the appearance was very natural. It might be possible to have something like this prepared in your area if you cannot find a source.

Packed stone dust or decomposed granite is a popular path surface and has been used in gardens for centuries. Stone dust and similar fine materials, even compacted earth, are traditional for paths in Italian gardens.

Obviously, permanent materials like gravel and stone pavers may be used in the driest spots. Gravel and stone, of course, are fairly low maintenance, although you probably will have to weed the gravel or in between the stepping-stones in the areas that are not quite so dry.

For gravel, I prefer the small $^3/_8$-inch (1-cm) multicolored, rounded river stones, or speckled pea gravel, as opposed to what most suppliers call gravel, which is crushed rock. Crushed rock is usually one color and has sharp edges.

Larger stones will not look good, or feel good underfoot. Worst of all is white quartz. Fortunately, this bright material, which used to be seen everywhere, has fallen out of favor.

Steps can be made from cut stone, recycled composite plastics (synthetic wood), or wood. Planks, or what are usually called railroad ties, can make useful and relatively inexpensive steps, but in a moist situation, real wood can become slippery and a host to algae or moss. I covered my steps made of 4-by-4-inch (10-by-10-cm) and 6-by-6-inch (15-by-15-cm) wood with hardware cloth—small-gauge wire fencing—stapled in place. The "cloth" is made with one course of wires placed in one direction and then another set in a perpendicular track, and welded where the wires cross. Be sure to lay the cloth down so that it grabs. It must be placed with the wires on top parallel to the width of the tread—the direction of the walker. Otherwise, it will be very slippery indeed.

OPPOSITE ABOVE Non-living materials for the landscape at the Brooklyn Botanic Garden's Native Flora Garden include a bark path and a low wooden bridge.

OPPPOSITE LEFT Frog's Leap, Elsie Freeman and Kip Neale's garden in Maine, has an area created in the Japanese style. In it, pebbles and raked gravel are used as a non-living ground cover.

OPPOSITE RIGHT Frog's Leap also has a gently sloped wood boardwalk leading through a setting of rocks and trees.

PART 6

PRACTICAL HELP FOR MAKING A SHADE GARDEN

THE GOOD EARTH

In addition to light limitations, shade presents other challenges. These start with the soil. In this section, we'll look at shade-specific issues around existing soil, and knowing when to leave well enough alone. We'll also investigate what might be the most precious resource—water—and how to help your soil become more capable of accepting and retaining moisture.

In shade gardening, we are often trying to plant near the roots of trees and shrubs, and that is a very specific kind of environment—quite different from a raised vegetable bed, for instance, or an open island bed cut into a lawn.

Before planting in the shadows where there may be competition for moisture and nutrients, we must do some investigating.

What Is My Soil Makeup?

Our analysis begins by observing soil texture and makeup, looking for clues about drainage as well. Topsoil can be described as being sandy, silty, clayey, or loamy. Sandy soil is frequently identifiable because the sand is visible. That soil drains so well that it may not hold enough moisture and nutrients for most shade plants. Clay soil has very fine particles and tends to hold too much moisture. Clay feels sticky or slippery when moist and becomes rock-hard when it dries (it's what bricks are made from). Dry clay may be difficult to remoisten—the water just runs off. Silty soil has a mix of sand and clay. Natural loam is a blend of clay, silt, sand, and organic matter—a good place to start.

The way to fix clay or sandy soil and help silty soils is the same—add organic matter.

Most living things in soils, including plants, insects, bacteria, and fungi, are dependent on organic matter, which is around 50 percent carbon, for nutrients and energy. Organic matter holds soils open, allowing the infiltration of air, and may hold as much as twice its weight in water. When we want to add organic material, we add it to the surface and let nature do its thing, what we call the "no-till" method. More on this later.

Will Soil Prep Be Needed?

The woodland soil that supports many of the plant species of the forest floor is often less than a foot (30 cm) deep, and may be as thin as 4 inches (10 cm). The surface mix of loose-leaf litter is referred to as the forest duff. Even though not deep, it is ideal for many desired shade-garden plants. Duff is the result of decades of falling leaves, dust and soil particles carried by the wind, animal bones, dry and moist fruit, bits of bark and branches, feathers, and organic matter of all sorts that have built up and been processed by fungi, bacteria, arthropods, and creatures of all types into the most delicious planting material. After sufficient time, the ultimate product of this decomposition—humus—moves downward to a distinctive organic layer below

PREVIOUS SPREAD The Garden of the Gods at Greenwood Gardens in Short Hills, New Jersey, has an edge planting of ostrich fern and giant old American rosebay rhododendrons (*R. maximum*) in the acidic soil.

ABOVE Virginia sweetspire (*Itea virginica* 'Henry's Garnet') likes a somewhat acidic soil. The leaves will be pale green in neutral soil, and darker in soil with an acid level they favor.

the newly added material. That layer below the duff is what we might think of as rich topsoil—a mixture of organic matter and minerals. That kind of topsoil is shade gardeners' gold, but usually we don't have it.

If you are in a new housing development, your future will be even more challenging. While you have an opportunity to place the trees and shrubs in the landscape where you want them and plan for varying amounts and angles of light and areas of shade, the soil may have been compromised. The top layer of earth is often removed during construction. Losing the forest duff and humus that took decades to form—well, that is the saddest situation. After construction, contractors will bring in "clean fill," which is subsoil from other construction sites that has been screened to remove the larger stones but is rarely anything that resembles quality topsoil and is nothing like the woodland.

Put Your Soil to the Test

Soil chemistry is also important for the success of the desired plants. The pH of your soil is its rating for alkalinity or acidity. You may have heard the terms "sour" and "sweet," standing in for acid and alkaline (or base). There are fourteen numbers on the pH scale of soil acidity, with 7 being neutral. The scale is logarithmic, so pH 6 is 10 times more acidic than neutral. The right pH for a given plant allows it to absorb the nutrients it needs for growth.

Most of our ornamental plants like a neutral to slightly acidic soil: 7.5 to 6.5. But many of our woodland charges prefer a more acidic soil. For example, the ericaceous plants like rhododendrons and blueberries prefer soil acidity of 5 to 6 and 4 to 5, respectively. Other acid-loving plants include wintergreen, bearberry, sourweed, mountain laurel, and camellias.

The general way to test your soil's pH is to take multiple samples from each of the places where you plan to grow shade plants, and mix those samples together to create one larger sample. If you suspect the areas may have different types of soil, you can, of course, take individual samples. Label each of these as to location and send them off to a private soil-testing laboratory, or, in many states, the cooperative extension service associated with the state's land-grant university (http://www.csrees.usda.gov/Extension/USA-text.html). You can also buy a home soil testing kit and follow the directions for a general analysis.

The Nutrient Bind

The sandy soil in my New Jersey garden is neutral, but the water from the well is alkaline, so when I irrigate to establish new plants, I have a problem. I find that some plants do not grow as large as they normally would. Issues like that have to be considered. If you are planting next to the foundation of a new building, the concrete could affect soil pH, making the adjacent earth alkaline. Rinsing the building with white vinegar could help.

Adjusting the soil pH is possible. The best way to lower it, to make the soil slightly more acidic, is with the addition of acidic organic materials, for example, oak leaves, pine needles, aged sawdust, or composted coffee grounds. (Be warned,

SOME GOOD NEWS

Some new findings present a surprising bit of good news. The Marin Carbon Project, in association with the University of California, Berkeley, has been investigating the potential for specific land management practices to bind atmospheric carbon dioxide. Plants absorb CO_2 through their foliage, and when their leaves fall or when they die, they transfer it to the soil through their roots. Peter Byck, director of the film *Carbon Nation*, described how adding ½ inch (1.2 cm) of compost on top of the soil increases the sequestration of soil to 4,000 to 5,000 pounds of carbon per acre over a three-year period. As he puts it, "the soil gets turned on." It is what organic gardening is; it is what agriculture used to be. The soil is doing what it evolved to do—be a massive carbon sink. Another bonus is that "the soil becomes able to retain 27,000 gallons of water." Byck claims that soil holds the answer to America's CO_2 problem.

SAVE THE SOIL, SPARE THE TREE

If there were any old trees on the site prior to construction, undoubtedly some damage will have been done to their roots. In almost every case, if you have not been around to tie yourself to a tree or lie down in front of the bulldozers, the future is uncertain. Workers like to park in the shade, and heavy equipment on roots can kill trees—the soil under them is often irreversibly compacted. The best thing to do might be to top dress the area with a thin 2- to 3-inch (5- to 7.5-cm) layer of compost or leaf mold. Water the area under the tree deeply, and all the way out to the edges beyond the drip line (the imaginary circle corresponding to the spread of the branches above). Water again, especially if nature doesn't cooperate with frequent rains.

RIGHT To help the enivornment, we can plant trees that clean the air, and absorb and store carbon dioxide. Old trees like this one are nearing the end of their lives; best to plan and plant their replacements before they die, especially in cities where benefits to human health are priceless.

OPPOSITE LEFT A baby toad makes its way across dried leaves that will contribute to the soil of the future.

OPPOSITE RIGHT Over the years, the natural cover of autumn leaves has been incorporated into the humus-rich soil at Garden in the Woods. Here mulching an interrupted fern (*Osmunda claytoniana*).

GARDEN IN THE WOODS'S SOIL MODEL

Years of falling leaves and other organic materials decomposing and building the fertile forest soil made woodlands attractive for agriculture, which is one reason there aren't a lot of original deciduous forests left in the United States. Almost all of what we think of as "old" woodlands in North America is second-growth forest that grew up after farms and pastures were abandoned. These trees, mostly deciduous in the eastern half of the country, may still represent the widest variety of original species.

At the Garden in the Woods in Framingham, Massachusetts, the headquarters of the New England Wild Flower Society (the oldest native plant organization in the United States), leaves have been spread on beds for decades. Tests today reveal that the resulting soil is a near perfect medium for growing the plants we hope to have in our shade gardens. Nate McCullin, the garden's former senior horticulturist, described the process of making that soil in three steps. In the fall, they remove 75 percent of the leaves that have fallen on the garden beds. The 25 percent left on the planted areas is for insulation and erosion control. Nate believes that removing most of the leaves is important since it gives the soil a chance to breathe and prevents the leaf litter from getting too dense and packed down. The leaves that are taken away are shredded and piled in mounds throughout the garden, where they sit and age through the winter to turn into leaf mold.

At the end of the winter, the aged leaf mold from the piles can be spread over the entire beds before the spring ephemerals emerge. Those plants coming up from dormant crowns—bulbs and other forms of underground storage units (modified stems collectively called geophytes)—are accustomed to pushing the leaf litter of the forest floor aside. This process provides all the fertilizer that's needed at the Garden in the Woods, with the possible exception of new plantings, which get a boost from compost or compost tea.

The recommended home version of compost for woodlanders: Collect leaves from your property, but not all of them. Allow a quarter of the leaves to stay where they fall beneath the trees. Rake up leaves off of paths and the lawn, if there is any, and put them through a shredder if you can. If you do not have a machine to chop the leaves, spread dry leaves on a patch of lawn and run over them once or twice with a bagging mower (preferably electric).

Remember, if you are spreading this as a mulch after plants have emerged, do not let the material touch the stems of any plants, including shrubs and trees, because it will keep them wet and encourage rot. If you do not have a readily available source of leaves, you can use compost. If possible, top-dress the compost with a sprinkling of some shredded leaves (borrowed from neighbors or from the local leaf dump) to help break the force of raindrops and keep the compost from splashing about or drying and repelling water. The light mulch of leaves will help in getting moisture down to the plants' roots.

you'll have to drink a heck of a lot of coffee to have much of an effect! Many coffee shops are happy to give the stuff away, however.) For even more impact, you can use elemental sulfur. When using sulfur, a little goes a long way (see page 200).

To make the soil less acidic, there are organic additives. You can use ground-up eggshells (tons of them) or dried crushed oyster shell. Hardwood ashes from the fireplace will have a bit of a temporary effect. The quicker organic fix is the addition of dolomitic lime (calcium-magnesium carbonate). Before adding anything to your soil, read packages and carefully follow directions for rates of application, and remember that in most cases, we hope to have shade-garden soil that is neutral to a bit acidic.

Making radical changes to the pH does not seem like a logical thing to do. Since I do not have acidic soil, I do not grow very many rhododendrons, for example, except under a pine tree that drops its needles and helps lower the pH.

To Till, or Not to Till?

The ultimate goal is to incorporate organic matter into the soil—humus—which, in the natural forest community, happens slowly over time. In nature, nobody comes in with a spade, let alone a tiller. In garden beds, the old methods for improving soil are still adhered to, for the most part. "Double digging," the process of digging down 2 feet (60 cm), mixing in amendments, and turning over the soil again has pretty much been discredited. The new thinking is that this amount of disturbance causes problems: Air spaces in the soil may be eliminated, microorganisms are disrupted or killed, and weed seeds that have laid undeveloped in the soil for years, perhaps decades, are brought to the surface where they can germinate. And besides, among root systems of established woody plants, deep digging wouldn't even be possible.

Instead, in most cases when you need some improvement, you will be amending the soil in a different way—by applying a layer of organic mulch, best done in the fall, if possible. For preparing a bed, you can spread up to 4 inches (10 cm) of humus on the surface and let the natural cycles of cold and heat, as well as microorganisms and plant roots, slowly homogenize the material. This "no-till" method is a bit more like nature's way.

Continue to add organic matter, such as chopped leaves or somewhat composted leaves (leaf mold) again every spring and fall. Adding a layer of coarse organic material such as a mulch on the surface of the garden keeps moisture in the soil, keeps it cool, and discourages weed seeds from sprouting. The mulch should not bury the crowns of the plants or touch their stems; it should go just up to them. Mulch the area closer to plants with 1 to 3 inches (2.5 to 7.5 cm) of the organic material.

As previously stated, if you do not have access to leaves, or enough leaves to shred and spread for a new planting area, consider other materials that will eventually incorporate into the soil and promote growth in the garden beds. Mix chopped leaves with aged sawdust, well-rotted cow manure, or composted grass clippings. Mulch has to have an open texture in order to allow rainwater to percolate

A MULCH IN COLD WINTER

We've learned about using mulch to improve soil, conserve moisture, and minimize weeds. There is another kind of mulching that is done to protect some plants in the winter. If you think about it, snow is the best winter mulch in cold climates. But we cannot rely on a guaranteed cover.

Contrary to what might seem intuitive, a mulch in winter is *not* put down to keep the ground warm, but to keep it cold. This is a useful treatment for newly planted herbaceous shade perennials and woodland wildflowers. The point of the winter mulch is to shade the ground, although it isn't a blanket of material like the chopped leaves, but a loose, open tented cover, for example, made of pine boughs lightly placed over the area.

If the frozen soil thaws when it is struck by sunlight under deciduous trees, for example, and then refreezes, bad things may happen. The soil expands, contracts, expands, and plants may be damaged during this process. It creates an upward movement of the soil called frost heaves and can push plants—especially newly planted ones—right out of the ground. The freeze-thaw cycle also seems to toss my plant labels out of the soil.

I gather branches from discarded Christmas trees in the neighborhood if they do not have tinsel, cut them into 1- to 2-foot (30- to 60-cm) pieces, and use them to protect areas prone to ground heaving. Then, in early spring, I remove the branch mulch and take it to the compost pile.

WEED-SMOTHERING SOIL PREP

My soil has been disturbed hundreds of times over the years by people moving earth or by floods bringing sand and seeds to the garden. Pulling the weeds causes even more disturbance. To reduce the weeds in some open areas away from trees to be used for future beds, I smothered them (along with the grass) by covering the areas I wanted with four layers of newspaper or one layer of corrugated flattened cardboard (I used old shipping boxes with staples and tape removed). I moistened the paper or cardboard and covered every inch of it with a mulch of leaves, when I could get them, or compost. The paper and cardboard breaks down and becomes incorporated into the soil. Be sure to cover all of the paper or cardboard, for if any is exposed, it will wick moisture away and stop decomposition.

With this method, annual and perennial weeds and even grass were smothered, and I was left with an organic layer without causing a great deal of disturbance. It is best to undertake this method in the fall, so the soil will be ready for planting the following spring. But it can be done at any time and even planted through.

LEFT Lawn or weeds can be smothered with layers of moistened newspaper or cardboard, covered with a mulch of leaves or compost, and planted through in new beds. Here, ramps (or wild leek), a popular but threatened foraged plant, is being cultivated in a native edibles garden.

....

MAKING YOUR OWN COMPOST

To process garden wastes and fallen leaves into soil-improving material, you can make compost in bins or open piles. There are two general methods, cold (or slow) composting and hot (or quick). I make mine slow and cold in three or more working piles in an out-of-the-way area of the property on high ground. The current heap has the freshest, newest material; the next one is aging; and the third is ready for use. I simply layer the green and brown materials, such as green clippings and dry leaves—that is, ingredients high in nitrogen or carbon, respectively—leaving the heap be. This cold method is sometimes called the "let-it-be" method, and it takes about a year to produce useable compost. The cold compost will have to be sieved or screened. Add the large leftover pieces, sticks and twigs, to one of your other processing piles or bins to continue breaking down.

If you need to keep things nice and tidy, you can buy or make bins—divided containers that can be as simple as wire fencing attached to posts driven into the ground.

For hot or quick compost, the material going to be used is chopped up first, then put into a bin or pile that is about 4 cubic feet (0.1 m³). Start with a thin base layer of coarse twigs and stems for drainage and air circulation. Some recipes call for a specific ratio of 30 parts carbon to 1 part nitrogen. Sources of carbon are usually brown and could include cardboard, dried leaves, or straw. Organic sources of nitrogen (and carbon) include grass clippings, food waste, seaweed, and various animal manures. As examples, wood chips have a carbon to nitrogen ratio of about 400 to 1. The ratio in chicken manure, on the other hand, is about 12 to 1.

Build these materials up in thin layers until you reach about 4 feet (1.2 m) and saturate the pile until water pours out the bottom. Keep the composting material moist but not sodden (a dry pile will not "cook," nor will a very soggy one). Leave the pile for about four days, and then turn it to blend the contents every other day.

In a short time in summer, longer in the winter, the composting material will heat up to something between 140 and 150 degrees Fahrenheit (60 to 65 degrees Celsius)—hot enough to kill weed seeds and most pathogens.

Mix the material as best you can, and moisten it if it is drying out. Turning the compost will add oxygen, which the organisms need to do their work. Try to plunge a hayfork into the pile and fold as you would when making a soufflé, bringing material from the bottom up to the top. When the pile begins to cool off, turn it again, bringing material from the center to the outside, and leave it to rest to finish composting.

If the pile smells foul, there may not be enough oxygen. Try to punch holes in the pile. If you test the temperature of the interior and it does not seem hot, add more nitrogen, perhaps even well-rotted cow manure, and water.

Hot compost can be made in around eight weeks—or even as quickly as three.

The outcomes of cold or hot composting are pretty much the same. Hot is for the impatient DIY type who loves to be involved in the process. Hot compost requires much more attention, but for a shorter period of time. Hot looks like soil and smells like earth when it is finished.

Cold takes longer but requires less work and attention. Cold compost will have to be sieved to remove the larger twigs and vegetable matter that may not have broken down. Cold is for the busy gardener with less time. It's your call. You might do both if you have the space.

COMPOST TEA

Expert gardener Andrea Filippone, a partner in F2 Environmental Design with Eric T. Fleischer, bases her management techniques on encouraging and maintaining the natural living systems through soil management techniques, applying custom blends of compost and liquid biological amendments, which are often referred to as "compost tea."

Some modern gardeners believe that the proper application of compost tea could be about the most important practice in horticulture in the future, but others disagree. The benefit of the tea, proponents claim, is that not only is the soil improved, but also the pH can be altered and diseases eliminated. A tea with a high bacteria count would be good for lawn; a different tea with a high fungal count would benefit the ornamental plants we hope to grow. These different teas depend on the original source of the compost used in the brewing. Advocates claim that soil that has been destroyed after years of modern agriculture practices can be brought back and that nitrogen can be made available without the use of synthetic fertilizers.

One minor drawback to applications of tea (or any other nutritional input) could be that it makes weeds healthier right along with the desirable plants. Skeptics claim that applying regular compost is just as effective as the liquid preparation—stay tuned for further developments in this discussion.

One can try to brew compost tea at home, but it can be tricky, and the process is very specific. It is not a simple matter of adding some finished compost to water and watering plants with it. The tea is made by steeping compost that is put into a fabric bag and then submerged in water that is vigorously agitated with pumps and oxygenated with aerators, feeding the microorganisms so that they grow, and grow fast. The finished tea, which might be ready in as little as one day, depending on temperature, has to be used within twenty-four hours of having been brewed, which makes it even more challenging for a home gardener.

Companies are springing up around the country promising to apply a useful brew on trees, lawns, etc. It is important to determine how the tea is being made and that it is super fresh. Bottles of compost tea that you might find for sale could not really be filled with the living organisms that are necessary. Nate McCullin brewed tea at GITW, bottled it and gave it to members ideally within four hours.

In the future, compost tea may be a familiar aspect of healthful gardening—or not. Time will tell.

LEFT Nate McCullin, the former senior horticulturist at Garden in the Woods, brews compost tea in massive vats with a giant tea bag filled with compost. Four air pumps constantly aerate and agitate the nutrient-enriched water.

down to the soil and not bead up or run off. Coarse compost could be used as mulch as long as it is mostly decomposed.

In general, screened compost from a commercial source will be too fine to prevent weed seeds from sprouting and keep moisture down below. If finely screened compost dries out, it may actually repel water before it becomes moist and permeable again. For that same reason, and because it is not environmentally sustainable, never use peat moss as a humus source (see the box, The Trouble with Peat, page 224).

If you have no good soil for making a new planting bed, in the case of construction fill, pure clay, or pure sand to a depth of 1 to 2 feet (30 to 60 cm), you will have to bring in new soil. The best thing would be to find high-quality topsoil or loam, perhaps from an old farm field. To generalize, topsoil is something like 45 percent sand, 25 percent clay, 25 percent silt, and 5 percent organic matter. Loam might have up to 25 percent humus, perhaps in the form of compost. Try to buy loam from a very good source that makes its own compost.

The woodland soil has even more organic matter, which can be added to the surface of the new, clean loam as described above, with chopped leaves and leaf mold.

Making Your Beds?

The depth of the layer of organic material to be added to a garden-bed-to-be depends on where you are planning to plant—out in the open or among the tree roots. You also need to know whether you're creating beds, borders, or other kinds of plantings.

An island bed is pretty much what it sounds like—a planting that is open on all sides, in the shaded middle of a lawn or surrounded by a path or low edging. For a shade garden, the bed would be made in a spot away from tree roots.

Organic material such as compost, leaf mold, and other sources of humus can be piled about 8 inches (20 cm) thick at the center of the bed, sloping down to 3 or 4 inches (7.5 to 10 cm) at the edges. You may make a retaining border of stones, metal edging, logs, or other material, or feather the humus or an organic top dressing of mulch down to the ground of the surrounding area, which may remain lawn if there is enough light, moss, or path material. An edge can be cut into lawn, creating a shallow trough that will stop grass from entering the bed.

You will need to place stepping-stones within the island bed for access to plants, to weed, to deadhead, etc. Try not to have any plants farther than 3 feet (1 m) from an access path.

A border is a long version of the island bed and is usually one sided—open to the path, for example, with low plants in the front and tall plants at the back. The border may be made up against a wall, a hedge, the house, or another building. Organic material should be piled throughout the border, from 4 to 6 inches (10 to 15 cm) thick.

Beds and Tree Roots

In my experience, you can add around 4 to 6 inches (10 to 15 cm) of well-draining organic material over about one-quarter or less of the root zone of an established

OPPOSITE A woodland bed, edged by a gravel path, features Virginia bluebells, yellow wood poppy, and cinnamon fern. The bluebells will fade completely after they bloom. The wood poppy blooms longer, and if the faded flowers are pinched away, it will go on for months. If you let the wood poppy blooms fade without pruning them, attractive fruits take their place.

and even mature tree. Picture a triangular shape on the ground, kind of like a slice of pie with the point a couple of feet from the tree trunk and widening so that the crust is the edge of the bed. That edge might be at the tree's drip line (an imaginary circumference on the ground corresponding to the outer spread of the branches). Again, the material should not touch the trunk or cover exposed roots.

The place where I made my pie-wedge beds in my garden had been covered with piles of ¾-inch (2-cm) crushed rock. I took away as much as I could, but didn't fret that there was a bit left. I figured it would contribute to drainage. I used finely shredded and composted hemlock bark, which happened to be available in my area, blended with composted leaves and some topsoil. (Composted redwood bark can be found on the West Coast.)

If you have shallow-rooted trees, like beech and many species of maple, topping the area beneath them is not a good idea. The roots of mature beech trees, for instance, may be visible on the surface for what could be several feet from the trunk in every direction. Besides competition for moisture from shallow roots, some trees may produce fine branching feeder roots that could grow into the new organic material if you try the pie-wedge method.

Some gardeners have tried to thwart feeder roots by laying down synthetic woven landscape cloth before adding organic material. I have not heard good reports about this method. People often lose their tempers with landscape cloth—it gets caught on tools, tears but does not degrade, and may work its way to the surface to show itself. The roots of the woodland plants tend to grow into the cloth, making it difficult or impossible to lift them without disturbing the cloth when you want to divide them and make more. Although it's unlikely, tree feeder roots could even grow into the fabric and form a thick, water-resistant mat.

Planting in the Shade of Trees

When planting in the shade under trees, the form or size of plants used to start with can be just as critical to success as what species or varieties are chosen. Before putting the first plant into the soil, it's important to do some careful examination of the spot and have a plan for aftercare in place.

Examine the root zone first. By and large, it is not a good idea to mess with the roots of any tree. Bark is the protective layer of a tree, like skin. If that covering is breached, water, pathogens, and creatures may attack the vulnerable interior tissue.

Oak trees tend to have deep roots, so planting there or making pie-wedge beds is not very risky. Some of the mature trees growing on your property with roots exposed at the surface, however, could have some plants carefully inserted into little pockets among the roots.

The entire root may not be visible. If you see roots flaring out from the trunk, follow these as they move away from the tree and sink into deeper soil. Brush away a little soil or leaves with a whiskbroom to get a better look.

Note: For garden spaces beneath those mature tree species with many roots at or just below the surface, I opt for plants in containers raised up on bricks for air circulation and drainage, rather than planting over or among the roots (see page 128).

Every plant needs attention. One might imagine that a native plant will do well on its own. After all, it survives in the wild without attention. But buying a wild plant—even one identified as ideal for your location and conditions—then planting it and leaving it to fend for itself will most likely be a fruitless venture. All plants need help becoming established.

Start small. Whenever possible, plant from seeds and install young plants, bulbs, dormant rhizomes, and tubers. Baby plants and miniature spring-flowering bulbs may be plunked into holes in the existing soil if they are made carefully and without damaging tree roots.

Larger plants from the nursery that have been grown in delicious conditions with plenty of water and fertilizer and often more sun than they will get in your garden may not catch on right away. They may need a long period of adjustment and plenty of TLC to become established. For the most part, that means water, water, water when you plant and throughout the first growing season or longer.

Some drought-resistant ground covers, such as Mrs. Robb's spurge (*Euphorbia amygdaloides* var. *robbiae*), bishop's hat (*Epimedium* species and hybrids), and bigroot geranium (*Geranium macrorrhizum*), can be squeezed into small spaces between tree roots. Sections of the stems of the semievergreen bigroot geranium break off easily. If collected early in the growing season, the stem ends need only to be slipped into a hole in the soil and watered. The leaves may wilt for a while, but the plants will soon root in, and new leaves will grow.

As mentioned earlier, some mail order companies sell "liners" and "plugs"—baby plants in flats. These might be local plants, ferns, etc. Young plants will most likely produce more vigorous specimens that grow faster and stronger and soon catch up to their pricier counterparts from larger pots.

Limit your use of annuals. A good rule of thumb when trying to be water-wise is to plant more trees and shrubs and fewer annuals—and to start with small ones, which can adjust gradually to the conditions. Long-lived woody plants have deeper roots and, once established, can withstand longer dry periods. Conversely, annuals by their very nature start out small each spring with shallow roots, and if they hit a dry spell too soon after planting, they will never grow well (if they survive).

The best place for annuals might be in your planted containers or in the vegetable garden. (Additional how-to specifics on working with containers and even making your own from hypertufa are on pages 230–233.)

OPPOSITE Very little will grow in the shade of beech trees. Their massive shallow roots take all the moisture out of the soil, but they're beautiful in their own right.

ABOVE In early spring, pieces of the stems of the bigroot geranium (*G. macrorrhizum* 'Album') can be broken off and squeezed into spaces between tree roots, where they will catch on and grow into a weed-suppressing cover.

ABOVE A pot of three-year-old *Arisaema sikokianum* seedlings with their snow-white pestle-like spadixes. Sown seeds sometimes result in variations like the mottle leaf of one of these plants.

RIGHT To get mail-ordered dried seeds of *Arisaema fargesii* to germinate, they have to be rehydrated by soaking them in water that is changed several times a day for two weeks. I used a toilet tank to help with the water changing, and they all came up.

PROPAGATION TRICK: REHYDRATING SEEDS

In the early 1990s, it wasn't easy to find jack-in-the-pulpit (*Arisaema*) plants. Why? I can only guess. The local species was too common to be held in high regard. The flowers are either green or green-and-brown—not showy enough for most growers, who typically think color is what attracts customers. Too many sellers underestimate the attraction of weird but lovable oddities. Other reasons were that the more unusual Asian species were not well known (some had yet to be discovered in the wilds of China). These plants were rare in mail-order nurseries, and if you could find them, expensive. It can take many years for them to flower from sown seed, and time means money when a plant is taking up space in a grower's greenhouse or nursery bed.

It was the Asian species that I hoped to add to my collection, and seeds of some were available from plant societies and through mail-order suppliers in other countries.

Every plant's seed has a mechanism to keep it from germinating at the wrong time and in the wrong place. For example, seeds do not sprout at the end of summer just because rain moistens their faded flower heads. They need to be on the ground and at the right temperature. Some, like the hardy cyclamen, even need to be in the dark. Others need to have been cold before they respond to the warmth of spring, and some even need to be warm, then cold, and then warm again, like the winter aconite. In the case of jack-in-the pulpit, the plant's means of delaying germination is the moist fruit with pulp that coats each seed and which needs to disintegrate over the winter to allow germination. Unfortunately, however, seeds from moist fruits must not only be cleaned but dried for shipment.

As a result, my attempts to grow exotic species from the seeds that arrived by mail from overseas suppliers failed. I was familiar with growing the domestic species from plants in my own garden; I'd harvest the seeds when the stem of the plant's red-berry laden fruiting club shrivels and falls over. Nature uses winter's freeze and thaw to degrade and strip the seeds of flesh so they germinate in spring. If I cleaned the seeds and sowed them in pots indoors, they would germinate in about three weeks.

Yet when I sowed dried mail-ordered seeds for the Asian species in a clean medium with moisture and warmth, like my freshly cleaned seeds from the woodland, nothing happened. So I asked a member of the Rock Garden Society how he did it. "Oh, you have to rehydrate the seeds," he said. "Place them in water for two weeks and change the water four to six times a day." I wasn't able to do that for practical reasons, but soaking the dried seeds is key, and freshly replaced oxygenated water reduces the chance that the seeds might grow mold and rot, which they very well might in still or stagnant water. To carry out this directive, I found an organza gift bag like the kind one receives, filled with candy, at a wedding, and placed the seeds inside. I then hung the bag with a bent paper clip in the tank of the toilet. That way the water got freshened several times a day. After two weeks, I sowed the seeds, and they all came up.

This method will most likely work for similar situations: when seeds of hardy perennials that originated in moist fruit are purchased from mail order suppliers, and they arrive cleaned of fruit and dried. Dry seeds from dry fruit like peas from pods do not need hydrating. But all seeds need the special treatment that will get them ready to germinate, which for most seeds, thankfully, is just moisture and warmth.

....

SUMMERING HOUSEPLANTS
IN THE SHADE GARDEN

All indoor potted plants enjoy a vacation outdoors. Most of them do not want to be in full sunlight, and none of them care to go directly from the indoor garden to the blazing sun. Without the protection of glass windows, which filter a good deal of the light, they'll cook. Fortunately, we're looking to decorate areas in the shade.

I bring the plants out when all danger of frost has passed and nighttime temperatures are consistently above 50 degrees Fahrenheit (10 degrees Celsius). Some plants, like begonias, like it even warmer than that. Gradually place the pots in places with varying degrees of sunlight. Start by taking the plants to full shade, and in about five days, as they become acclimated to brighter light and moving air, you can move them to their summering spots in filtered light, medium shade, etc. It's a good idea to move any plant that wanted a south-facing window inside—a cactus, for instance—to the sunniest spot outside, and any plant that was away from the windows—interior decorator plants such as palms and Dracaena, for instance—to deeper shade.

If there is an area that you use for recreation—for example, the patio near the grill—you have a good spot for arranging plants in containers for temporary color, texture, and life, as well as for their own health.

I like to stage the containers so that some are elevated above others. Stairs are good for this if the pots do not block their use. I had an outdoor fireplace that was great covered with pots in the summer. You can also invert empty clay pots and use them to lift the containers of other plants. Nearly any waterproof prop can be used—for instance, metal milk crates or stacked concrete blocks.

You may find that you need to water frequently in late summer as the big plants have filled their pots with roots and temperatures are high. Don't use saucers under plants in places open to the sky since they can fill with rain and leave your plants sitting in stagnant water where roots may rot.

Your plants can stay out all summer long but should come back inside before the first frost of autumn or, even better, before the heat goes on inside. In other words, when the kids go back to school, the plants should go back inside. Don't be surprised if some of the plants drop leaves when they make the stressful transition back to the dry indoor air of the window garden. It is natural, but take my advice and be careful not to over-water at this time.

Now, there could be an issue with hitchhikers—critters that want to come inside along with the plant. Look under leaves. I never put pots directly on the ground. Worms could come up through the drainage holes and wreck havoc in the confined space of the container. Examine the plants as you move them inside. If you suspect there might be something in the soil besides plant roots, soak the pot in a bowl or pail of water for an hour, The soggy soil will chase most bugs out of the planting medium. It is a good idea to leave that plant outdoors for a few more days so the soil will dry out a bit.

Don't give up making the annual move to the "country." The plants will grow strong and healthy in the warm days and cooler evenings, with air movement, bright light, and occasional rains washing their leaves clean of dust and most of the pests that invade the indoor garden.

OPPOSITE I repurposed an outdoor fireplace as a staging platform for my summering houseplants. The plants love their "vacation" and I enjoy the decorated seating area beneath the sun porch (page 107).

· ·

POLYMER CRYSTALS

In order to help new plants become established and stay hydrated in a difficult spot, I mix potassium-based polyacrylamide water-absorbing crystals with soil. If you have ever used these products, you know that a little goes a very long way. The dry crystals look like kosher salt. These granules absorb around 300 times their weight in water and plump up. If you add dry crystals to potting soil when planting and water as usual, you may find the next day that the soil and polymer nuggets have created a volcano in the garden or poured out of a planter.

To avoid this problem, I prehydrate the crystals and add them to excavated soil when planting. Add about a tablespoonful of hydrated crystals to a cup of excavated soil mix and use that around the little transplant. The package says the crystals will degrade—they do seem to disappear in a year or so.

As with all newly planted plants, water well—deeply and often—as the little charges become established, and visit them frequently during the first year.

· ·

POTTING MEDIUMS FOR SHADE CONTAINERS

Most commercial potting mixes are peat based. I don't use them, for reasons I'll explain later. American Soil & Stone in Richmond, California, is one of the few commercial suppliers I know of that produces potting mixes without peat. Their ready-to-use Ultra Potting Mix comprises coir, sand, red lava, dolomite lime, nitroform 38-0-0, iron sulfate, triple superphosphate, and calcium nitrate. Coir is shredded coconut husk, a recycled byproduct of the coconut processing industry, and is the moisture-retaining organic ingredient in the mix. Basically, Ultra Potting Mix includes organic matter to retain moisture, a material for drainage and aeration in the form of sand and crushed red lava rock, organic fertilizer, and trace elements. I envy gardeners near Richmond.

A potting medium can be pretty simple, like my lazy version, or as fine-tuned as you care to make it, like the Ultra. The most important ingredients are moisture-retaining organic matter and those that promote drainage and aeration. For my homemade mix, I use coir and sieved aged compost for the moisture-retaining medium, along with readily available lightweight perlite (puffed volcanic glass) for drainage. The ratio is about four parts organic matter (equal amounts coir and compost) to one part perlite. I adjust the proportions as required, adding more perlite for plants that need extra drainage, less for plants that like damp roots. I do not always mix in fertilizer, lime, or trace elements.

I rely on nature and compost to fertilize my shade garden for the most part, but in the closed environment of the pot with no real soil, or loam, I need to add nutrition. Compost provides nutrition in the beginning, but I might add a naturally slow-releasing material such as bone meal for phosphorus and green sand for potassium when I know the plants are "gross feeders." Dehydrated cow-manure pellets may be used, as well, and as the season progresses, liquid kelp or seaweed. You want a balanced mix with nitrogen, phosphorous, and potassium. Follow the manufacturer's recommended rates, and if anything, err on the light side.

If I lived near Richmond, California, I would definitely go to American Soil & Stone, but there is nothing like that place near me. It is even hard to find coir. I usually get it from mail-order suppliers. Coir is shipped compressed and dry and must be rehydrated. Directions usually suggest placing the brick, block, or "tile" of coir in a container like a wheelbarrow and adding water. If you need the coir in a hurry, use hot water—and stand back. The last coir tile I bought measured 11 inches (28 cm) square and 5 inches (13 cm) thick and weighed 11 pounds (5 kg). Once hydrated, it expanded to 17 gallons (64 L) of organic matter and nearly filled the wheelbarrow.

THE TROUBLE WITH PEAT

In the United States, peat moss is almost exclusively used by the horticulture industry. Peat is the partially decomposed remains of sphagnum moss, which is found in bogs on all continents. It is highly acidic and breaks down quickly when used away from its anaerobic origins, compressing and squeezing air out of the soil or potting medium, creating an unhealthy condition for plant roots. Yes, it is organic, but it is a poor choice as a soil amendment, not only for the health of your plants, but also because the harvesting of peat damages the environment. Peat moss is mined from bogs, which are ecosystems full of plants like sundews, pitcher plants, butterwort, cranberry, and bog rosemary, and a host of rare and endangered animals like dragonflies, frogs, and birds, not to mention the living form of the moss itself (sphagnum). Of course, the moss can grow back if a bog is restored after mining, but the aged peat moss product can take tens of thousands of years to form.

Harvesting this material even destroys archaeological and anthropological artifacts and human and animal remains that have been preserved for many centuries in the anaerobic bogs. Ancient CO_2 is also preserved in these bogs, trapped in the moss, but released into the air when mined. In fact, peat bogs store about 10 percent of all fixed carbon on earth.

Most of the peat is mined in Canada and transported hundreds of miles, often when it's damp and heavy, which adds further to the fuel required for shipping. Although coir is also shipped, it is greatly compressed and dried, so it is lightweight and a lot can be packed into smaller spaces. When moistened, the compacted coir expands many times its volume.

If more people demand coir, compost, or other alternatives to peat, there will be greater, and higher-quality, supplies of these options. The ideal would be locally produced compost everywhere. Many municipal waste stations make compost from collected leaves and give it away to residents, but you cannot guarantee the cleanliness of the product. I've found pieces of plastic in a batch of compost, and a grower I know found a bicycle. But things are improving as demand increases. A company near me sells a good-quality compost made mostly from the vegetable waste discarded by the local supermarket—the proprietors of which are thrilled to have the stuff picked up and taken away.

LEFT The surface layer of living sphagnum moss (seen here) has to be scraped off when peat moss is mined. The young plants (like white *Thalictrum thalictroides*) and animals that live in this special plant community are displaced or killed in the process. This is just one of the environmental impacts of harvesting peat moss for horticulture.

How-to Planting Tips

Use a dibble (a pointed wooden stick made for planting) or a similar tool to make small holes in the ground next to the roots. Rotating the handle of the dibble in a circular motion will enlarge the hole. When the hole is made, drop a miniature bulb into it and fill the cavity with compost and soil. Similar holes may be made for small-rooted plants, plugs, as mentioned previously, or ground covers. These baby plants catch on fast and will often grow into quart-pot-sized specimens in a year. It is important to keep up with watering during the first growing season.

When planting from a nursery container, moisten the soil first. Then knock or slip the root ball out of the pot. Before you plant in the ground, tease the roots apart, to loosen them. In the case of a woody plant, like a shrub, do not be afraid to score the root ball with a knife. Roots branch when cut, just like twiggy top growth does, and they will venture into their new environment sooner if they are released from the tight soil of the restrictive quarters.

Time your transplant. You can move just about any plant, even a tree. The move may be needed for a number of reasons—putting in a new utility line, for example, or if something just isn't doing well in one spot. Perhaps it simply needs more or less light. Of course, there are also aesthetic reasons.

You can dig up a plant to transplant, elsewhere. It is best to dig and move trees when they are dormant (in winter) or when perennials are just waking up in the spring. It is great if you know of the impending move a year in advance and can do some judicious root pruning around a tree or shrub in the late winter a year ahead of the move. But it's not always possible to plan that way. If I cannot move a plant when I would like to, I take extra care when it has to happen. For example, a herbaceous perennial can be moved during the growing season, as long as the top growth—leaves and sometimes stems—is cut back to compensate for roots lost in digging. When the plant arrives at its new home, transplant it, water it well, and keep the soil moist. If the plant is being moved into a sunnier spot, consider making a canopy of a translucent material, like an old sheer curtain stretched across stakes, to shelter the transplant for the first week. Watering is very important, and in hot weather, you could even set up a sprinkler to add a gentle spray a few times during the day.

Use soaker hoses. To help plants become established in my shade garden, I irrigated the first season, attempting to deliver the equivalent of at least 1 inch (2.5 cm) of rain per week. Porous soaker hoses (made from recycled automobile tires) work very well and last a long time. In sandy soil like mine, more hoses are needed, and they have to be placed fairly close together since the water tends to go straight down. In slow-draining clay soil, the hoses can be farther apart, as the water is inclined to spread near the surface.

Designing in Containers

When I put together a mixed-plant container, I follow the advice of most designers: I use one showy tall plant at the center for a pot that will be viewed from all sides, or at the back for a planter that will be placed up against a wall or near a tree trunk and enjoyed from one vantage point. This plant is the "thriller." I use a few sprawling plants to trail over the edge of the pot ("spillers"), and a few more in between to complete the planting—"fillers." In general, the chock-full planters will contain annuals and cold-tender perennial plants that will be killed by an autumn frost.

Another way to design planters is to have only one kind of plant in each container and cluster them for an arrangement. These pots may be homes to cold-hardy perennials and woody plants, even trees. Choose plants that originated from at least one hardiness zone colder than the place where they will live. With one kind of plant, you will be able to pay more and better attention to each species or variety to meet its needs. If you intend to have the plants in the containers permanently, be sure the pots and tubs are weatherproof. In cold climates, the freeze-thaw cycle will crack most terra-cotta and even concrete if the medium is too moist going into winter.

OPPOSITE ABOVE A dibble is a pointed tool for wiggling small holes between tree roots for planting seeds, small bulbs, or baby plants.

OPPOSITE BELOW When I started the woodland garden beds, I laid a zigzag of porous soaker hoses for irrigation during the first year to help establish the young plants.

LEFT In some challenging areas beneath trees, I turn to containers. Containers allow me to have a garden of tender and hardy perennials in pots elevated on bricks set between the roots.

ABOVE Containers can be made of almost anything, including wood barrels, plastic or metal buckets, or terra-cotta (clay), the traditional material. I make containers out of concrete in the antique faux bois or fake wood style.

To help prevent questionable containers from breaking, try to keep the medium on the dry side toward the end of the growing season. To help the pots endure, you might tip them on their sides so that they will not be exposed to rain or snow, or get them under the cover of a roof. Conical containers, shaped like traditional flower pots, have a better chance of surviving, because if the material expands, it may move up rather than out. You can cover the soil in a container that must be stored outdoors, one that formerly had seasonal plantings of annuals that are now gone or perennials that are completely dormant; make a plastic "shower cap" and hold it in place with rope or a bungee cord. Remove the cover when the danger of freezing temperatures has passed and before perennials emerge, if they are in the medium. (This is not the best method for perennials in containers in sun, as the medium will warm up and the dormant plants emerge too early.)

To prepare my homemade concrete containers to be able to withstand freezing, I line them with one or two layers of thin plastic bubble wrap before putting in my soilless potting medium. The bubble wrap compresses to allow for the expansion of the mix inside the pots and, so far, I believe this practice has helped keep these pots from breaking.

You can also make your own containers using a weather-resistant medium called hypertufa, a mixture of cement, perlite, and coir. Plants love to grow in these constructions, usually rectangular troughs, because they have excellent drainage, and air passes through the porous walls. In most cases, the troughs will last for several seasons, even years. (See directions for making troughs on page 230.)

. . . .

Some Tender and Hardy Genera to Look for When Designing Shady Containers

Acorus—sweet flag

Alocasia—elephant ear

Asparagus—asparagus fern (tropical houseplant varieties)

Astilbe—astilbe

Begonia—begonia

Browallia—bush violet, browalia

Buxus—boxwood

Caladium—caladium

Carex—sedge

Dichondra—dichondra

Hedera—ivy

Heliotropium—heliotrope

Heuchera—coral bells

Hosta—hosta

Impatiens—impatiens, busy lizzy

Lamiastrum—yellow archangel

Lamium—dead nettle

Liriope—lilyturf

Nephrolepis—Boston ferns

Ophiopogon—mondo grass

Oxalis—sorrel, shamrock

Philodendron—philodendron

Plectranthus spp.—Swedish ivy and others

Primula polyantha—primrose

Strobilanthes dyerianus—Persian shield

Tiarella—foamflower

Vinca major—bigleaf periwinkle

Viola—violet

OPPOSITE When designing a container garden, a balanced arrangement might contain one special tall plant (cardamom, *Elettaria cardamomum*) surrounded by lower plants. The recommendation is often to have a tall thriller, a spiller that drapes over the container edge, and fillers for the spaces in between.

ABOVE Flowering begonias are colorful choices in containers for light shade and filtered light.

BELOW Tender plants may also be included in container plantings for their fantastic foliage, for instance, the palm-like stunner *Begonia luxurians*.

MAKING YOUR OWN TROUGHS

For decades, gardeners have recycled hewn stone troughs to use as planters. The troughs were originally carved to make watering containers for animals and sinks. Rock gardeners found that troughs cut from extremely porous lightweight tufa rock, a variety of limestone, gave plant roots access to the oxygen they needed, and they grew extremely well. Tufa is not an unlimited resource and can be expensive and hard to find, so some people have been making an artificial tufa rock called hypertufa.

Hypertufa troughs are often used to grow alpine plants that love excellent drainage. But we can use troughs in the shade as well, filled with container media and small hardy plants like dwarf hostas (5).

Hypertufa troughs are fun to make and a great project to take on with friends. How about a hypertufa weekend! Originally, hypertufa was made with peat moss and cement. The super-acidic peat neutralized some of the alkalinity of the cement. But instead of peat I use coir, which is neutral. After several years, I have not seen any negative effects from this substitution.

MOLDS AND REUSEABLE FORMS FOR HYPERTUFA

The moist hypertufa mixture can be formed over an inverted plastic bowl or any sturdy but flexible container—one that the material will not adhere to. If in doubt, the mold can be smeared with petroleum jelly before the moist hypertufa mix is patted onto it. The material can also be pressed into the inside of a very large plastic bowl to make a similarly shaped container. Make the walls at least 1 inch (2.5 cm) thick. Be sure to use something to make drainage holes—for example, four wine corks can be pushed into the soft hypertufa in what will be the bottom of the container. After 24 to 36 hours, depending on temperature, the mold can be carefully removed from the inside or outside of the hypertufa "pot." When the hypertufa is fully hardened, the wine corks can be drilled through for drainage holes.

Frames can be made as molds. These can be built out of wood planks, or 2-inch- (5-cm-) thick rigid Styrofoam insulation (available at home improvement stores), or a combination of both. Basically, you will be making a box that is open at the top and bottom and whatever size you want your trough to be. For example, ours is approximately 10 inches (25 cm) high, 12 inches (30 cm) wide, and 12 inches (30 cm) long.

To make a reuseable form out of rigid Styrofoam, cut the pieces so the two long sides overlap the ends of the two short sides, or stagger equal-length sides so they overlap at the corners, as shown (1). Push large nails in from the sides to hold the corners (2). Then run two strips of duct tape around the boxes, covering the nails and holding the box tightly (3, 4).

If the frame will be set on a plastic-covered piece of plywood during construction, wood two-by-fours can be temporarily attached to the plywood with screws to help hold the Styrofoam box in place (5, page 232).

5

Hypertufa Trough

This recipe will make one or more medium-sized troughs, about 1 to 1½ inches (2.5 to 4 cm) thick and approximately 10 inches (25 cm) high, 12 inches (30 cm) wide, and 12 to 18 inches (30 to 46 cm) long. Yield will vary based on characteristics of your materials.

Dry Ingredients (to be measured with a scoop or plastic deli container):

12 quarts (11 L) hydrated coir (or peat moss as a last resort if coir cannot be found)

12 quarts (11 L) perlite

2 handfuls synthetic reinforcement fibers (these are usually made of alkali-resistant plastic or glass and are found among masonry supplies)

8 quarts (7.5 L) Portland cement (look for OPC, or Ordinary Portland Cement, not concrete or a mortar mix)

Liquid Ingredients:

4 quarts (3.7 L) liquid acrylic admixture or bonding agent (called concrete liquid additive, bonding agent, and/or acrylic fortifier)

4 quarts (3.7 L) water, or more if needed

Supplies:

Dust masks

Rubber gloves

Sieve such as a commercial soil riddle or homemade construction consisting of ½-inch (1.2-cm) wire hardware cloth stapled to a wooden frame

Mortar box or wheelbarrow

Scoop or garden trowel for dry ingredients and for mixing

Quart (or liter) measuring container (for example, a half-gallon plastic milk jug with the top cut to make a larger opening, with the handle retained, and the container marked at the quart line)

Plastic sheeting to lay over the work surface and become the bottom of the trough

Wine corks or short sections of PVC pipe for drainage holes

Brace for frames

Duct tape

Nails (16d to 20d-penny, 3½ to 4 inches [89–102 mm] long)

Plastic wrap

Spray bottle with water

Wire brush, grater, or file, for distressing surface

Electric drill to make drainage holes through corks

Instructions:

Wear a mask and rubber gloves!

Sieve the coir fibers into a mortar box or wheelbarrow. You do not want to have clumps (1). Add the perlite to the coir (2).

Fluff and separate the synthetic fibers by rubbing the strands between your fingers to loosen them; they usually come in very tight bunches and should be divided as best as possible into individual strands—one small bunch, about a teaspoonful, could fluff into a handful. Add them to the dry materials, making certain the downy fibers are distributed evenly throughout the mix and do not end up in clumps.

Add the cement and thoroughly mix with a trowel or gloved hands (3).

Add the liquids and mix thoroughly. The consistency should be fairly dry, like friable garden soil. When a handful is squeezed, it should hold together in a ball (4), but no liquid should drip out. Don't be surprised if you need to add more water to achieve this.

Lay out the plastic sheeting on a flat surface and place the Styrofoam form on it. Position short 1- to 1½-inch (2.5- to 4-cm) sections of plastic pipe or wine corks at the bottom of the form where the drainage holes will be. If you have wider pieces of pipe, you may use as few as two (5), but you'll probably need about six if you're using corks. Large holes may be covered with screen later, but good drainage is essential.

Carefully trowel the mix into the bottom of the form, making sure that the drainage-hole molds remain upright and in place. Add enough material to make a thickness of 1 to 1½ inches (2.5 to 4 cm). Thickness may be judged by cork or pipe section height, or by piercing the moist mixture with a cake tester or unbent paper clip.

Next, build up the inside walls of the trough to a similar thickness. The mix should hold itself in place as you pat it up against the insides of the form (6).

Leftover concrete mix can be formed inside or on the outside of a plastic bowl for a small hypertufa container (7).

Once the trough has been made in the mold, it must be left to begin curing, while remaining moist. Cover the form with a piece of plastic wrap and shade if necessary.

After twenty-four hours (in temperatures between 50 and 70 degrees Fahrenheit/10 to 21 degrees Celsius), the form may be removed. If you used wooden reinforcements, unscrew them first. Remove the tape, pull out the nails, and drop the planks of foam away from the new trough. Avoid lifting the trough by its sides if at all possible. At this point, it should hold together but will still be soft enough to distress with a wire brush or a cheese grater.

If you used pipe for drainage molds, you can carefully tip the trough on its side and gently tap and pop them out (8, 9). Remove the Styrofoam form.

Roughing up the outside of the trough makes it look more like the carved stone original that is the model for the hypertufa troughs. Distressing the outside also makes a more hospitable environment for moss to grow in time. Use a wire brush or cheese grater (11).

By the second day out of the form, a wire brush or grater will no longer make a dent, and if you need to distress the trough further, you will have to use a file or power tools (12).

Keep the trough moist as it cures for at least two weeks. Concrete doesn't dry, it hardens, and the longer it is moist the harder it will be. The idea is to not dry it, but cure it.

If you have used corks, bore them out with a spade bit on a cordless power drill.

If there are any hairy parts from the fibers, these can be burnt off with a lighter or a blowtorch flame quickly grazed across the surface. Plant the finished container (13).

Moss likes an acidic environment, yet with time it seems to grow on super-alkaline concrete. I am not sure exactly why, but I suspect that after enough time and rainstorms, the concrete surface neutralizes yet still stays just damp all the time—something that mosses like. There are kits for growing moss on surfaces, and you might like to try one. I haven't, and I am not directly aware of success with coatings of yogurt, buttermilk, or beer to encourage moss.

13

Planting Trees

The old saw used to go "plant a fifty-cent tree in a five-dollar hole." The idea was that preparing soil was more important to the future of a plant than the plant itself. Oops—that's not true. When an extra-large hole is dug and the soil is improved and used to "backfill" the hole when the tree is installed, the roots tend to grow vigorously into the amended soil and then stop. The procedure is somewhat like making a container in the old soil. It has been proven that planting a tree in the soil that it will grow in for its entire life actually makes for a more successful specimen.

A tree should never be planted too low. The root flare is the place where the trunk meets the roots and widens. That should not be underground, and it's often better to plant it a bit too high, since there is usually some soil settling. As you dig the hole, lay a long stake across the opening at ground level. Then lower a yardstick into the hole and note the height at the point where it crosses the horizontal stake.

Some trees are purchased "B&B"—this is when they have their root ball dug and wrapped in burlap. Back when trees were hand dug, the root ball was really shaped like a sphere. Now machines called tree spades are most often used to dig cone-shaped root balls. Some growers add soil above the root flare to make the ball look more traditional. Be careful to brush or scrape away any of this soil so that you don't inadvertently plant the tree too low.

When you see newly planted trees, you often see two stakes with guy wires holding the tree so that it will not move in the wind. That is another old procedure that has been shown to not help the tree. Moving a bit in the wind makes the cells of the trunk stronger, in the same way that exercise builds muscles. If a tree is planted in a very windy location or on a slope, then stakes might be useful, but very often, the people who install the wires do not return to the scene to untie them, and the tissue of the young plants can actually grow around and include them, or worse, be constricted to death by the wires.

All wire, nondegradable string, and as much burlap as possible should be removed when planting a tree. The old method was to leave the burlap, which, being organic, would eventually degrade. But the fabric is sometimes treated with chemicals to retard decay, and it is often tied in a knot around the trunk well above the soil line. The fabric left above ground might wick moisture away from developing roots and retard the decomposition of the burlap. The knot of material above ground could take years to disintegrate, and by then, it might have strangled the tree.

People in the west and the far south of the United States might be thinking, "What the heck is all of this B&B stuff?" Most trees and plants in those regions are grown in containers and sold that way. The growers do not often have clay soil that holds together for a good ball, but also, since there isn't a freeze/thaw problem in the warmer areas along the coast, plants can stay above ground for years growing in a soilless medium in containers.

One thing applies in all cases: Newly planted trees should be watered—not just once, but frequently and thoroughly as they becomes established. There should be a well built up around the base of the tree to hold water. This construction is like a

....

PRUNING TREES

At times, you may want to remove the lower limbs of trees to allow more space below them, and so more light can reach the plants below. You can buy a guide to pruning, and I suggest that you do to help you know what you or someone you are hiring should be doing. There has been a lot of research in the last few decades that's turned tree pruning on its crown. The old idea was to make the cuts invisible. That was the "flush-cut" theory. Then paint the wound with tree dressing. This is bunk. Flush cuts allow disease organisms to attack and decay the main parts of the tree, and tree wound paint seals the cut, keeping it moist and hospitable for the bad guys. Those are just a couple of examples of why it's important to have up-to-date information (and keep a sharp eye on the utility company when they come to trim trees).

SOME GENERAL THOUGHTS ON PRUNING

Large tree pruning and dead tree removal should always be left to a professional who comes highly recommended, is a certified arborist, and has proof of insurance.

Prune for health first. Remove diseased branches and older, lower branches that may shade newer ones.

Trim branches that cross each other and scrape together. Leave the branches that grow out, away from the center of the tree, and aim for an open vase shape. If limbs grow too close together, or if there are competing leaders, there might be a weak branch crotch that is susceptible to splitting. One limb must go.

The general recommendation for ornamental flowering deciduous trees (and shrubs) is to trim them right after they blossom. That will give them time to set flower buds for the following year.

Most major pruning on mature trees is best done in late winter before flowering or new growth begins. You will miss some blossoms, however.

There are exceptions to the "rule" above—for example, many magnolias and crabapples will push suckers or watersprouts, resulting in multiple new shoots from the cut area. Fewer shoots may sprout if these trees are pruned in summer.

In shade, most evergreens will be the broadleaf types. Many of these can be pruned year after year and have an ample reserve of dormant buds to add new dense growth. We use shade-tolerant ones like boxwood for backgrounds, hedges, and even topiary. On the other hand, many needle-leaf evergreens will not produce new growth at all if incorrectly pruned.

Cutting down a tree to make a garden should be one of the last things you do (especially in a shade garden). But if the tree is growing poorly or is threatening to fall on your house or car, call a professional. Do not undertake a big saw job without a witness poised to call 911.

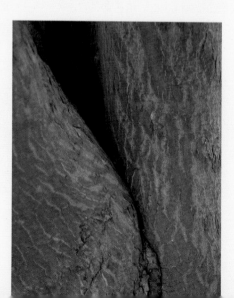

RIGHT A bark inclusion occurs when competing branches grow too close together. This is a vulnerable spot where the tree may split. In this situation, one branch may have to be removed.

STEPS FOR PRUNING

Years ago, the idea was to make the site of a removed limb seem to disappear, with little or no trace of its ever having existed. That's changed. Thanks to the work of the late Dr. Alex Shigo and others, we have come to realize that healthful pruning is not invisible pruning. Shigo, called the father of modern arboriculture, performed autopsies on hundreds of trees and discovered that cutting too close to the main trunk damaged the "branch collar." This prevented healing and allowed diseases to enter the live tissue of the tree, often leading to the tree's death. On the other hand, leaving a stub that's too big does not allow a tree to grow new tissue to close off or compartmentalize the wound. Bad pruning is dangerous, but good pruning can be therapeutic.

Look carefully at the tree where the branch meets the main trunk. There is usually a flare and often some different-looking tissue—a circular band that could clearly be the collar. There are some trees where this collar is hard to see, and others where the growth is obvious. The collar should be left intact after pruning.

Cutting away a living branch involves three cuts. The first one is an undercut made beneath the branch and up about a third of the way through the branch and 4 to 6 inches (10 to 15 cm) away from the trunk (1). This undercut is made so that the falling branch will not tear the healthy tissue. The next cut is down from the top and just a bit farther away from the tree than the first cut (2). When you've gotten about halfway through, the heavy branch will break away, but it will not tear the bark because of the first cut (3, 4).

The last cut is to trim the branch stub so the complete and undamaged branch collar remains (5). In time, the cells at the branch collar will grow and may completely close off the site of the removed branch.

crater with a large reservoir in the center, or a big doughnut with the tree trunk in the hole. The soil or mulch should not actually touch the bark tissue.

Dealing with Deer

The gardener's options for preventing deer from grazing begin with spray deterrents. There are numerous repellents on the market for treating your foliage. One that has done very well is a concoction of rotten eggs, garlic oil, and cayenne pepper. That recipe is similar to homemade concoctions; however, the manufacturers say, "It's all in how you rot and blend the eggs." The smell is an issue: this popular brand will keep deer out of the garden, but it may keep you out as well.

Another brand I've tried has an acceptable scent of garlic and clove, and the odor fades quickly. I found that using this product monthly was very effective . . . until it wasn't. Deer may get used to one deterrent or another. One key to these products seems to be swapping them from time to time. Alternate between two to three sprays.

There is another repellent that was developed in Scandinavia for the forestry industry. This one is among the few that contain smell and taste deterrents that can be used in the winter. This spray seems to contain mostly rehydrated dried blood, and when you use it, it does clog the nozzle, which can be easily washed clean, but it also covers your plants with unsightly red dots. Still, these quickly fade or wash away while leaving the product's effectiveness intact for a few more weeks. (It's understandable if the blood ingredient turns you off. Vegans will want to opt for other preparations.)

In all cases, new growth remains unprotected, so diligent reapplication is called for in the spring. Regardless of what spray you use, applications should be repeated every three or four weeks to maintain an effective level of smell and taste defense.

Other deterrents include a motion-sensor sprinkler head called "Scarecrow," which has been reasonably successful. When anyone, be it deer, neighbor's dog, or spouse, enters the guarded area, a burst of water sprays a strong stream toward the intruder in order to frighten it away. However, the deer (and others) may become accustomed to the spray, and it could lose its effectiveness. Another mechanical deterrent is an electronic ultrasound machine, which emits a high-frequency sound. I've heard that these do not always work over time, because the deer seem to get used to the sound like they do to the water spray.

The last mechanical control is the best solution: a fence that is at least 8 feet (2.4 m) high around the planted areas of the property. A wooden post and plastic netting arrangement may not be very expensive. My fence is galvanized pipe set into concrete with netting stretched between the vertical members and heavy wire at the top and bottom to keep the netting taut and close to the ground (deer, especially fawns, will go under a fence otherwise).

Eight-foot (2.4-m) heavy-duty plastic netting can be placed around the perimeter of a property and attached to posts hidden behind trees. Gardeners in deer country always say they love their fencing, no matter how it looks, and tend to turn a blind eye to it in time. Posts or galvanized pipes (after a few months of aging) can

OPPOSITE An 8-foot- (2.4-m-) tall plastic-net deer fence runs along the boundary of most of my property. In summer, my concrete urn and pedestal get planted, and that, along with perennials, shrubs, and trees, completely disguises the fence.

also be disguised with what I call the invisible paint—my old standby, Cabot brand opaque stain in the shade called Spanish Moss, which is the color of bark and dirt and virtually disappears.

As for how you are getting inside the fence, of course you can get to the garden from the house, but how about coming up the driveway if that area is also fenced? If you do not want to have a gate that has to be opened and closed at the entrance, you can install a cattle grate—a simple arrangement of pipes set at ground level with spaces in between and a drainage pit below. Deer (and cows) won't walk on the uneven surface.

Water, Our Most Precious Resource

We must be as conscious of water use as we are of energy consumption. Water is a threatened resource, and we have to use the best practices now. It would be great if we could collect all the rainwater, for example runoff from the roof, for use later. Theoretically, you could collect water in a climate such as Seattle's through the winter, when the garden doesn't need it, and then use it in the summer when it doesn't rain for weeks. But the mini-garden rain barrels on the market are woefully inadequate for more than a token gesture on that front. A lot of them hold less than 30 gallons (115 L) of water, not much more than a large garbage can's worth. That amount will be used up in the garden in no time at all.

A hundred years ago, houses were built with cisterns in the cellar, a room with a watertight floor and walls. Water from the roof was directed to the underground cistern where it could be used for the household. I wish we could bring that back.

When I started the woodland garden in New Jersey, I built a 5-foot- (1.5-m-) high wooden water tower stand and placed a 33-gallon (124-L) garbage can on top of it. A hose led from a valve on the bottom of the tank to the soaker hoses and gravity watered the garden slowly. The water tower was designed to be used for weekly watering during the first year of the garden as the local plants were becoming established. In the fall, I stopped it.

The most wonderful cistern I ever saw was one designed by James David in Austin, Texas. The tank was huge—at least 1,500 gallons—and stored water drained from the roof. That kind of construction wouldn't be practical for everyone. For now, the hope is for more municipal recycle and reuse water-treatment plants and enforced restrictions in places where rain is infrequent and during times of drought, so none is wasted and some is available in the leanest times.

To make the best use of every drop, we can take some simple steps. For example, water the garden in the early morning or evening when there will be less evaporation. And perhaps you can at least help to recharge the aquifer: in other words, collect water when you have it, and send it underground. The most exciting technique we can use to that end is rain gardens.

Rain Gardens

When it rains, water runs off roofs, streets, landscapes, or driveways, mixing with dirt, dust, settled air pollutants, fertilizer, chemicals, oil, garbage, and bacteria. The tainted water usually enters storm drains or runs off lawns and land to eventually make its way to nearby streams, rivers, and ponds, where it accounts for more than half of all pollution. As gardeners realize the importance of water, not just for irrigation but also as a resource, some people are thinking about how the water could be cleaned and returned to recharge aquifers through rain gardens. Compared to a conventional lawn, rain gardens allow for 30 percent more water to soak into the ground.

Conventional gutters and downspouts, as well as sump pumps, can be channeled into underground perforated drains from which some of the water will seep into the earth as it travels to the rain garden. Water that is directed to these con-

structions gets filtered through the soil before it seeps deep into the ground. Some of the accumulated water can evaporate and return to the atmosphere, but leave the particulate matter to the plants that use the moisture and remove some pollutants and convert them to less harmful substances. Plants absorb chemicals from the soil. In the root area, microbes turn volatile organic chemicals (VOCs) into food for the plant. Most of the water will seep into the ground to recharge the aquifer and none will leave the property.

A rain garden is not a water garden. Nor is it a pond or a wetland. Conversely, a rain garden is dry most of the time. It typically collects water only during and following a rainfall event, and since the water drains away in less than forty-eight hours, it does not promote the breeding of mosquitoes.

A rain garden is a special area located in the lowest part of a property. It should be placed at least 10 feet (3 m) away from the building foundations and should not be located where water historically collects for long periods of time. If the soil is heavily compacted, or if it is poorly draining and mostly clay, a new medium has to be developed. The new medium should be moisture retentive but well drained, for example consisting of roughly 25 percent garden loam, 25 percent compost, and 50 percent very coarse sand.

As for width and length, recommendations call for an area about 20 percent the size of the roof, patio, or pavement that will be draining into it. A rain garden for a typical suburban residential home or small building is between 100 and 400 square feet (9 to 40 m^2). Regardless of the size, every rain garden can have an impact.

Shade plants selected for this area must be able to tolerate periods of wet and dry: local wildflowers, sedges, moisture- and shade-tolerant shrubs and ferns. It might be best to not include trees, because they tend to take up too much of the water too quickly. As with every consideration, and every effort, in the making of our shade gardens, striking the right balance is the key.

OPPOSITE This location in a low part of the landscape might be a good spot for a shaded rain garden. Rain gardens can be planted with local perennials that can withstand both wet and dry conditions. The water is filtered through the soil and cleaned by plants before it reaches the aquifer. If the soil is heavy or clay, it should mixed with compost and sand so that it is moisture retentive but well drained. You don't want a lot of trees, since the water should not be carried up into masses of leaves where it will evaporate into the air.

LEFT Native to much of North America, the tall goat's beard (*Aruncus dioicus*, flower detail) is the kind of herbaceous perennial we want for rain gardens since it originates in moist places but can tolerate drier soil as well.

AFTERWORD

A WORD ON SUSTAINABILITY

PREVIOUS SPREAD **PREVIOUS SPREAD** One of the magnificent plantings in filtered light at the Elisabeth C. Miller Botanical Garden in Seattle includes shrubs like the spider azalea, *Rhododendron stenopetalum* 'Linearifolium' and chartreuse Japanese forest grass.

ABOVE, CLOCKWISE FROM TOP The open flowers of Chinese mayapple, *Podophyllum pleianthum*, seen from below; strawberry begonia's cousin, the foamflower, *Tiarella wherryi*; deep-shade-tolerant strawberry begonia—*Saxifraga stolonifera* 'Red Form'.

OPPOSITE In many ways, shade itself is sustainable. There is much less evaporation in the cool shade and therefore less irrigation. The demands for fertilizer are also reduced in this tranquil place.

The words *green* and even *organic* have been overused to the point where they have nearly lost their meanings. Now we hear the word *sustainable* over and over. Sometimes a fad becomes a trend and especially in this case—a way of living. I hope sustainable is here to stay.

What does sustainability mean? We've just learned how water, a precious and threatened resource, can be capitalized on and in the process conserved. We can strive to design and create outdoor spaces and develop maintenance procedures that will not compromise future generations and the planet. The goal is to protect and enhance the ability of the land to become self-supporting, one garden at a time.

Nature, undisturbed by human intervention, is self-sufficient and self-sustaining. For the most part, when we make shade gardens such as the ones discussed in this book, we are mimicking the practices of nature to reduce care, minimize disruption, and respect energy requirements for a healthy environment. This objective requires avoiding invasive species and promoting native plants, adapting to the local weather and climate, water resources and geology, and more. Here are some pointers to keep in mind while you're planning your environmentally friendly shade garden.

Plant trees: We need to plant trees whenever possible to help clean the air. Deciduous trees can provide shade in summer and let in sunlight in the winter. Evergreens can be planted for windbreaks, to conserve fuel for heating the home, and for helping protect other plants from harsh, desiccating winds and winters. When possible, plant trees that grow, or grew, naturally in your area. Trees are also CO_2 sinks that help sequester this greenhouse gas.

Build better paths: Consider permeable surfaces for all paths, never mortared

block or other solid materials, so that water can percolate down into the soil and not run off. Use a rake and broom instead of a blower for leaves and dirt on pavement.

Reduce lawn area: The lawn is one of the most energy-hungry areas of our landscape.

Conserve water: Lawns need about an inch (2.5 cm) of water a week, but native and site-appropriate plants may not, once established. You can provide some water and let nature help with the rest, adding water only when the garden needs it. A moisture meter might be useful; these are inexpensive probes pushed into the soil. When you water, water deeply but less frequently, which encourages plant roots to grow deep and be more drought resistant. If you use a sprinkler, water very early in the day or late in the evening to avoid losing moisture to evaporation.

It is much better to use drip irrigation and soaker hoses than overhead oscillating or impulse sprinklers.

Collect and use rainwater as much as possible—some is better than none. Set up at least one rain barrel to use for hand-watering containers. If possible, consider a cistern. If you are building a new house, include water capture and storage in the basement.

Develop swales and hillocks to direct water. Try not to let any rainwater leave your property. Plant a rain garden. Research whether you are allowed to use gray water on gardens in your area as well.

Consider more natives: I can't emphasize this enough—do not plant potentially invasive species. Use native plants that are known to have coevolutionary relationships with animals like birds and butterflies. Make habitat for birds and beneficial insects when possible, including letting fallen logs, as well as standing snags, remain in the garden. Do not feed local shade plants with anything more than their mulch of leaves or compost and leaves. Too much synthetic or even organic fertilizer will encourage rapid and large growth that will require more water and food to sustain. Unused fertilizer can run off into nearby waterways.

Increase your critter tolerance: Try to get used to some damage on leaves from insects, rather than striving for impossible perfection in the garden and using harsh methods to achieve it. Find resources that help identify good bugs and bad ones. Very generally, local good bugs that do cause damage will not kill their favorite food source. Holes in leaves might be signs of exotic pests, since the more clever local pests will eat from the edges of leaves so that birds do not have a clear sign of where their next meal might be dining.

Reevaluate how you deal with weeds and waste: Pull weeds by hand instead of using hazardous chemicals. Recycle plastic pots; take them back to the nursery or check with nearby public gardens to see if they have a pot-recycling program.

Use mulch and compost: Mulch all beds to keep soil cool and moist. Use fallen leaves as your main source of mulch. Collect all yard "waste" and make it into compost that will increase your soil's moisture-holding capacity, improve tilth, and even add fertility.

The bottom line: We want to leave the shady places where we garden (and relax or play) just as we found them—or even better.

OPPOSITE The early days of my woodland garden, a lush oasis in the shade of a giant white pine tree. There, some favorite plants grow, like lavender-blue *Phlox divaricata*, ground covering mayapple (*Podophyllum peltatum*), white foamflower (*Tiarella* spp.), pink wild geranium (*G. maculatum*) and a baby silverbell tree (*Halesia tetraptera*). When worries about our changing climate become overwhelming, this verdant retreat is where I go to rejuvenate.

INDEX

ACKNOWLEDGMENTS

My great appreciation goes to my editor, managing editor, and the associate art director at ABRAMS for their unfailing commitment to making this book as good as it could possibly be. We even had fun! Thank you, Andrea Danese, Emily Albarillo, and Darilyn Carnes.

Special thanks to Margaret Roach and Louis Bauer for their assistance and support.

My gratitude goes to gardeners, friends, and great gardens that contributed to this book: Tony Avent, Bellevue Botanical Garden, Brooklyn Botanic Garden, Hilary and Michael Clayton, Coastal Maine Botanical Garden, Bill and Melissa Cullina, Kris Dahl, James David, Kristin DeSouza, Marcia Donahue, Susie Egan, Elisabeth C. Miller Botanical Garden, Andrea Filippone, Michael Ferreri, Bill Fidelo, Eric "T" Fleisher, Elsie Freeman, Frelinghuysen Arboretum, Kathy and Ed Fries, Garden in the Woods, Karl Garlid, Diane Genco, Noel Gieleghem, Jim Golden, Greg Graves, Greenwood Gardens, Steve Griffin, Jill Hagler, Ellen Hoverkamp, Brenden Huggins, Richard Iversen, Dan Jaffe, Tom Koster, George Lasch, Ruth Levitan, Paul Licht, Ellenn and Duncan McFarland, Nate McCullin, Mary Meyer, Kip Neale, New York Botanical Garden, Riz Reyes, Diana E. Ruark, Amy Ryan, Alber Saleh, Gene Schaefer, Kristin Schleiter, Patti Shea, Eric Slovin, Richie Steffen, Leslie Stoker, Marco Polo Stufano, Henriette Suhr, Barbara and Robert Tiffany, Brandon Tyson, Mark Veeder, George Waffle, Richard Weber, Wave Hill, Jeanne Will, Kimberly Williams, Charles Yurgalevitch

PAGE 1 The shade-garden story is one about leaves. Mounds of broad hostas and masses of feathery ferns demonstrate the varied scale and textures of our plants.

PAGES 2–3 The view across the sod covered bridge in my New Jersey garden is of the shade plantings where foliage, color, and texture reign.

PAGES 4–5 The wide grass path through hosta collections at the Gardens at Mill Fleurs, in Pennsylvania, created by Barbara Tiffany around the home that she shares with her husband, Robert.

Published in 2015 by Stewart, Tabori & Chang
An imprint of ABRAMS

Copyright © 2015 Ken Druse

Library of Congress Control Number: 2014942983

ISBN: 978-1-61769-104-1

Editor: Andrea Danese
Designer: Darilyn Lowe Carnes
Production Manager: Denise LaCongo

The text of this book was composed in Proxima Nova and Stymie

Printed and bound in the United States

10 9 8 7 6 5 4 3 2 1

Stewart, Tabori & Chang books are available at special discounts when purchased in quantity for premiums and promotions as well as fundraising or educational use. Special editions can also be created to specification. For details, contact specialsales@abramsbooks.com or the address below.

THE ART OF BOOKS SINCE 1949

115 West 18th Street
New York, NY 10011
www.abramsbooks.com